THE
GREATEST
WORTH

THE GREATEST WORTH

Finding Oneself as
a Single Member of a
Family-Centric Faith

KEVIN L. BAKER

Copyright © 2019 by Kevin L. Baker

All rights reserved. No part of this book may be reproduced or used in any manner without written permission of the copyright owner except for the use of quotations in a book review.

For more information, address: theldssinglesguy@gmail.com

First paperback edition February 2019

Illustrations by Ius Yunias
Edited by Stephanie Heilman and Brooks Becker

ISBN 978-1-7327877-0-4 (paperback)

Scripture quotations from the Bible are taken from the King James Version.

The author made efforts to utilize references that are in the public domain or protected through fair use. The author will be happy to rectify any omissions or mistakes brought to his attention.

The events and conversations in this book are recounted to the best of the author's knowledge and ability, although some names and details have been changed to protect the innocent as well as their privacy.

WARNING: The author is highly single. Do not think about the author near fire, flame, or sparks as incidents of spontaneous combustion, while rare, have been known to be reported. Thinking about the author may potentially affect an individual's mood as even the slightest deliberation can lead to an extended or prolonged state of extraordinary euphoria. The author represented on the cover may be cuter in person but must be dated for the full effect! Any such activity, however, may have the unintended consequence of bringing time and space into one continuous medium for the involved individual. Finally, while true that thinking about the author may give one a strong sensation of flying, such thoughts will not actually give that individual the ability to take flight. Please consider responsibly.

Published by The LDS Singles Guy Publishing LLC, a Minnesota LLC

www.theldssinglesguy.com

For my wife
(Wherever and whoever she is)

Contents

Introduction
ix

1
What Single Adults Experience as Latter-day Saints
1

2
My Story
15

3
Recognizing Shame—The Effects of Emotional and Relational Trauma
31

4
Moving Forward and Establishing Yourself as a Single Adult
51

5
Upon What Do We Base Our Relationships?
79

6
Relational Expectations
113

7
Considering the Needs of Single Adults
145

8
Developing an Eternal Perspective Despite the Challenges of Being Single
187

9
Being and Becoming Saints of God
211

10
The Opportunity of One
259

11
Moving Forward: Understanding and Relating with Single Adults
281

End Note
289

Notes
291

Introduction

I was once in St. Louis, Missouri, for an important work meeting. Having a few extra hours, I decided to go to the St. Louis temple for a session. The problem was that it was the middle of the day on Wednesday. Although the temple was open, there were literally no patrons in attendance at that time. As I sat alone in the chapel waiting for the temple session to begin, I noticed one of the temple workers walk in, look at me, look at his watch, and walk out.

This occurred several times, with an increased look of frustration coming over his face each successive time. I am sure he was stressed and worried about filling needed assignments for the temple session, and the fact I was alone did not help the matter. After a short while, he walked up to me, placed his hand on my shoulder, and quietly whispered, "Brother—is your wife coming?"

I smiled and quickly replied, "I don't know, but if you see her, point her out. I will gladly take care of the rest!"

I have been a single adult most of my life. I have experienced the hope and joy of prayed-for relationships and the agony and trauma associated with the failure to maintain or develop healthy relationships in a gospel context. I have also faced the difficult problem of finding personal validation in a religion that maintains marriage as a covenant necessary for exaltation and as one of its highest forms of worship for each member.

As the Church of Jesus Christ of Latter-day Saints grows and becomes more relevant in society, it faces an increased challenge of loving and accepting those of its members who are single. More and more people are single today, whether by choice or by circumstance. How well single adults incorporate themselves into the church and how the church and its membership receive them is critical to the development and spirituality of single adults.

Recently, I visited a popular church bookstore in Salt Lake City, Utah. After asking for the location of the books covering topics and issues for single adults, the salesperson directed me to a section where the books (of which there were many) related exclusively to having and developing a healthy marriage relationship.

"This isn't what I need or had in mind," I stated, but the only other book the salesperson could find on the subject dealt with how to be successful at dating. In this moment, I felt I was experiencing insanity as some humorously define it: continuously repeating the same action and expecting different results or outcomes.[1] My definition of insanity is much simpler: trying to get married in the church, failing, trying again, and then having those around me incessantly tell me how to improve my effort or opine on how I should accomplish a marriage.

As single adults, we are often overstuffed or satiated with a multitude of theories and advice about correct dating techniques and how to best become and remain happily married. Yet there is little advice or help for us on how to be single. Often, I ask myself why this discrepancy exists, why being single is not discussed more fully or openly in the church, and why there are few available resources on this topic for single adults.

The purpose of this book is to help fill this gap. It is not to assist or advise single adults on how to date or to become married. Its purpose is to uplift, aid, and comfort those who are struggling as single members of the church; to give context, perspective, and understanding about single-adult issues for married members both in and out of the church; and to provide relevant facts and points of discussion about relationships and other topics for everyone so that all may feel welcome and loved in the gospel environment.

The thoughts, depictions, and impressions contained in this book are my own and do not reflect, nor are they intended to detract in any manner from, the teachings of the Church of Jesus Christ of Latter-day Saints. This book is written on the same principle given to Oliver Cowdrey, whom God instructed to write by way of wisdom but not by way of commandment.[2] If any inconsistency to the doctrines of the Church of Jesus Christ of Latter-day Saints or the teachings of its prophets is found, such inconsistency is a result of inadequacy on my part. This book is intended solely to enrich and elevate those who read it and is not to be dispositive of any religious doctrine or its application.

1

What Single Adults Experience as Latter-day Saints

> Wherefore comfort yourselves together,
> and edify one another, even as also ye do.
> —1 Thessalonians 5:11

It's early on Sunday morning. The alarm goes off, and as I begin to wake, I look at the ceiling and wonder if I have enough energy to go to church. Sundays are always the most difficult day of the week for me because I wrestle with my motivation as a single adult in the Church of Jesus Christ of Latter-day Saints attending a family ward. Sundays can feel like the movie *Groundhog Day*, where I repeatedly relive the same experience over and over and over again with slight modifications and adjustments.

After hitting the snooze button several times, I say my prayers, roll out of bed, and start preparing for the day's activities. As I get dressed and make breakfast, I turn on the TV or radio not because I am interested in listening to it but because it penetrates and fills the quietness of the house. A surreal silence permeates my surroundings otherwise. There is no one to whom I can say, "Good morning," no one with whom to eat breakfast, no one to give a hug or compliment, or with whom I may even argue. Some people might wish for quiet moments like these; however, after many years of beginning days just like this, the quietness can be deafening as it reminds me of the unrelenting and unremitting loneliness I have felt and continue to experience.

Arriving at church early, I find a seat in the back of the cultural hall. I usually sit in the back because I feel a sense of discomfort sitting where people can see me. I do not do this because I feel guilty, or unwelcome, but I feel different because I am a forty-seven-year-old male who is divorced without any kids. Sitting in the back is also easier on me because I don't know by whom I should sit. It can be unwieldy or cumbersome asking to sit with someone each week, as families and parents are busy wrestling with kids. Even if they are happy to sit by me, I wonder if I am imposing on their family time in church. As a result, the easiest and most comfortable option is to grab a seat somewhere in the back.

Invariably, a family running late will see the open chairs next to me and sit down. I feel a sense of relief that I am not alone anymore, but the feeling quickly fades when they ask if I can move down to accommodate all their kids. There is no meanness or rudeness in their request; however, the first thought I have is one of selfishness, telling myself that my seat is just as important as the other. Still, I don't want to separate the family, so I grab my belongings and slide to a different seat or move to a different row.

After sacrament is over, a priesthood leader approaches me with a smile on his face and hands me a ward temple schedule. "Will you please give this to your wife?" he says. Somewhat stunned, I stammer in reply, "I am not married." The priesthood leader's look is one of consternation and dismay. I am not sure whether he is simply embarrassed to have made an incorrect assumption or if he is uncomfortable to learn that I am unmarried. Irrespective, I don't know how to respond to the situation except to say, "Thanks." I start to feel shame not for who I am but for what I am not. A part of me is also embarrassed that I have been in the ward for a long period of time but have still not publicly disclosed or explained my marital status. I try not to be hurt or angry at these questions as they happen all too frequently and in many different and varied ways. In truth, what hurts the most isn't that people don't know or understand my relational situation; it's that the inquiry triggers deep feelings and emotions within me that are challenging to carry.

After church, there is a busyness in the halls as ward members try to collect their families and go home. I stand in the hall hoping to say hi or have a conversation with someone, but an appropriate moment never arises, and I end up leaving as quickly as I arrived. Upon returning home I reflect on the speakers and the lessons I heard. I know I felt the Spirit and that I enjoyed being at church, but I am also disappointed that the talks and lessons were not engaging. Once more, they related almost exclusively to families, the raising of children, and other issues not as relevant to me or pertinent in my life.

I love the church. I have been an active member all my life. My parents both joined the church before I was born, and I was fortunate to have the chance to gain a personal testimony early on. I faithfully served a mission in

Zurich, Switzerland; I was blessed with the opportunity to attend Brigham Young University; I have been given meaningful callings to serve with bishoprics, stake presidencies, various stake and ward Sunday schools, institute programs, and scouting programs. These have enhanced my spirituality and given me greater understanding of who I am and where I belong. Yet I find myself in a situation I never anticipated, that of being both single and divorced in the church.

My purpose in sharing this actuality is not to be negative or to complain. Neither is it to denigrate the church, nor to be thought of as a victim. Rather it is to point out the reality I have experienced in actively attending the church as a single adult over several decades. I have encountered and found natural barriers stemming from different lifestyles, personal interests, and life priorities that may at times impede normal connections and deep friendships between single and married members of the church. As a result, it can take great effort and motivation for single adults to remain active in the church and to practice our faith.

Describing or conveying what single adults encounter in the church is extremely difficult, for how do we describe insular feelings of loneliness, bitterness, or despair, especially when we feel them while we are standing in the middle of a familiar and crowded room?

I once had a conversation with a man who was a member of a different faith and who had resided for a time in Salt Lake City, Utah. I asked about his experience there and whether he enjoyed it. His answer surprised me and gave me something to think about. He said all his neighbors were friendly, nice, and upstanding members of the church. He praised the quiet, safe, and comfortable lifestyle found in the Salt Lake Valley, but he also said he felt tremendously alone while living there. He stated most of the social and community activities were run through the church, to which he did not belong. While he felt welcome and invited to participate in these activities, he felt a separation or feeling of not belonging because he was not of the same faith as those around him. In other words, despite the warm hospitality and friendship extended by members of the church, he felt like an outsider because of the circumstance he faced. In many ways, the experience of single adults within the church can parallel the feelings and sentiments this good man expressed to me. The issue isn't whether single adults feel invited or welcome but whether they feel they fit or belong in church situations where they are not part of the majority.

In her *Ensign* article, "Singles in the Ward Family," Sister Kathy Grant compared being single in the church to joining a stargazing club. The problem, as Sister Grant describes, is that as a new club member you do not yet have the club jacket the other members do, which helps them to withstand the intensity of the cold outside. In Sister Grant's analogy, you ask about getting a jacket and you are told not to worry, that you will be able to acquire one at the proper time. At club activities, you notice that most of the conversations center around the use, maintenance, and care for these jackets. Without thought, the other club members ask why you do not have a jacket or insensitively tell you that you really should have a jacket for these activities.[1]

Perhaps Sister Grant's analogy is a simplification or generalization of what single adults may frequently encounter in the church; however, it does express the innate awkwardness or sense of longing that single adults may sometimes sense in a family-centered environment, especially as single adults face the questions of where we belong or how we fit in the church. It also demonstrates the less-than-tactful approach many well-meaning married members of the church may utilize when approaching single adults. As a result, single adults may be easily lost, or at least feel misplaced, in a traditional family ward when we do not belong to a family or have a family of our own.

I have observed many members of the church relate or connect with each other through their own family relationships. Conversation topics within the church typically center on the raising of children, family events, or specific family issues or concerns that need additional thought or counsel. People with children will often make efforts to stop in the hallway to chat with others who have similarly aged children. Oftentimes, playgroups or church activities are coordinated to facilitate the social needs of families or children. These are good and proper as people develop needed and meaningful friendships, connections, and support with those around them.

Think for a moment, though, on the single adult who may not have children or a significant other with whom to participate in such activities. What does a single sister with no children say when she attends a Relief Society dinner where the only conversation amongst those in attendance is about children? How does she connect? Does she leave feeling alone and wanting while others have felt loved? How does a single brother feel when a stake has a couples' dance on Valentine's Day? Does he go? If so, will it be awkward for him and others in attendance? These church events are not wrong, neither are their intended purposes contrary to the principles of the gospel, yet single adults may struggle to find acceptance and connection within the body of the church because of our current relational status or because our opportunity to connect is diminished through the program or structure of the church.

Part of the issue for single adults affecting both our opportunity and participation in the church is that the lifestyle needs and circumstances for us are diverse and different from those of married members. Because of these differences, the church, its leaders, and its members must have more understanding and sensitivity to these needs for single adults to feel accepted or connected within the church.[2]

Elder Oaks taught that families and the church have a symbiotic, or mutually reinforcing, relationship. He states:

> The theology of the Church ... centers on the family. Our relationship to God and the purpose of earth life are explained in terms of the family. We are the Spirit children of heavenly parents. The gospel plan is implemented through earthly families, and our highest aspiration is to perpetuate those family relationships throughout eternity. The ultimate mission of our Savior's Church is to help us achieve exaltation in the celestial kingdom, and that can only be accomplished in a family relationship.[3]

The church's correct and proper emphasis is on the family. The church's fundamental purpose is not, however, to ensure each of us finds an eternal companion; rather, its function is to enhance our personal spirituality and to prepare each of us to receive exaltation. While entrance into the highest degree of the celestial kingdom requires a temple marriage, one does not enter as a result or consequence of that marriage. Entrance into the celestial kingdom is predicated not on whether we are married or whom we have married, but rather on who we are and what we have become. Because of this, the principles and doctrines of the church are open to all, single or married, and it is up to each of us individually to come unto the Savior, to partake of the redeeming effects of the atonement and be saved. For those of us who may not have the opportunity to marry or remarry in the temple, God has promised to judge us according to the desires of our hearts: "For I, the Lord, will judge all men according to their works, according to the desire of their hearts."[4] Whether married or single, faith is required that temporary separations will have eternal opportunities in the life to come.[5]

Having said that, there are few of us in this life who want to wait until the next life to receive and participate in the blessings of marriage and eternal companionship. When asked what his greatest fear about being single was, a good friend of mine commented that becoming a ministering angel was staring him down like a freight train. I have rarely met a single adult whose life's ambition was to remain unattached or unaffiliated to someone else; however, the weight of remaining single and the belief we will someday be held accountable for the duration and length of that condition is a tremendously heavy burden for single adults to shoulder. Additionally, becoming married is not a sure-fire recipe for accelerated personal growth or a panacea for individual happiness. It is also not as simple as entering a candy store and selecting that which delights you most. It involves timing, opportunity, risk, and, most importantly, the exercise of another's agency in choosing you. Perhaps this is one reason the scriptures offer little doctrine or insight into how to get married, but rather focus on the type of individual we must become in a successful marriage relationship.

Sometimes unrealized and unintended insensitivities may occur toward single adults from married members of the church. I once attended a single-adult activity hosted at the local stake center where this was the case. The activity was a game night and there were several people of different ages around the table playing the game Apples to Apples. In the middle of the game, a single sister arrived. From my perspective, this looked to be her first single-adult activity and she appeared anxious about being there, almost as if she were asking herself, *How did I get into this situation? Do I belong? Should I stay?*

The high councilman in attendance immediately stood up, smiled, offered his chair and stated, "Please take my seat and play. I am married and I am just here to supervise." The single sister stayed briefly but ultimately left before anyone could talk to her. I knew there was no intended offense or malfeasance in what the high councilor said or did. I am certain he envisioned this as an act of acceptance and love, yet his actions and language set himself apart from the single adults present.

What he failed to realize in this moment was an opportunity to connect and interact with this single sister, leading to an unrecognized and less satisfactory outcome. This sister didn't need to have her relational status called out or offered as a point of difference. Neither did this married member need to feel a sense of duty or responsibility to be at a single-adult activity. This high councilman should have invited this single sister to participate as an equal, accepted her for who she is, and given her an opportunity to connect with others allowing her to feel a sense of belonging, irrespective of her relational status.

On the other hand, single adults must learn and recognize that the church as an institution is not intended for, nor is it designed to satisfy, the individual needs of each member. I have observed that those single adults who attend the church solely for a social experience are often left disenchanted, wanting, and disappointed. Those single adults who attend the church to grow, to repent and partake of the sacrament, and to increase their faith tend to have a greater sense of spirituality and have more satisfaction in their church activity.

I once attended a combined Priesthood and Relief Society session during ward conference where I was the only single adult in attendance. The purpose of the meeting was to discuss the strengthening of marriages and the consequences of divorce today. Admittedly, these discussions are hard topics for me whenever they occur, and walls go up inside of me that make it more difficult for me to feel the Spirit. I know, however, this topic is an important one to discuss and the church should not stop having these types of discussions because one or more of the participants is single.

As the stake president began this discussion, he read verbatim from the *Church Handbook* some of the doctrine as it pertains to single adults. A debate among the family members of the ward ensued, regarding whether the church should be more careful and mindful of its single members when discussing such topics. I was grateful for the stake president's introduction as well as the ward members' concern and sensitivity toward single members, yet despite this effort I found myself wanting spiritually. As I pondered on why this was, I realized the doctrines of the church were not the issue with which I was wrestling. In fact, I take great comfort and joy in knowing eternal possibilities exist outside this lifetime.

The difficulties associated with being a single adult in the church have very little to do with the church or its doctrine. Rather, the difficulties with which single adults struggle lie to one degree or another with a lack of connection or attachment within the church's programs. This deficiency or depletion of connection and attachment may result in feelings of low self-esteem or low individual worth in the church. It may also result in feelings of inadequacy relating to individual expectations or feelings of not measuring up to gospel standards. If the greatest success in the church is a righteous family, the single adult, rightfully or wrongfully, may perceive the inability to achieve that goal as the greatest failure.

Single adults, especially those who are older, may feel like we are stuck, prohibited from achieving happiness in the gospel based solely on the fact we are not currently married. Some of us may feel incomplete not only in the church but also in ourselves because we do not have a companion with whom we can enter the temple and be sealed. God intended men and women to progress together toward exaltation.[6] It's a companionship exercise enabling us to walk with each other in a mutually supporting and reinforcing relationship that is perpetuated throughout eternity. As a result, part of God's purpose for the natural difference between men and women is so we can complete each other on a fundamental and spiritual level.[7] Perhaps this is the reason why President Russell M. Nelson taught, "In God's eternal plan, salvation is an *individual* matter; exaltation is a *family* matter."[8]

I have not met many single adults who would disagree with the church's doctrine on marriage, feel it's incorrect, or advocate for a different interpretation of it. Yet this doctrine is complicated for single adults because the condition of being single is at odds with who we are really and who we are really intended to become. Whenever someone is not in a marriage or committed relationship, feelings of shame, isolation, and fallibility are an intrinsic byproduct of the condition in which we find ourselves. Single adults may feel that although we may achieve salvation, exaltation is something that is less likely, if attainable at all. Additionally, the lack of attachment or connection with others over time is comparable to an exposed emotional nerve that becomes instantly active once it's touched. I have seen too many single adults become inactive or leave the church altogether based on a self-imposed perception that they are of little worth or they have failed spiritually because of their current relational or life status. As a result, it becomes easy for us to question our place within God's kingdom, for us to let go of the iron rod, or for us to lose our faith entirely.

I know God is truly concerned with the trials and circumstances of single adults and He is mindful of the many remarkable contributions we make. The opportunity for all of us is, as Paul states, to become "no more strangers and foreigners, but fellow citizens with the saints, and of the household of God."[9] The challenge of this charge for the church and its membership is not in the sincerity, devotion, or desire for its fulfillment, but rather in its application and implementation. The underlying, and crucial, question becomes how the church and its membership incorporate and include single adults into full fellowship so that we feel welcome and are given opportunities to spiritually progress.

Some single adults feel we have few friends or acquaintances within the church. What a heartbreaking feeling and unhappy state of life. Commenting on this problem, Gerald A. Speedy stated, "Think what it would be like to not have a single friend. It is almost impossible to comprehend. Without a friend, a person is in a state of crisis."[10] To assist single adults in feeling more accepted in the church and in coming to the Savior, friendship and fellowship must reach far beyond the few hours of church each Sunday or a cordial handshake at the doorstep. Do members of the church try to truly befriend single members? If a true friend does not exist at church or its activities, might single adults be demotivated from attending and thus self-exclude ourselves from the edifying and uplifting social activities we so desperately need? Single members need great self-motivation to participate at and to be active in the church. Without a friend in the ward or branch, single adults can be encouraged or inclined to satisfy social needs in ways that may not be in harmony with gospel standards or that may not be conducive to the Spirit. A good network of friends is an important impetus and resource that allows single adults into the comforting fellowship offered by the saints of God.

Often in the church, we prioritize our relationship with God over all other types of relationships. This emphasis and practice is understandable as it focuses on our spirituality and our goal of achieving salvation. The single adult's relationship with God is incredibly important, yet the relationships and connections achieved with other people in mortality are likewise important. Church members and church leaders should equally consider the importance of both when engaging single adults. It is easier for married members to focus on their relationships with God because they have constant and sustained relational validation both in and out of the church through their existing marital and family ties. For single adults, who have limited or no relational validation, this focus is much more complex than for married members. The lack of social interaction and opportunity, even when we have a strong relationship with God, may lead to spiritual impediments in the long term.

Why do single adults struggle in family environments to make meaningful friendships and connections? Many times, our ability to foster true friendships is hindered by a lack of understanding between married and single members, or by the two groups' differing priorities. Stated differently, how married members regard and treat single adults in a family environment has a direct bearing on how we feel and incorporate ourselves in the church. Are single adults invited as friends to non-church activities? Do we have people to sit next to if we come to church? Do we have people with similar interests to talk to and communicate with in the ward or branch? Are members cognizant of our needs outside the church during holidays or other important times?

While single adults are largely self-sufficient, we may need helping hands just to accomplish day-to-day tasks that are not apparent to those around us. Sometimes just being in a church meeting or activity where married men and women are holding hands, scratching backs, or showing small acts of kindness toward each other may be difficult if we do not have that comfort in our life. Additionally, single adults sometimes struggle to find relevance in a church where the programs themselves are designed to heighten or enhance family—not individual—experiences. Married members may not fully understand or appreciate why single adults may be less than willing to intensify our commitment to these church programs and objectives when we are already struggling just to attend and be part of them.

On the other hand, single adults ourselves may hinder opportunities for true friendship through complete social withdrawal, angry or embittered feelings, or strong entitlement mindsets. When reaching out to others, single adults should not behave as though we are victims or believe church leaders don't understand us. Nor should single adults say to the members of the church, "I'm here. Take care of me." What is truly needed is an increase in love and understanding by all. How grateful I am for members of the church who make extra efforts outside church activities to socialize with and befriend those who are single. How grateful I am to single adults who courageously reach beyond our areas of comfort and establish significant and lasting friendships regardless of our marital status or station in life.

One final point as it pertains to the fellowship of single adults: Single adults have a tremendous ability to love and to serve, especially in the church. I am truly amazed to see this practiced as single adults attend activities and other church functions. When we have meaningful opportunities to serve, we reach beyond ourselves and we are stretched in capacities we never imagined.

That said, church leaders should carefully consider the welfare and social needs of single adults in the specific callings and service opportunities we are assigned. Several years ago, upon moving into a new ward, I was called as a Sunbeam teacher and I faithfully accepted. Even though I enjoyed my service in this calling, my church experiences each week consisted of going to sacrament and spending two hours with young children in a small room. I loved these children, yet teaching them did not give me the social interaction I desperately needed. While I was diligent in the calling, it became very difficult for me to have such limited interaction with ward members over a long period of time. I didn't know anyone in the ward and they had little opportunity to know me. Even though I was serving in the church and striving to maintain my relationship with God, I was losing out on my interpersonal relationships with others; all of these are crucial for the spiritual health and well-being of single adults.

As we give voice to the challenges and struggles of single adults in the church, we begin to understand the dilemma single adults encounter in choosing to participate in the church or to leave it altogether. My justification and reasoning for remaining active in the church is about a personal desire to develop and practice faith and to better understand my value to God as well as my place and worth in society. That said, I have often asked myself what is the value and worth of single adults in the church.

When Abinadi stood before King Noah, a wicked and degenerate priest posed a fundamental doctrinal question to him, a question this priest did not fully understand, nor care to hear answered:

> And it came to pass that one of them said unto him: What meaneth the words which are written, and which have been taught by our fathers, saying:
>
> How beautiful upon the mountains are the feet of him that bringeth good tidings; that publisheth peace; that bringeth good tidings of good; that publisheth salvation; that saith unto Zion, Thy God reigneth.[11]

Abinadi's insightful answer has touched my soul in ineffable ways and helped me to find worth and meaning as a single adult in the church. Abinadi responded that the Savior saw His seed when He undertook the magnitude of the atonement and offered Himself for our benefit. Abinadi then posed this question, "And who shall be his seed?"[12] He answered this question by stating that all those who listen and hear the prophets of God, who believe in the Savior, and who look forward to receiving the benefit of His atonement are His seed. Abinadi further explained that the prophets themselves and those who labor and strive to bring others to the Savior are also His seed. Abinadi concluded, stating:

> And these are they who have published peace, who have brought good tidings of good, who have published salvation; and said unto Zion: Thy God reigneth! And *O how beautiful upon the mountains were their feet*! And again, *how beautiful upon the mountains are the feet of those that are still publishing peace*! And again, how beautiful upon the mountains are *the feet of those who shall hereafter publish peace*, yea, from this time henceforth and forever!

And behold, I say unto you, this is not all. For *O how beautiful upon the mountains are the feet of him that bringeth good tidings, that is the founder of peace, yea, even the Lord,* who has redeemed his people; yea, him who has granted salvation unto his people; For were it not for the redemption which he hath made for his people, which was prepared from the foundation of the world, I say unto you, were it not for this, *all mankind must have perished.*[13]

Abinadi's answer to the priest's question is meaningful and significant to single adults. His answer expresses both the individual value and the intrinsic worth of each of us, for each of us, whether single or married, is the seed of Christ. Abinadi's answer demonstrates how beautiful each of us is in the sight of God and the value and importance He places on His relationship with us. It makes plain the exquisiteness of the Savior's atonement, that His condescension below all things allows and gives us opportunity to partake of eternal life. It further explains that the effects of His atonement will be beautiful for us not only in this life but also in the next. It expounds that each of us, single or married, has a role and a responsibility to be actively engaged in the work of God, to declare His message and to participate in building His kingdom so that all may partake of the fruits of the gospel. It also establishes that we all have standing before God and that the ties of our faith are not what separate us but what bind us together to bring peace, joy, and contentment. How beautiful that truly is.

For single adults who labor to find acceptance or toil to fit in a family-centric religion, who sometimes may question who they are or wrestle with where they belong, I say, oh how beautiful upon the mountains are they who endeavor to participate in and partake of this work to bring salvation to themselves and to others. Whether our efforts as single adults are great or small or whether we exercise maximum faith or are still developing it, each effort and each individual is welcome and accepted in the gospel and in the church. Despite the challenges to single adults, the gospel is not a married-only religion, and there is room for all to participate in the benefits thereof.

Only through the gospel do we come to know the Savior and accept the great things that He has done for us. Only through the gospel do we understand the importance and effect of ordinances and covenants in our lives. Only through the gospel can we lift ourselves up, can we overcome our own deficiencies and feelings of inadequacy and find happiness in the manner and capacity that God has apportioned to us. And only through the gospel do we learn that we are not cast off forever, that we are not alone in the universe, that winter will turn to spring, and that the night will surely turn to day; for the greatest worth to God is each of us.

2

My Story

*Then I saw, and considered it well: I looked upon it,
and received instruction.*
—Proverbs 24:32

Several years ago, I coordinated the publication of the annual ward picture directory for the local single-adult ward. During this process, the institute director approached me and requested that I include him and his wife in this publication. Thinking this a great idea, I set a time immediately after church to take their picture. After the service concluded, the institute director found me in a busy hallway and with an anxious and bewildered look, stated, "I know my wife is around here somewhere, I just can't find her." With a wry smile and a twinkle in my eye, I quickly responded, "Don't worry, I have the same problem."

As I look back and reflect on the course of my life, the most challenging and distressing difficulties I have faced came while developing and maintaining personal and intimate relations with the opposite sex. I have faced intense personal loneliness and feelings of low self-esteem for extremely long periods of time. Telling my story publicly is not easy, because those feelings of shame and disappointment still exist. I used to joke that my dating life was a romantic tragedy of epic proportions and if Shakespeare were still alive, he would have written *The Life and Times of Kevin Baker* rather than *Romeo and Juliet*. I am telling this part of my life openly to let you know and understand the social awkwardness and the relational barriers I have encountered as well as the heartache I have felt.

I truly do understand the emotions and feelings associated with being a single adult in the church. I hope the experiences and stories I articulate are not looked on as negative or depressing, but rather as a guidepost for further discussion about single adults. I don't look on these experiences as sad, yet they occurred, and they are an important part of my life. Despite my adversity, today I realize Heaven has constantly and ceaselessly watched over and cared for me. That knowledge has given me the ability to find joy in my life and blessed me with tremendous hope and courage to face the future.

When it came to dating relationships, fear was the greatest obstacle I faced. The fear of rejection, the fear of being laughed at, and the fear of not knowing how to act or what to do were all things I struggled with. Growing up, I was not blessed with great size, physical acumen, or athletic prowess. In fact, I was smaller, quieter, and shyer than most kids. My father was a popular and good-looking man, a champion athlete whose strength, skill, and abilities I did not inherit. In fact, his athletic abilities were the means and impetus for his joining the church, as he earned a full baseball scholarship as a catcher to BYU. He excelled at college, both on and off the field. I often felt embarrassment growing up because of my small size and lack of athletic ability, wondering if I disappointed my father or others because of this, even though I excelled in different areas such as academics, scouting, and music.

In my first year as a young boy playing fast-pitch baseball, I was terrified. Each time I went to the plate, I thought, *What if the pitcher hits me? What if I swing and miss? Will people laugh at me*? I didn't even know how to swing the bat and internally I felt so scared and afraid. All I could do was stand in the batter's box, tightly gripping the bat, and shrink down as low as possible. Truth be told, I felt much smaller on the inside than my stance was on the outside.

Ironically, for the first time, I found great advantage in my size, as it was difficult for the pitchers to throw a strike. As a result, I was walked on a regular basis. This seemed to work for me. I went the entire season getting on base without swinging at a pitch, never taking a risk, and never really feeling any sense of accomplishment or satisfaction. Fortunately, at the last game of the year, for whatever reason, I found a small glimmer of confidence, closed my eyes, and swung at a pitch. I still have absolutely no idea why or what came over me. To my surprise, the bat hit the ball. Not only did I make contact, but the ball went into the outfield and turned into a double. I think the shock for both myself and my coach was overwhelming; neither of us knew what to do when it occurred.

Dating always made me feel like that small kid gripping the bat so tightly in the batter's box, not knowing what to do, not understanding where to go, and not having the courage, skills, or expertise to be successful. When

I went on my first date, I was nervous, surprised, and did not know how to comport myself. The reality was, while I was in the game, I was never really playing and thus never really making any progress. I was the ugly duckling, not understanding myself, surrounded by different people, and wondering why I didn't fit in.

Though shyness and fear were initially significant obstacles, I gradually became more confident with age. Even though fear became less of an issue, I still faced continuous and repeated rejection in the church dating environment. Despite being academically and professionally successful, despite being an active, kind, and spiritual person, I found that I was not someone who engendered or sparked attention from single women in the church. My opportunity to date was thus greatly constrained. It was common for women to tell me I was not tall or attractive enough for them to make a connection with me or to be interested in dating me. This happened so frequently that I began to anticipate or expect it in my interactions with women. This viewpoint increased the already high level of difficulty for me, while simultaneously decreasing my willingness of trying to date.

I remember one girl I was interested in after my mission. She lived in my dormitory complex on campus. Even though she was aware of my interest, she came to me and asked me to drive her from Provo to Salt Lake City (about forty miles) for a date she had with a different person. I remember agreeing to drive her there in the hopes of spending some time with her, yet on the way home I felt disappointed and ashamed because she was not interested in me from a dating perspective.

I have thought a lot about this experience, because it is representative. When I did gain the courage to ask someone out, the women I tried to date were generally interested in other people. These women did not view me as a bad guy, but they always had other options available to them who had a higher dating or relational priority.

Dating felt like I'd thrown my name into a hat along with every other eligible single guy. I watched the single girls draw name after name and I anxiously waited for my own name to be pulled. I was disappointed that it never was. If I was fortunate enough to have a girl agree to go out with me, I would find her emotionally guarded on the date. It seemed to me in most cases, the girls I asked out had predetermined they were not attracted or interested in me and had only agreed to the date out of courtesy. As a result, the interactions that occurred on these dates were more rigid and superficial, affording little chance or opportunity to develop any deeper or longer-term connections, let alone a second date.

Throughout my life, many of the women I encountered and became interested in were happy to have me as a friend; however, the moment I showed interest in dating or creating a higher level of relationship with them, barriers went up almost instantaneously. For me, these barriers were insurmountable and often discouraging. To compound matters, priesthood leaders continually told me that if I did not have a marriage relationship, it was my fault. I found these leaders gave great empathy to the single women in the church, but to the single men they gave unsympathetic treatment or little, if any, quarter. This paradox left me with a flawed but real choice: do I try to date and risk not having any friends, or do I try to be friends and not worry about dating?

My first real memory in the dating world occurred when I was fourteen while attending my first young men and young women's church dance. Part of the church's program for young men and young women is to teach them the sanctity of marriage and the virtuousness of intimate relations that are shared only between spouses; yet, at that age I didn't fully understand the concept of sex or what dating meant. What I understood about girls was that intimacy or sex is bad and it was something to be feared. At that time in my life, the church prohibited dating prior to the age of sixteen. Even after that age, dating was strongly discouraged, highly supervised, or conducted in a group setting. The church considered dating an advanced or higher form of courtship to be reserved solely for potential marriage partners. As a result, the church frowned upon all interactions that had even the appearance of dating prior to the age of sixteen, and it tightly controlled or scrutinized dating activities thereafter.

Because of this proscription and forbiddance, I did not date prior to this point in my life. Also, I did not have any close friends of the opposite sex, nor did I have or develop the social skills necessary for dating success. I did not have a support system in place to guide me, to encourage me, or to show me what to do as I matured and grew.

Being dropped off at the church for my first dance was like being dropped into the deep end of the pool without any swim lessons or training. I had entered a foreign arena, and I was ill-equipped to handle it. I don't remember much about that activity except standing around the side wall watching others dancing, feeling shy and embarrassed. I regularly attended church dances from that point on with mostly the same pattern. Over time, I did begin to ask girls to dance, but it was as painful as fingernails on a chalkboard. I usually ended up dancing in groups or with those whom others did not regularly ask to dance.

I was seventeen years old when I finally went on my first date. By that time, I was interested in girls but I still did not relate with many or understand how to go about dating. I was also acutely aware of my body and that it had not developed in any impressive way. I was exceedingly skinny, weighing less than ninety pounds, and had no real muscle structure. I still distinctly remember my high school swim coach, during my senior year, pointedly asking me when I was going to get bigger and stronger. I was not the cute or popular guy at school, and I knew it. Additionally, there were not many members of the church in my school. Other students didn't understand the church and negatively thought of me as a "Mormon." At that age, I was still learning about my religion and my faith and I didn't fully understand what it meant to be a member of the church. This, combined with other peoples' perspectives, made me that much more different and worsened the social clumsiness I already felt.

Dating was not something I did, not because I didn't want to but because I neither had the opportunity nor the skill set to do it. The first time I mustered the courage to ask a girl out was for my junior prom, an act that took me weeks to even talk myself into doing. I had decided I wanted to go to my junior prom and I didn't want to go by myself. When I finally did ask someone to go with me, I felt like running away and hiding. I would have rather had a mountain fall on top of me than to have gone through that experience. She was not a member of the church and she did not go to my school. These facts made it easier for me to ask her out; if she said no, no one would ever know. To my great surprise, she said yes. When the junior prom arrived, I had no idea what to do, how to act, or what to say. The date was awkward for me and most likely for her, too. Still, I was proud of myself for having asked, but I did not have an opportunity to talk with or to date her again.

I wish I could say that experience propelled me into a life of asking more girls out. The opposite occurred, as I slinked back into my emotional hiding place and didn't resurface until my senior prom. By that point in my life, I was eighteen years old and I was beginning to become ashamed of the fact I had never had a girlfriend, never held anyone's hand, never kissed anyone, and did not know how to achieve that goal. If people found out about this, I was laughed at and teased. It became something I hid and buried deep inside. It seemed everyone else around me was easily and effortlessly entering relationships, and I didn't know where to begin.

A year later, when my senior prom arrived, I remember again wanting to go. I was interested in a girl at school who I thought was cute and I had heard she did not have a date. Like previously, it took me many days to garner the courage to ask her out. She sat right behind me in history class. When the bell rang, I approached her during the commotion of students leaving and asked if she would like to go with me to the senior prom. My asking was more blurted than graceful, imposing like a far-away car horn honking on a busy and crowded city street. In her defense, I was inarticulate and untimely and probably caught her completely off guard.

She politely declined, and I was crushed. It was the first time someone had turned me down, and I was embarrassed. All my fears were realized in that moment. Fortunately, a friend of mine set me up on a blind date for the senior prom, and we enjoyed our time together. But again, no connection occurred and the date quickly ended. High school graduation came and went, and the sum of my dating experience was a whopping two dates. Still, I was proud of myself for doing that small amount and I often wonder how I would have felt had I not gone to either of my high school proms.

My freshman year at BYU was a new experience—it was the first time I was out of my parents' house and on my own. With high school behind me, it was a fresh opportunity to try again. I was more outgoing and doing better at making friends. That everyone around me was a member of the church greatly assisted, as I no longer felt socially isolated because of my faith. For the first time, I started to feel like I belonged. I participated in all church and school activities and I was busy with my classes and schoolwork. Despite this, I still struggled with talking to girls or asking them out. Like a sliver I could not find or remove, it bothered and wore on me: constantly pricking and infecting my soul about things I could not change. I began to feel that I was not valued as a person because of my inability to connect with girls on a personal or intimate level or to have dating relationships as effectively or as readily as others around me. It seemed as if there was a constant hole inside of me that, no matter my effort, I was not able to fill.

As a freshman, I met a girl named Natasha who was in my family home evening group. It's fair to say I fell in love with her almost immediately, but she did not reciprocate those feelings. I tried for over a year to date Natasha, and I made many mistakes; however, our relationship never went further than being just good friends. I suppose I believed if I kept trying and never gave up, things would eventually work out. Natasha was my first real failure in a relationship. I know today that I was single-minded about Natasha and I did not seriously try to date other people. I am not sure why I ignored other potential opportunities, but I believe it was because of my strong feelings for Natasha and my inexperience.

While I was trying date Natasha, a difficult experience occurred that led to great personal and public embarrassment. After discovering I had never kissed anyone, my college roommate both teased and laughed at me. He knew I liked Natasha and so he decided to create some motivation to help me kiss her. He proposed the idea of a group date, however, the catch was that if I didn't kiss Natasha by the end of the date, I had to run around the dormitory square, in the middle of winter, in a Speedo. I took the dare because I felt shamed by his initial reaction and because I hoped that by having his help, it might work. Unfortunately, the date did not go as planned.

When the date arrived, I made dinner for a group of friends and we all went dancing afterwards. Natasha seemed distant and standoffish the entire night. All my hopes went out the window early on and I did not push things with her. I accepted what was happening but felt like a failure inside. When the date ended, she jumped out of the car and ran into the dorm before I even had a chance to say goodnight.

That night, I fulfilled the bet with the full dormitory watching and laughing at me. I tried to shrug it off as no big deal, but I felt enormous embarrassment and humiliation inside. I later found out that someone had told Natasha, in advance of the date, about the dare. I was angry and hurt, but mostly I was afraid that I had ruined my chance at a relationship with her. I held myself responsible for what had occurred and I did the only thing I could: I walked over and apologized for what had happened. My apology rescued our friendship, yet I was not able to be more than good friends with her going forward, even though the strong feelings I had for her persisted for a long time.

My first year at BYU ended without fanfare and I prepared to serve a two-year mission in Switzerland. I was truly excited about the opportunity, but the fact I still hadn't kissed a girl or had a relationship weighed heavily on me. It impacted my confidence, and I questioned my own abilities to face the future. I told myself, if I couldn't even summon the courage to kiss a girl, how in the world was I going to serve a mission in a far-off country? The sting of not having a dating relationship with Natasha also bothered me. Perhaps this was the wrong sentiment for me to have, but it was how I felt.

Fortunately, several weeks before I left on my mission, I met a girl named Jane. I asked her out, and we started to date. She seemed to like me in a way that previously no one ever had. Things seemed easy, and I enjoyed being with her. The hurt I experienced with Natasha began to wash away, and I was happy. Jane was the first person I ever kissed, and it is still one of my life's favorite memories. I felt a sense of relief and a new found courage that carried me into my mission.

Leaving Jane was extremely difficult for many reasons. Even though our relationship lasted only a few short weeks, I had found a sense of self from being with her. She embodied the type of person I had hoped to be with and I truly loved her. I hoped that she would wait for me while I was on my mission and that we could continue our relationship going forward; however, that hope did not come to fruition. One of the great ironies to that point in my life is that Jane went to BYU as a freshman shortly after I left for Switzerland and lived on the same floor where Natasha was a resident assistant. I received co-written letters from both at the beginning of my mission, which was both joyful and awkward at the same time. When I returned from Switzerland, Jane was engaged and I only saw her once at BYU, for five minutes. She was uncomfortable when she spoke to me, probably because she had other priorities in her life.

While I understood that, I was deeply disappointed. I am grateful for her because she gave me a measure of confidence in my life at a time when I was lacking. That confidence allowed me to move forward on my mission and grow as a person. I did also see Natasha again, but I had changed and so had she. The spark I previously felt was not there. Still, I was grateful for the chance to see her again as a friend. At least it offered some closure to the feelings I had years before.

After my mission, I had high hopes of meeting someone and getting married. My mission president counseled me to get married, and I felt an obligation and a sense of duty to do so. I thought that I had served an honorable mission and God would bless me with a relationship and a spouse within a relatively short period of time. All I can say is that I tried for years to date, attempting both small and grandiose things, mostly with little or no success. Sometimes I could get a girl to go on a first date with me, but never a second. Dating became just as much a mystery to me as it was before I left on my mission. It wasn't the fault of the women; all I know is that I tried and was unsuccessful.

As the years went by, my stress increased and concern grew that I might never find someone to be with me in my life. Graduating from BYU at the age of twenty-five was supposed to be a happy life moment, and although I was proud of my accomplishment, I left BYU feeling a failure. I had not met anyone or had the opportunity to get married.

After BYU, I entered graduate school at the University of Oregon, where I earned both a Master of Business Administration and a Juris Doctorate. I reasoned that because I was not married, I had both the time and the opportunity to earn these two degrees. I quickly found out that the rigors of simultaneously earning two graduate degrees were massive and time consuming. Yet I still attended institute and tried as hard as I could to have a social life. I served as the elders quorum president and later as the executive secretary for several bishoprics.

I was twenty-five when I met a girl named Rebecca. It was my first year of graduate school and she had recently joined the church. We started to date and she would be the second girl I kissed in my life. For the first time in many years, I was again excited someone cared enough about me to include me in their life; however, several weeks later she showed up to church holding a friend's hand. I suppose that moment is when I found out she didn't want to date me anymore. I was hurt, shocked, and disappointed not only from the manner of the break-up but also from the failure and loss of the relationship. This experience set me back emotionally, and I focused again on the demands of church and school. I did continue trying to date people, even outside the church, but I encountered similar rejection and more failure.

By the time I was twenty-six, Natasha, Jane, and Rebecca represented the sum of my personal relationships through this point in my life. Each of these were of very short duration and none had any real chance of progressing into marriage or the establishment of a family. I was attracted to and loved other women from afar more deeply than I care to get into. I tried my best to develop quality relationships with them and experienced the pain of rejection on a regular basis. I used to comfort myself by wishing them happiness in the relationships they chose, knowing full well they would not be choosing me. As I look back on it, I am certain there were individuals who may have been interested in me whom I either did not recognize or did not consider. For that, I am sad. My self-confidence was low and I didn't know what to do or where to go; I had served faithfully in the church in meaningful leadership roles and developed beneficial talents and skills, all of which I had hoped would attract someone in my life, but I was still without success.

After graduating from law school and business school, I entered the professional world in the hopes I would be successful, which I was. I took a job in Gillette, Wyoming, as a commercial lawyer with Rio Tinto, a large international mining company. I was good at what I did, I worked hard, and after only three short years, I was promoted to general counsel, where I had management responsibilities over several lawyers. This opportunity was unique; normally a general counsel has significantly more professional experience than I did at the time.

I was grateful for the opportunity and for the responsibility; however, it came at a considerable social cost: living for almost ten years in a place that had little to no opportunity to date. At that time, Gillette had a population of nineteen thousand people and was remotely located. I used to joke that there was a pretty girl behind every tree in Gillette, the joke being there were no trees in the heart of the prairie. The largest metropolitan area with any meaningful single-adult wards or activities was Denver, Colorado. The problem was that Denver is a six-hour drive from Gillette; it was too far away for me to have any reasonable or consistent activity with those single adults.

Part of my initial rationale for accepting employment in Gillette was that I had lived most of my adult life in areas where there were many single girls in the church to date, and been unsuccessful. I felt living in Gillette, where there were few, if any, dating opportunities could hardly be different. My optimism and sureness for a relationship were fading. I recognized that I had passed most of the prime opportunities I had to meet and date good women in the church.

It was a sobering realization that I was left behind when all my friends have moved on with their lives. In Gillette, the only opportunity I had to meet single women in the church was over the internet. I tried that venue for long periods of time without success. I would write or attempt to connect with many different women online, but would receive little or no response in return. If I ever did receive a response, it was perfunctory at best. As a result, I found the same type of rejection occurring online that I previously encountered in person, but this time it was on a more frequent and rapid basis.

In many respects, my experiences with internet dating are like the age-old tradition and practice of tracting on a mission. Tracting in the Switzerland mission was a required activity, one where missionaries spent six to eight hours a day, six days a week proselytizing. At that time, we didn't have pass-along cards, TV ads, or other forms of referrals from the church or its members. To a large extent, the missionaries were dependent upon their own efforts for finding and teaching people in an area that was generally not receptive to missionary activities. The mission taught, and the missionaries understood, that tracting itself was not a productive means for finding people to teach. The problem was, there existed few if any practical proselytizing alternatives. Consequently, missionaries knowingly spent a large amount of time and effort engaged in ineffective means for finding people, all while believing that such finding methods were not acceptable in the church's missionary program. This condition would lead to disappointment, discouragement, and despair.

My use of and experience with internet dating is exactly like this. I spent a lot of time viewing profiles, sending emails, and trying to make connections with people, but with little or no success compared to the time and effort utilized. Said differently, the return was not high for the required investment. Like tracting, internet dating felt like it was the only available or viable means for me and I participated knowing that my opportunities to find someone were low and likely not to improve. Still, I was grateful for the forum as it gave me some hope I was at least trying, and I was, in a small way, engaging in the dating process.

There was one humorous benefit to starting online dating while it was in its infancy, when people were still unsure about it. I signed up for several sites offering lifetime memberships for low introductory amounts. After almost seventeen years of use, I haven't decided whether it's positive that I got my money's worth!

Despite my lack of dating opportunity, priesthood leaders or other church members would admonish me to be more productive in my efforts, for which I had little or no means to accomplish. This not only heightened my sensitivity but also aggravated my feelings on the matter. I would be formally interviewed or informally asked about my dating life, counseled to try church activities in distant places, and told to be less selective in my dating criteria. When this did not work, I was counseled there was a purpose in my being single, that this time would give me experience to be a better husband later, and I should be more faithful in my church activity. I dreaded each of these discussions, as I had no good or acceptable answer. I felt different and misunderstood, unable to achieve something everyone wanted me to have. I wished people could see my life and my experiences through my eyes rather than through the program or expectation of the church.

Years went by in Gillette, and I filled my life with work and church responsibilities. I was called as the stake executive secretary, where I served faithfully with two stake presidents for six years. I also simultaneously served for eight years as the institute teacher and as the advancement coordinator for the local Boy Scout council. I loved these callings, as they distracted me from the loneliness I felt. They also gave me meaningful opportunities to help and serve others, which brought me great joy. Irrespective of this, my loneliness neither dissipated nor went away. The intensity of my church service over such a long period, combined with the rigors of work and the difficulty of being single, wore on me.

Just prior to my thirty-fifth birthday, the stake presidency was scheduled to be released. The stake had a vibrancy and a pronounced anticipation relating to this, as two members of the Quorum of the Seventy were assigned to visit Gillette for stake conference. As the stake executive secretary, it was my responsibility to meet with these general authorities, to discuss individuals they may want to interview, and to coordinate their schedules. When I arrived, these general authorities had a form to fill out that included a box on the top indicating whether you were single, married, or divorced. Thinking nothing of it, I checked the single box and went into the meeting.

I handed the completed form to one of the general authorities and, before I could sit down, he looked at me, pointed his finger, and sternly asked, "Where is your fiancee?" Not expecting the question and somewhat taken aback by his tone, I replied that I did not have one. He then leaned forward and forcefully stated, "That is not what I asked you." I knew exactly what he was telling me: I needed to be married and there was no excuse for being single. I was stunned. The years of failure, loneliness, and desperation instantly flooded over me, and I could barely keep my emotions in check. Exasperated, I looked at the other general authority, who leaned back in his chair and said, "Brother Baker, take it to the Lord." I was upset, hurt, and angry from this exchange. My first thought was, *Hello—I have prayed every day for nearly twenty years for such an opportunity*.

I think what bothered me most about this exchange was there was no dialogue or attempt to understand why I was single and no thought or empathy given to the lifelong struggle I was still experiencing. It was as if the church at its highest levels did not care about me or what had happened to me; it only cared that I was not married. Still, after some deep breathing, thought, and reflection, I went home that evening and prayed to Heavenly Father. I poured out my heart and told Him that He knew exactly what I had gone through. He knew my trials and tribulations and knew that His servants had commanded me to get married. I had no idea what to do and I was putting everything in His hands.

Several weeks later, I met a girl online who chatted with me and showed some interest in me. She was beautiful and a member of the church. I hoped that a relationship would develop. She lived in Denver, and by happenstance, I was working on a multi-billion-dollar commercial transaction that required me to be in Denver on a regular basis over an extended period. I traveled down to Denver for at least two weeks of each month and, rather than stay at a hotel, I would stay at her parents' house in their guest bedroom. This allowed me to work in Denver and come back and spend time with her in the evening. It was an answer to a prayer that had I prayed for a long time, and I viewed it as God responding to what His general authorities had instructed me. My excitement and expectations were high.

We dated for about six months before I asked her to marry me. In truth, the long-distance relationship we had, coupled with the fact I dated her in her home environment, disguised many of the relationship problems we would later encounter. I remember dismissing or overlooking relational issues that arose as we dated, believing they would all work out once we were married. Also, I believed marriage was the solution to my own deficiencies and feelings of inadequacy. Sadly, the marriage itself lasted less than four years before she left. Even though we had no children, the divorce proceedings were prolonged and acrimonious. I did not want to be divorced and I did not want her to leave, but I had no choice in the matter.

The problems we encountered began the very night we were married and thus began a steady pattern of rejection, failure to connect, and inability to bond in a normal and healthy manner. It is easy to point the finger at each other and say the other was at fault. The truth is that we were both at fault. Each of us had past underserved traumas that scarred our lives and impacted our ability to appropriately bond with one another. As a result, we both entered the marriage on disparate footing, not really prepared to accept and to love each other as we should. The inability to connect or bond with my wife, however, revived and intensified the loneliness and shame I had previously felt as a single adult.

Part of me struggles with how to describe the circumstances that occurred in our relationship. While I often talk generally about the type of relationship we had and how that relationship affected me, I have concluded that discussing the actual events is not important, as I often viewed them subjectively, I don't want to embarrass or publicly harm my ex-wife, and they are in my past and I choose to look forward. I do say, though, that our relationship was unhealthy and dysfunctional from the beginning, that she rejected it, and that I had little or no say in what occurred. I also realize no matter how much I gave, how desperately I held onto the relationship, what I changed, or who I became, our relationship was ultimately going to end despite my sincerest efforts, hopes, and wishes. That is both a comfort and a burden I carry.

The walls in the relationship were so high, so thick, and so well defended that it prevented a normal attachment or bonding to occur. I used to think the relationship itself was a lot like the city of Jericho. I thought if I tried hard enough, prayed long enough, and changed myself enough, eventually those walls would come down, yet to my great despair and personal shame, they never did. Like Joshua and the Israelites of old, I marched around and around those walls with focused purpose and intent. I shouted, made noise, and did everything in my power, but they never came down. I began to wonder what Joshua would have done if Jericho's walls never fell. Would he give up? Would he just abandon a land promised to his forefathers? I just didn't know. Because of this struggle, I began to look at my own failures and weaknesses, and doubt who I was and what I wanted to become. I lost myself and didn't know where to go.

As I was wrestling with the enormous weight of these things, I found myself in the Salt Lake City airport waiting for a flight. I had a long time to wait, so I pulled out my Book of Mormon and placed it by my side. I had intended to read it, but I was so emotionally exhausted that I put my feet on my suitcase and closed my eyes for a short nap. When I woke, I was startled to see Elder L. Tom Perry and Elder Quentin L. Cook from the Quorum of the Twelve Apostles sitting directly in front of me.

That is the last time I take a nap in the Salt Lake City airport, I thought. Elder Perry looked at me, leaned over, and asked me what I was reading in the Book of Mormon. I hesitated to tell him, so I mumbled I had just started reading it from the beginning again. He smiled, and we talked briefly about small things.

The next two days I felt guilty because I had read something in the Book of Mormon that I was pondering in my heart and didn't have the courage to tell him. So, I wrote him a letter and told him what scripture I had read and what I was thinking about. To my surprise, he wrote me back and said the following:

> When we were in the Marine Corps and had to run the obstacle course, there was a big wall where you had to run as fast as you could and act like you had a step, to step vault you up and then you would crawl over the top and slide down the other side.
>
> There was always a wall you had to get over. But I guess the more you practiced running hard and hitting that wall just the right way, the more you could vault over the top and go through the rest of the obstacle course.
>
> Some things require practice, discipline, and obedience.
>
> I would encourage you to find a way to vault the walls that are holding you back so that you can move forward into the great blessings the gospel has in store for all of us, if we only will be faithful.

I tell you this story because my marriage was something that couldn't be saved, no matter what I did or who I became, but I was holding on to it irrespective of that. I also tell it to you because I know Heavenly Father loved me enough to send one of His apostles to talk to me and counsel me in a time of great trouble and doubt. For that I will always be grateful.

I do not enjoy being single and I try every day to have hope, to give love and forgiveness to those around me, to take control of my life, to not be a victim, and to develop healthy relationships. It has been several years since my divorce was final, and I again find myself in the world of dating. I am experiencing many of the same paradigms, challenges, and obstacles as I did previously. Dating is a Gethsemane to which I did not want to return. I am finding the opportunities to date single adults in the church are just as infrequent and as difficult as they were for me prior to my marriage. Yet I approach it with a different attitude and perspective. I know that my marriage taught me an essential lesson about relationships and about myself that I am trying to carry into the rest of my life. I have more confidence, courage, and self-worth today than I did previously.

One of my favorite paintings, *The Singing Butler* by Jack Vettriano, hangs in my house. It depicts two people dressed in evening wear joyfully dancing with each other on a cold, rainy, and windy beach with a devout butler and a worrying maid frantically trying to hold umbrellas to protect and keep up with them. This couple does not have a care in the world and they are happy and grateful just to be with each other. It makes me smile every time I look at it because it reminds me of the grace, beauty, and joy we may have in our individual relationships despite everything that goes on around us. I think that is what relationships are about. My true hope is that someday I will have the opportunity to have a healthy, functioning relationship, and until that day, I am learning and continually striving to be happy with myself and with those around me. I have learned to accept myself despite difficulties and hardships, and despite long-term loneliness. This understanding and self-awareness is the basis for my ability to be happy as a single adult in the church.

The scripture that I was pondering and sent to Elder Perry was something Isaiah wrote, "Behold, I have graven thee upon the palms of my hands: *thy walls are continually before me.*"[1]

I know no matter what circumstances and difficulties we face, no matter how insurmountable or hard it appears, no matter how far and high we must go or for how long we must do it, that we are understood, watched over, and cared for, and that we have the capacity and capability to move forward despite the walls and obstacles we encounter.

3

Recognizing Shame— The Effects of Emotional and Relational Trauma

Hope maketh not ashamed.
—Romans 5:5

For single adults, recognizing the effects and realities of relational and emotional trauma is important, especially for those who are single for long periods of time. Many times, our incapacity to have a current relationship or the damage we received at the hands of a past failed relationship may cause shame impacting our readiness, willingness, and capability to appropriately connect and bond with others. As a result, it negatively affects our ability to develop successful and healing relationships both today and in the future. In a very real sense, these traumas self-perpetuate themselves, contributing to or causing repeated failed relationships and long-term pain or depression.

The renowned opinion and advice columnist Abigail Van Buren, better known as Dear Abby, once received a letter from a married couple who constantly argued and bickered about whether food should be covered when in the microwave. The arguments between this couple about this were so sharp that shouting matches regularly occurred. Their question to Dear Abby was how they could resolve their conflict without getting rid of the instigating and offending appliance. She answered by offering specific actions they could take to alleviate the conflict, most likely saving an unsuspecting microwave from certain doom and destruction.[1]

I suppose we can all laugh at the topic and manner of this couple's argument, perhaps because we empathize with it or we have experienced something similar ourselves. Maybe we see it as a market trend or an investment opportunity in microwave appliance makers. Even though Dear Abby's advice to this couple was specific in nature, her advice taught me the need for better understanding, greater tolerance, and more acceptance for those with whom we have personal relationships.

Disagreements are nothing new in the evolution of personal relationships. I was recently intrigued by an article about the ridiculous things couples have argued about, which ranged from the correct and proper technique for making grilled cheese sandwiches and who would turn out the light at bedtime, to how to spend hypothetical lottery winnings, what paint color to choose, and whether candy corn was a vegetable.[2] Many of these arguments were so piercing, so bitter, and so caustic they nearly ended the respective relationship.

What makes me sad about all these stories is not the minutiae and details of the argument, who was right or wrong, or the corrective actions taken, but that, for whatever reason, these couples in those moments were not able to create a healthy attachment or bond between themselves. As a result, a tear or snag occurred in the fabric of their relationship, leaving each pained and wanting. When we strive to have a better understanding of, a higher tolerance for, and a greater acceptance of ourselves and others—especially those with whom we have personal relationships—it will go a long way in preventing or at least softening many of the relational difficulties we experience. By doing this, we help to mitigate the degree of emotional and relational trauma we encounter and lessen the amount of shame we feel.

Emotional and relational traumas are the unseen but very real hurts and pains resulting from an inability to have healthy connections, attachments, or bonds in our lives. From a psychological perspective, emotional and relational traumas impact our ability to feel safe and secure with ourselves and with others.

Trauma shows up in the young woman who tries out for cheerleading and is told she is overweight and not able to be on the team. Later, she develops an eating disorder as a coping mechanism. It shows up in the young man who tries out for sporting or other teams and is told he is too small, too weak, or not good enough. As a result, he turns to substance abuse or other addictions to cope with the pain he feels. Trauma shows up in our childhood when we try to engage with others but are socially ostracized from connection or friendships, if we are teased or bullied for being different, or told through a myriad of ways that we do not belong in the group. It shows up in husbands and wives who are not able to sufficiently give or receive, preventing healthy connections between them, or between them and their children, leaving families shattered and lives broken. It also shows up in single adults who are not able to form lasting or meaningful friendships and relationships over prolonged time periods, leading to dejection and hopelessness.

The wounds that occur from the lack of healthy connections and attachments, or from exposure to abusive or deriding conditions in our lives or in our personal relationships, may rob us of our sense of self-worth and cause significant despair, discouragement, and despondency. In short, they cause or lead to our feeling shame. This shame can validate within ourselves Satan's greatest lie that we, as individuals, are of no value or that we are not worth loving either from those around us or from God.

It is my observation that those of us in the church who experience emotional and relational trauma are often counseled to merely throw our burdens on God and believe He will take care of it. I want you to know that I believe this, but I also believe this sentiment ignores the underlying problem. When we experience long-term relational trauma or emotional abuse, we often do not know *how* to or more importantly *what* to throw onto God. As a result, we need to learn to grow and strengthen ourselves as individuals to accomplish what God would have us do and to achieve the healing we so desperately need.

The martyrdom of the saints in Ammonihah and the impact it had on Amulek has given me a lot to think about. To legitimize their physical succession from the Nephites and to justify their spiritual apostasy from God, the people of Ammonihah "brought their wives and children, and whosoever believed, or had been taught to believe in the word of God and caused them to be cast into the fire."[3] When Amulek saw the torture and suffering of those consuming in the fire, he was "pained." In other words, he experienced an emotional trauma.[4] Having lived and worked in Ammonihah, Amulek knew many, if not all, of these people. It is also possible his own wife, children, or other family members were included in this martyrdom.

Amulek's first reaction was to request the power of God to prevent this tragedy altogether. Perhaps this reaction is understandable at any time a significant or hurtful event occurs, yet Alma responded to Amulek by stating the Spirit constrained them from acting and the suffering of those martyred had a divine purpose. After hearing this, Amulek responded, "Behold, perhaps they burn us also."[5]

I have often thought about the intense feeling and consuming emotion of that statement. Amulek's cry is not one of fear or anxiety for his personal safety but one of tremendous inner grief for those he loved and a sincere desire to stand with them in their pain and suffering. Alma understood this when he replied it was up to God whether they would also be burned, but because they still had a work to accomplish, it would not happen.

Sometimes the emotional hurt inflicted on those who behold is greater than the physical hurt inflicted on those who endure the act itself. In this sense, it's easy to think to ourselves, *I would rather experience a physical trauma than to endure what I am right now*. Those people who were burned suffered horribly, yet their suffering was but a moment and God blessed and received them. Amulek's suffering was not of body but of mind and spirit. This type of trauma is caused not by the event itself, but by the self-inflicted misery that comes afterward as we reflect on the event and ask ourselves why it occurred or allow ourselves to doubt our own sense of self-worth. Such feelings last much longer and often break upon those suffering like waves on a beach. Even Amulek himself needed time, love, guidance, and support to overcome his difficulties. After the martyrdom occurred, the scriptures simply record Alma took Amulek into his own house and ministered to him in his tribulations and strengthened him in the Lord.[6]

The Savior's example to us when dealing with and overcoming emotional trauma is instructive and useful. The trauma of Golgotha and Gethsemane had both a physical and a spiritual impact on the Savior. The scars He carries today are a reminder of the agonizing sacrifice He made, yet He is happy, not because of *where* He is but because of *who* He is; He does not allow the experience of the past to affect His present or His future.

I think anyone who is wrestling with an emotional trauma can learn from this example. Sometimes our troubles, tribulations, and difficulties are meant to develop positive thinking, positive outlooks, and positive perspectives in our lives. We learn to patiently endure, to calm our souls and our minds to the swirling events of our lives so we may gain experience. We see things for what they are and accept ourselves in ways only God can see. We become humble and vulnerable, which leads us to have hope not only in ourselves but also in the Savior. As a result, we can be happy and obtain healing from the emotional effects of whatever difficulties (great or small) we experience in this lifetime.

Amulek was one of the greatest men in the Book of Mormon. He experienced great abuse and emotional trauma yet through his faith and the help and understanding of others, he overcame and blessed the lives of many.

WHAT IS SHAME?

Shame is nothing new and it is inextricably tied to our experience here in mortality. In fact, the essence of shame is embedded in the events directly after the fall of Adam and Eve from the Garden of Eden. After the creation of the world, Adam and Eve were given dominion over the Garden of Eden, where they lived in direct communion with Heavenly Father and the Savior. They were naked yet they felt no shame.[7] Sometimes in the scriptures nakedness is representative of personal want, need, or depravation (i.e., "naked and ye clothed me"[8]); however, in Adam and Eve's experience I have often viewed their nakedness not as an individual burden or need but rather as an outward manifestation of the lack of shame each had in the presence of deity. Because God had created them and placed them in that condition, there was no reason or influence that should cause them to feel different about who they were, how they were living, or what they were doing.

From time to time, I hear members of the church compare the nakedness of Adam and Eve to the innocence of a small child, the idea being they lacked an understanding and ability to perceive and appropriately react to current conditions and events. Personally, I like to think of Adam and Eve's nakedness more as a genuine acceptance and comfort with oneself, with one's standing with God, and with one's surroundings. It is the definitive demonstration of vulnerability between themselves and God.

Directly after Adam and Eve partook of the fruit of the Tree of Knowledge of Good and Evil, their eyes were opened and they understood or perceived they were naked.[9] Interestingly, their first action or impulse was to cover themselves and to hide. Adam and Eve did not feel shame as a result of their actual actions of partaking of the fruit but rather by and through their cognizance and recognition of their current individual status and condition. Stated differently, they felt shame for who they were in relation and comparison to God and their surroundings. Their nakedness, which was once viewed as sacred between them and God, had now become a significant failure and an embarrassment to them.

Undoubtedly, Adam and Eve felt guilt for their disobedience; however, it was their shame in who they were and in their own impressions of their standing with themselves and with God, that caused them to cover their nakedness and to attempt, unsuccessfully and futilely, to hide from Him. Oftentimes shame has the same effects in our own lives. We look around us, longing for acceptance and connection, but our perception of our differences and inadequacies may cause us to feel shame at who we are as individuals. As a result, we numb our feelings and hide who we are, not only from ourselves and those around us, but also from God.

I truly love how Heavenly Father addressed Adam and Eve after they hid themselves in the Garden. Heavenly Father called unto Adam and Eve, saying, "Adam, where art thou?"[10] I have often pondered why God would first ask Adam this question. Indeed, He knew exactly where Adam and Eve were, what they had done, and how they were feeling. Yet, He still asked Adam where he was. Perhaps God's question was less about the physical location of Adam and Eve and more about Adam and Eve's need to recognize within themselves where they stood spiritually and emotionally.

Heavenly Father also showed tremendous compassion and forbearance by not immediately passing judgment upon them, by allowing them to come out of hiding on their own volition, and by giving them opportunity to explain in their own words and views what occurred. Adam's response to God that he hid himself because of his nakedness brought two follow-up questions from Heavenly Father:

1. "*Who* told thee thou wast naked?" and
2. "*Hast though eaten* of the tree whereof I commanded thee that thou shouldst not eat . . . ?"[11]

I often think about the sequence and order of God's questions to Adam and Eve, and I believe therein is a heavenly pattern we as members of the church may overlook.

The first question God asks is directed at the *cause* of Adam and Eve's shame, while the second question is directed at their individual *actions*. When dealing with shame in the church, we tend to do just the opposite; namely, we focus first on individuals and their actions and pay little attention to or ignore altogether the origins, causes, and sources for the shame they are feeling. We instantly judge them based upon the sins we think they have committed and fail to demonstrate empathy for their own traumas and feelings of low self-worth.

God did not excuse Adam and Eve's actions because of the shame they felt, as He caused that they should be cast out of the Garden of Eden and face the difficulty and finality of mortality; yet, He showed tremendous love and restraint by first acknowledging and validating the sources of Adam and Eve's shame, and, second, by allowing them the opportunity to recognize it for themselves, thereby empowering them to overcome that shame so they could properly contextualize, positively view, and receive the consequences of their actions without additional trauma or suffering.

Shame is both the cause and result of many of the emotional and relational traumas we experience. Oftentimes we mistake or conflate shame with guilt, an inaccuracy that is understandable as both shame and guilt deal with separation. Guilt is a separation from God, while shame is a separation or disconnection from oneself, each other, or society. Guilt derives or occurs from what we do; it's a natural consequence of making mistakes or infringing upon God's commandments. It occurs as we live in a state of opposition to the way God intended us to live.[12]

True, the failure to appropriately understand guilt may have the same negative emotional effects on us as shame; however, when correctly understood, guilt can be a healthy motive in our lives as it allows us to look to God, rely on the atonement, and seek and find forgiveness. Shame, on the other hand, has the tendency to force us to look inward and to emotionally withdraw, a state from which personal growth and development for us is more problematic and less likely.

One of my favorite books on the topic of shame and overcoming its effects is *The Gifts of Imperfection* by Dr. Brene Brown. Dr. Brown is a noted researcher and popular author on shame. She explains that the difference between shame and guilt may be understood by recognizing the difference between the following statements: "I am bad" and "I did something bad."[13] Guilt is associated with the thought that my actions or behaviors were wrong or inappropriate. Shame, on the other hand, is about a basic and negative understanding of who we are in relation to our surroundings. Dr. Brown states, "Guilt is as powerful as shame, but its effect is often positive, while shame often is destructive."[14]

Shame is not about (or derives less from) the outcome of negative behaviors, the result of unwanted actions, or unanticipated events in our life. It is an internal and subjective feeling of separation from those around us. It is the incorrect idea that we as individuals are deficient, unworthy, faulty, unfit, powerless, or worthless and that we no longer have place in society or that we can no longer connect or bond with others. As a result, shame is highly individualized and subjective. It is also not correlative to the intensity or duration of any experienced event, trauma, or condition. It is subjective to the individual emotions we derive therefrom. This means the degree of shame we feel is a product of our individual perception; two separate people experiencing the same event or condition may have dramatically different levels or gradations of shame or emotional trauma. As a result, guilt is a more general or universal concept to all of us, while shame is adapted and customized to us individually. Understanding and overcoming shame is contingent upon how we as individuals manage or cope with the adverse and deleterious experiences or emotions that are specific and unique to us.

A great example of the difference between guilt and shame is found in contrasting the experiences of Alma the Younger and Amulek. Alma and the sons of Mosiah were privileged young men. They were born to good parents who were the spiritual and civil leaders of Nephite people; yet, they struggled with living righteous lives as they endeavored to shake the faith of those around them and to actively destroy the church. How sad they tried to ruin not only themselves, but also those who loved them the most. Perhaps this reason is why the angel who appeared to them corrected them by stating, "If thou wilt be destroyed of thyself, seek no more to destroy the church of God."[15] Upon hearing this, Alma recounts he fell to the ground in realization of what he had done. He states:

> I was *racked with eternal torment,* for my soul was *harrowed up to the greatest degree* and racked with all my sins. Yea, *I did remember all my sins and iniquities,* for which I was tormented with the pains of hell; yea, I saw that *I had rebelled against my God,* and that I had not kept his holy commandments.[16]

Alma further recounts he remained tormented by this recognition for three days until he remembered, or, better said, until he became willing to call upon the Savior and rely upon the atonement for relief.

Alma's pain was based upon his feeling of guilt for knowingly and intentionally living in a manner contrary to God's teachings. The depth and depravity of those feelings should not be understated; however, these feelings had a tremendously positive influence and outcome—leading Alma to repent, to lift his perspective, and to come to the Savior. This was instructive and helpful not only for Alma himself but also for the Nephite civilization as Alma later became a prophet and an influential leader among the Nephites. One of the points I have pondered regarding Alma's conversion is the immediacy upon which Alma's guilt was assuaged. I have often wondered whether Alma's suffering could have been reduced had he prepared himself to accept the Savior on a shorter time frame, or alternatively if his suffering would have lasted longer had he not accepted the Savior. While these questions may be academic in nature, Alma's experience represents a valuable lesson; namely, those who are suffering guilt because of their actions may find prompt relief by and through their willingness and humility to rely on the Savior and His atonement.

Contrast this experience with that of Amulek (discussed previously). Amulek experienced tremendous inner pain because of his trauma at the martyrdom in Ammonihah. Perhaps the pain Amulek felt was similar in fashion and scope to that of Alma, yet Amulek's pain was not a result of any personal sin on his part. It was a result of the circumstances and conditions he faced, the powerlessness he felt, and the loss he suffered. In other words, his pain was based in shame. Without question, Amulek called and relied upon God for relief and without question those around Amulek prayed for him as well. Still, his relief took much longer and was contingent upon other factors than those experienced by Alma.

My purpose in comparing the experiences of Alma and Amulek is to point out that there is often a difference between the causes for the feelings of guilt and shame. The feelings of guilt result from negative actions or activities. Shame, on the other hand, does not result from what we believe to be wrongful conduct but is generally a consequence of our surroundings, upbringing, and the ability, or, better said, inability to cope with situations that make us feel emotionally unsafe. Even though the effects or outcomes from feelings of guilt and shame may be identical, the basis for them and the process, remedies, and timing to overcome them may be dramatically different.

When it comes to single adults, shame is often an unrecognized factor in our ability to find happiness with ourselves and with the church. Take for example a young man and a young woman who are in a dating relationship that ends. In ending the relationship, one of the participants says to the other they are not the type of person they want to take to the temple. The reason given for ending the relationship is not about whether the relationship is healthy or a good fit but about the characteristics and worthiness of the other individual in that relationship. Perhaps many in the church would ostensibly accept this reason as a correct and spiritually based decision. Perhaps it is used to shield the one ending the relationship from dealing with the emotional effects and pain of ending it (i.e., "It wasn't me. It was the other person.") The problem is, because the reason given is not about the relationship but rather about the qualities of the other person in the relationship, it has a strong tendency to cause shame in the one receiving the criticism.

Not only does the possibility exist that the receiving individual will become distraught over the loss of the relationship, but it is also possible that individual will feel embarrassed the relationship has ended when their expectations and hopes were it would last much longer. Those who find themselves unexpectedly single again are immediately thrust into an emotional dilemma that is compounded by our shattered hopes and our unrealized expectations in the church. Additionally, those instigating the breakup, despite it being their choice or actions, may not be immune to shame's effects as they also face the prospect of being single again and starting over.

Oftentimes single adults become inactive in the church, lose faith, and struggle with our testimony not because we are unworthy but because we are embarrassed or ashamed to be single again. Because of this relational shame, we pull away from others and withdraw from God. I do not intend or mean to say every relationship should always continue. Neither am I suggesting the result of every failed dating relationship will end in shame or church inactivity. The point I am making is that is too often we confuse or conflate the relational shame that comes with a breakup (or other failures in dating or relationships) with guilt. As a result, the remedy we or others apply is not what is needed or appropriate for the circumstance and may have a less effective outcome than what we intended.

In dealing with or resolving these issues, priesthood leaders or church members will often approach a newly single member or someone struggling with relationships and encourage them to increase their faith, spirituality, and activity in the church, to focus on reading the scriptures, attending the temple, or service in their callings. While these recommendations are laudable and important to single adults in our spiritual development, they may not be the solution to the problems at hand as the issue was not a lack of spirituality or faith but rather the occurrence of shame in the loss of a relationship and in the condition of being single once more.

Stated differently, the effect or harm (inactivity) was unrelated to the cause itself (loss of the relationship). As a result, priesthood leaders and church members may wonder why single adults are going inactive and why they are unable to help us in our struggles. What is really occurring is confusion as to what caused the harm and the misapplication of the remedy for it. It is a lot like trying to pound a square peg into a round hole: what is needed is a customized and fit-for-purpose solution.

Just as Heavenly Father first dealt specifically and individually with Adam and Eve's shame after the fall, what is needed is a better understanding of single adults and our individual circumstances, a chance for us to be heard, and an opportunity and space to overcome our own shame on our own terms. In doing so, we are able to extend love and friendship to those who are feeling the impacts of shame in such a way that allows them a more effective opportunity than otherwise to accept and receive it in healthy and healing ways.

IS THERE A DIFFERENCE BETWEEN WORLDLY SHAME AND PERSONAL SHAME?

Once, while walking down a street in Washington D.C., I arrived at a busy intersection where several businesses were located. On the corner numerous people stood behind a large white banner with a sign stating, "SHAME ON" and then naming the alleged offending business, in red block letters. It was apparent that a labor dispute was ongoing between this business and its workers. While such disputes are common, it was clear this labor force was trying to motivate this business to act upon or to acquiesce to its demands by and through public shaming. What struck me is there was no basis given for the shame this labor force hoped to engender and impose. It was as if the use of the word "shame" alone would empower or achieve the hoped-for result. This experience made me wonder how shame is used as a motivator in our lives and how that shame impacts our perception of the world around us.

More and more, our society is turning to shame as a tool to persuade, influence behavior, shape choice or motivate action, stifle or censor ideas, muffle debate, dominate discussion, or exercise control over individuals, groups, topics, and issues. Opposing opinions are often met with a high degree of public scorn and ridicule just for presenting different views. Too often individuals are personally attacked, called names, put down, laughed at, or debased for voicing their countering beliefs or desires. These shame tactics do not focus on the accuracy or soundness of the policies or ideas posed but rather on the morality, character, and veracity of the individual advocating or presenting them.

Perhaps the greatest detriment to this type of behavior is its tendency to encourage a feigning or artificial conformity; we accept or tolerate activities or policies that are contrary to what we think or believe, because we are afraid of being labeled or shunned by those around us. The unintended consequence of this condition is the development of a negative mentality or perspective of individuals and groups. A feeling of anxiety or helplessness derives from such conditions—especially for those conditions we are unable to change or control. As a result, people or groups may sometimes see themselves as victims, having been or currently being wronged based on societal, ideological, or individual reasons. Believing they have been diminished or shamed themselves, the sad irony is these individuals or groups seek a remedy or a change through the same instrument they experienced: the shaming or putting down of anyone or anything they perceive opposed to their beliefs.

In my experience, such situations tend to make positive change and recovery more prolonged and difficult. I do not mock or ridicule powerful feelings of people who have been exposed to terrible things; however, I believe worldly shame is in part brought about by a negative mentality that ignores other positive avenues, beneficial compromises, or workable solutions. I also believe its use and practice can perpetuate or lengthen individual or societal problems and the attendant suffering.

Perhaps the most dramatic and familiar representation of worldly shame in the scriptures occurs in the vision of the Tree of Life.[17] Both Nephi and Lehi saw multitudes of people traversing the pathways of life striving to reach the tree, partake of its fruit, and obtain both peace and joy. Some people were unwilling to embark on the journey altogether, refusing to progress despite the call of those who loved them. Others joyfully began the journey but were not resolute, quickly falling away under the trial and pressure of the difficulty they faced. Some people made the journey, enduring its trials, reaching the tree to partake of its fruit only to later become ashamed. Because of this shame, they left behind the benefit of their journey to fall into misery and darkness. Others also made the journey to reach the tree and partake of its fruit and remained faithful.

One of the key elements of this vision is the depiction of the great and spacious building. This building represents the pride of the world, and it was foundationless. Lacking substance, perspective, and happiness themselves, the people within the great and spacious building sought to curtail the happiness of those around them by mocking, ridiculing, and deriding all within their sight. By continuously casting public shame to those around them, they successfully impeded and, in many cases, derailed the opportunity for countless people to receive and maintain eternal happiness within the gospel.

Shame is such a powerful influence on the lives of those impacted by it. With its increasing prevalence today and its effects on individuals both in and out of the church, I have often thought about whether there is a difference in how the church and its members view and treat individuals who experience or suffer shame. As members of the church, we are commanded to always pick up our crosses, to bear them with courage, and to "be not ashamed."[18] Rightly or wrongly, we can view or perceive shame itself as a sin. As a result, we may turn a blind eye to the fact shame can and does exist within ourselves or within members of the church, especially single adults.

Passively acknowledging shame or ignoring it altogether is a problem because the antidote to shame is in its recognition and acknowledgement. When we hide or gloss over shame and its effects, we are providing fertile ground for its increase rather than for its decrease in our lives and in those it impacts.

So how should members of the church recognize and treat shame, and is there a difference in the worldly shame described in the scriptures and the type of personal shame experienced in everyday life? In all honesty, this is a question I have pondered greatly and I do not have all the answers. Nonetheless, I have concluded there is a distinction between worldly shame and personal shame. Worldly shame represents humiliation toward, indignation from, and a lack of commitment to the Savior and the gospel. It comes from external sources like those represented in the great and spacious building. It is focused on us from the outside in.

Personal shame, on the other hand, is representative of the individual weaknesses that each of us experience during mortality. It is internal in nature and works on us from the inside out. While we may rightly view external shame, such as embarrassment for the gospel, its precepts, and its principles, as a sin, we should never view internal shame, especially as it relates to our personal weakness, as such. Understanding and recognizing the difference between worldly shame and personal shame will assist all to have sufficient compassion and vulnerability to confront and address its effects.

Irrespective of whether an individual is experiencing worldly shame or personal shame, the remedy is the same. Nephi's answer to the shame cast upon him from those in the great and spacious building was simple and effective when he stated, "We heeded them not."[19]

In truth the ability and courage to give no heed to shame in any of its forms may not be as easy for us as it was for Nephi. Sometimes the personal shame we feel will fuel and magnify the worldly shame that is cast upon us. Thus, we are prone to worsen or intensify all forms and types of shame in our lives. Still, the shame we feel must be recognized, accepted, and validated for us to move forward in a happy and healthy manner and to accept the joy the gospel brings for each of us.

HOW DOES RELATIONAL SHAME IMPACT US?

Recently, I was walking in a local mall and noticed two teenage girls wearing white paper dunce hats inscribed with the handwritten words, "I stalk boys on Facebook." This situation was uncomfortable for me personally and made me sad for these kids and for their parents. Sometimes we laugh at situations where parents publicly shame their children as a form of punishment. Perhaps we laugh because we ourselves are uncomfortable with the situation or are unsure how to act in response. While the results of these types of shame-based exchanges are not immediately seen and may be small in nature, their long-term impacts may be just as devastating (or even more devastating) as other types of punishment constraining both the development of our self-perception and our social awareness.

Shame is a learned behavior. Think about an overwhelmed parent who unintentionally shames their child in an attempt to achieve a desired outcome. If a child misbehaves and the frustrated parent states, "Why can't you be more like the other kids?" it may temporarily curtail the child's undesired behavior, thus giving needed relief to the parent; however, shame is the ultimate and unintended result for the child. If perpetually repeated, shame becomes routine and habitual in the lives of those we are supposed to protect, uplift, and reinforce.

To give illustration, the Lamanites had an "eternal hatred" for the Nephites.[20] This hatred was omnipresent and inescapable. It was passed down from generation to generation based upon the faulty perceptions of their parents. It permeated their culture, their thinking, and their decision making. It was originally founded upon a familial dysfunction between Nephi and his two older brothers, Laman and Lemuel, that they either did not or could not remedy. This hatred caused great hardship in future generations for both the Nephites and the Lamanites, leading to the loss of the gospel for the Lamanites and centuries later the complete destruction of the Nephites.

At least in part, the development of shame in our lives follows a similar pattern, passed down from parents to children because we are unable to deal with or properly respond to the relational difficulties we face. The consequences of this generational hand-me-down may not be the destruction of nations, but it certainly leads to the destruction of testimonies, the inability to develop healthy relationships, and the inability to appropriately cope in society.

One of my favorite examples of the effects of shame on individuals and on relationships occurred with Sariah, Abraham's wife. Sariah felt tremendous indignity and shame for her inability to have or to bear children.[21] Because of this inability, Sariah gave to Abraham her handmaiden, Hagar, to wife in the hopes that she and Abraham would have access to posterity in the future. Yet once Hagar gave birth to Ishmael, relational difficulties ensued between Hagar and Sariah to such an extent that Sariah dealt harshly with Hagar. Eventually, their destructive and unhealthy relationship eroded and failed; it became so corrosive, so hostile, and so acrimonious that Sariah demanded Abraham cast out Hagar and Ishmael. This he did leaving them with nothing.

Why did this happen? What is the cause of such relational dysfunction and lack of understanding for those who are faithful? Is not shame the underlying contributor to the relational difficulties experienced and the heavy-handed outcome demanded and implemented? Consider how Sariah must have felt about herself because of her infertility. Sariah viewed this inability as a "wrong" or deficiency on her part to such an extent that she was willing to allow Abraham to enter another marital relationship in the hopes of at least indirectly rectifying this perceived personal fault.[22]

Why would Sariah feel this way? She did not cause her inability to have children, neither did it result from anything she did. God did not fault her for this deficiency as it was a natural condition beyond her individual control. Still, she felt enormous personal shame because of her inability to bear children and how she viewed herself in this condition. Sadly, this perception negatively impacted her capability to have healthy relationships with those around her.

Think about that for a moment: Sariah wanted and desired Abraham to have a child with Hagar. There was nothing immoral or wrong about this desire or in the way it was accomplished; however, when the desired outcome occurred, rejoicing and joy was not the result; rather, jealousy, envy, and malcontent arose. Perhaps Sariah came to view the giving of Hagar to Abraham as a mistake. Perhaps Hagar felt elevated in status because she gave Abraham a child when Sariah could not. Perhaps Sariah felt threatened or at least diminished in her position and role as Abraham's wife. Whatever the cause, Sariah's personal shame greatly impacted her ability to appropriately deal with the situation. It escalated emotions, impacted perceptions, and prohibited alternative solutions. As a result, her relationships with Abraham, Hagar, and Ishmael suffered.

I am not casting blame for what occurred in this ancient family. Sariah was blessed of God and the mother to the Abrahamic covenant. No one may truly know the exact circumstances and exchanges that occurred between these individuals thousands of years ago. The truth is that Sariah, Hagar, and Abraham each played a role in the relational calamity that occurred. Irrespective of the negative outcome of their relationship, their experience is helpful and representative for us in identifying and recognizing the causes of shame and its impact on us and those around us. The root of personal shame is derivative of faulty perceptions of ourselves and our life conditions. This shame has a deleterious and profound impact on our ability to connect, to promote, and to maintain healthy relationships with others in our lives.

Shame is the origin and cause of many of the choices we make and the impetus for how we react to the outcomes of those choices. Shame prevents positive and productive viewpoints on life events and experiences, desensitizes love and empathy, and solidifies negative perceptions. These reverberate far beyond ourselves and our current relationships, adversely affecting those around us and our future generations.

Given the devastating and ruinous geopolitical and religious relationship today between the descendants of Isaac and Ishmael, I have often wondered if circumstances would be different if Abraham, Sariah, and Hagar had extended love and empathy toward each other rather than hatred, rejection, and discontent. Regardless, our task is to recognize the shame, hurt, and trauma we bring to each relationship, to understand and learn from it, and to reduce relational dysfunctions and deficiencies. In so doing we will enhance our ability to give acceptance and to receive love rather than to experience rejection, pain, and tragedy.

OVERCOMING RELATIONAL SHAME

When I was younger I swam competitively and worked as a lifeguard. One of the practice drills I used to undertake was to tread water in the deep end of the pool with a heavy rubber block held over my head. At first, I could easily keep the block high out of the water. As the drill continued, I would grow tired and become progressively unable to hold the block up. I would repeatedly drop down under the water and come up gasping for air, each time increasing in difficulty. Eventually the weight of the block and my hold on it dragged me completely under the water, and I was forced to let go of it to surface and to breathe.

My marriage relationship was a lot like this swimming drill. At first, the difficulty of the relationship was manageable. The joy of being married and the hope of an eternal relationship buoyed me up; however, over time, as the level of exertion required in the relationship increased, my ability to cope with the difficulties of the situation decreased and I began to be emotionally dragged down.

I tried to hide the effects of the relational trauma that occurred. I struggled as best I could to stay afloat, but I was ashamed by the circumstances and conditions I experienced. I frantically clung to the relationship hoping it would fix itself, believing everything would work out, yet I kept sinking deeper and deeper into pain and self-doubt. Indeed, it was like holding onto a dual-edged razor—the tighter I held on, the more difficult it became and the more hurt it inflicted. Eventually, I lost what was most precious, myself. I was forced to stand in my greatest fears and pains and let go. It was at that moment that I had a choice: I could stay in those feelings or pick myself up and work on getting better.

After my divorce, I kept hoping by some miracle my ex-wife would return and things would work themselves out, whether in this life or the next. I knew the relationship was unhealthy, but I continually asked myself questions such as: *Why did this happen? Can I live in a relationship that is out of balance? Should I continue to pursue or be in a relationship where there is little or no forgiveness or repair and where there is no connection?* I was also faced with the question of how to let go of someone I love. The real question I asked myself, though, is whether it was better to have an unhealthy relationship in my life or to have no relationship and live alone. I felt defective inside. I felt there was something wrong with me that was preventing me from having the healthy relationship I so truly desired.

As I look back and reflect upon it, I was suffering from a very real trauma caused by a long-term lack of connection and attachment. I was a good but imperfect man with a kind and gentle heart, who wanted to have a healthy relationship with his wife and family but was not able to do so. A large part of my issue was I pursued and sought for self-validation from having a relationship. In other words, I felt like I was nobody because I couldn't enter or sustain either a dating or marital relationship.

This was an unhealthy perspective on my part because I felt tremendous inner shame at the breakdown and loss of the relationship. I had been giving to the relationship for the sake of the relationship, but that effort was not received or reciprocated. When the desired, wanted, hoped-for connection did not occur, I would become hurt and angry. As a result, I would contribute to the relationship's dysfunction through emotional protests of arguing, withdrawing, or giving in to the situation. The intensity of my feelings and these protests increased as the relationship steadily worsened and deteriorated.

Part of my unhealthy behavior was not having the internal fortitude or strength of character early on to stand up for myself or to have the willingness to let go of a relationship that was not beneficial to my own well-being. From an outside perspective, this is difficult to understand or to explain, especially for the church and its members as it relates to the eternal nature of the marriage relationship. Yet I have observed these types of conditions happen all too frequently and in varied forms or degrees with too many people. The relational dysfunction of my marriage changed who I was, how I perceived events, and how I reacted to them.

I used to joke that I didn't swear for twenty years and then, when I got married, I swore like a sailor. Today, I better understand what happened and what my role and contribution was to that dysfunction. Because I recognize my own role in the breakdown of my marriage relationship, I can step back and recognize the truth and better accept it. I also know what occurred in the relationship and know that my reactions to it were not really a reflection of who I am as in individual. Rather, they were a response to difficulties and conditions I neither understood nor could change.

Fortunately, I had good priesthood leaders, counselors, friends, and family who put their arms around me, stood by me, and helped me pick myself up. My shame and hurt didn't change overnight, and my initial path forward was not clear. I recognized I had experienced something traumatic, but it took time for me to internalize it and to change how I felt about myself. The journey I have made and the internal process I experienced have strengthened me and allowed me to find joy and happiness despite a lack of a marriage relationship in my life. I still desire such a relationship, but I know better today who I am, what contribution I can make, and what allows me to find peace in this lifetime.

Today, I know I cannot simply focus on having or being in a relationship, particularly if that focus is at the expense of everything else. Having a healthy relationship is first about being healthy with myself and then about having the courage and capacity to risk becoming sufficiently vulnerable to someone else in healthy ways that benefit the relationship and enhance each other.

4

Moving Forward and Establishing Yourself as a Single Adult

> We are troubled on every side, yet not distressed;
> we are perplexed, but not in despair; persecuted,
> but not forsaken; cast down, but not destroyed.
> —2 Corinthians 4:8–9

How do we as single adults move forward in our lives, particularly after traumatic and difficult experiences? How do we find peace of mind, stillness of soul, and calm of heart after tremendous hurt, rejection, and failure? How do we turn something negative into something positive?

I found I needed to do two things: accept and remember my past, and develop enough internal character to make progress despite it. There is an old saying, "Put bad things in your back pocket and leave them there." For me, moving forward was about doing just that, keeping difficult emotions and feelings behind me instead of in front of me. It was about trying to view my difficulties, shame, and hurt as something from my past that strengthened me rather than something I constantly had to wade through or grapple with during each new experience.

It was no longer about slaying dragons I could never overcome but using these experiences as pillars of support that I could rely on in my journey. It was about not living in a constant state of fear but continuously learning and trying new things to develop the appropriate tools to be open to new opportunities, to look forward to new connections, to see things in a positive light, and to be satisfied with the results if I failed. I realize now the greatest gift I can give to myself is the ability to connect in meaningful ways with myself, with God, and with those around me.

After the House of Israel had completed their testing forty-year journey in the wilderness, they crossed the Jordan River on dry ground and entered their new life of pursuing and obtaining the Promised Land. Before continuing forward, they stopped and erected a unique memorial consisting of twelve large stones that they had carried with them from Jordan. The purpose of carrying these twelve stones was to remember the hardship of where they came from, the weight and burden of their journey, and to recognize and honor the promises, covenants, and blessings of God to the House of Israel.[1]

The symbolism of this effort represents the importance of recognizing not only the benefit of the opportunities and blessings we receive today but also remembering, in a positive manner, our struggle with the preceding difficulty we lived through. It is about carrying and shouldering the load and strain of the past, fostering the capability to objectively contemplate and remember it, looking ahead despite it, and progressing in constructive ways toward greater opportunities and purposes. It's about being forward-looking rather than backward-looking. It's also about being able to accept our past traumas in ways that we do not emotionally relive them.

Part of my journey in overcoming my own relational traumas was learning about who I was and being okay with that despite what previously occurred. There were many times when I needed to stop and reflect on the painfulness of my past, not out of sadness or shame, but to remember its importance and relevance in my life—to ground and remind myself I have value and I matter as an individual.

I learned to carry the onus and trauma of my past into my future. I established my own personal memorials or ebenezers to help me recognize where I stand today as compared to yesterday, to acknowledge the progress I have made, and to create a firm setting for my personal growth going forward.* These are reminders for me, like the heavy stones the Israelites carried from the trial of their past life into the peace of their new life, that God was in my life and a part of its details. They remind me that I have worth and purpose even as I work to recognize and receive greater blessings and op-

---

* Ebenezer means "Stone of Help" (see *Bible Dictionary*). After a great military victory over the Philistines that preserved the sovereignty and way of life for the Israelites, Samuel the prophet erected a large stone as a memorial and called it Eb-enezer (see Samuel 7:5–13). Like the twelve stones the Israelites carried over Jordan, it is a marker to establish the goodness of God and the triumph of our souls in overcoming the difficulties and trials of our lives.

portunities. They are core values and positive affirmations in my daily life, empowering me to stand each time I fall and motivating me to step forward even when I cannot or will not. They are the building blocks and the foundation for my turning darkness into light, difficulty into triumph, and bitterness into hope.

Whenever I struggled the most, I would write these core values on pieces of paper and physically stand on them just to remind myself in a small but personal way that I was okay, that I stood for something important, that I was loved, and that things would work out. Each of us should establish and raise our own personal and unique ebenezers to direct and guide our thinking and emotions, to anchor our souls, and to remind us of from where we have come so we may safely and confidently move forward.

The following are a few of the personal ebenezers I focused on, developed, and continue to apply in my life.

EBENEZER #1: IT'S OKAY NOT TO BE OKAY

In April 2014, CNN published an article about Adrianne Haslet-Davis, a professional dancer who lost her leg in the Boston Marathon Bombing.[2] The loss of her limb not only placed a physical impairment on her ability to dance but also caused significant emotional wounds that took a substantial amount of effort from which to recover. She indicated that after her injury, she initially felt she would just get her prosthetic leg and go on with her life; however, she found there was a tremendous amount of work she needed to do to get better. She said as the reality of her recovery unfolded she needed to take a hard look at herself and learn it's "okay not to be okay." I love the sentiment that it's okay not to be okay. It means we can connect and be present with ourselves, our emotions, and our spirituality so we are able to process them in positive ways, even when our feelings are negative.

Sometimes, as members of the church, whether single or married, we put on a brave face and smile even though everything around us is crumbling and in turmoil. We will tell ourselves how blessed we are on the outside but think something totally different on the inside. Occasionally, I will hear some individuals tell me that each day they have is the best day they have ever experienced. As a result, their life is a successive and unending calendar of days that are happier and more joyful than the previous. While I do not diminish the idea that happiness is a choice and that this sentiment expresses the importance of being happy each day, I often cringe when I hear statements like these as they can lead to the disregarding or de-emphasis of important feelings and emotions in our lives.

Our emotions interact with each other to create a balance in our lives. The problem comes when we try to maintain a controlled balance or to artificially generate an emotional outcome by diminishing the impacts of other emotions, to dampen emotions we deem negative in favor of those we deem positive. The consequence of valuing some emotions over others may lead to the destruction of our own emotional reality and the inability to cope in real time with real life situations.

The shortest verse in all of scripture is, "Jesus wept."[3] The brevity of this verse does not lessen its example or meaning, as the Savior himself felt sadness, disappointment, grief, and a multitude of other emotions that we ourselves may feel are negative. He lived with these emotions and expressed them in healthy ways without ignoring or discarding them in favor of other emotions. Life isn't about being happy without sadness; it isn't about having only positive rather than negative emotions. Life is about being happy through incorporating these things in positive ways into our lives so we may constructively experience and cope with the daily subtleties and complexities as they come. Ignoring or discounting our emotions and feelings, no matter what they are, impacts our perspective and our ability to cope with life's challenges in healthy ways.

Sometimes as single adults and members of the church we preoccupy ourselves with the idea of being perfect, but it is often more than that. We care not only about our ability to be perfect, but also to have others view us as such. We concern ourselves and fret over small details and forget that salvation is intended to be a process, a step-by-step approach to becoming sanctified. We worry we are not perfect right now and inwardly feel shame when the goal of perfection is not immediately achieved. We forget God gave us not only physical but spiritual weaknesses for the express purposes of learning humility and having the opportunity and motivation to come to the Savior.[4] Think about that for a moment: Do we view our weaknesses as a scarlet letter that must be shamefully borne or as a benefit to help us achieve salvation itself? The difference between the two views makes all the difference in our capacity to grow and be happy in our lives.

When I was a student at BYU, I taught for a short time at the Missionary Training Center. At that time, the Missionary Training Center taught a regimented missionary plan whereby missionaries would meet people interested in learning about the church, then teach and baptize them within a proscribed three-week period. Having served my mission in Switzerland,

I knew the Swiss people generally needed additional time for conversion, sometimes taking years before showing a desire to join the church. I struggled with teaching these new missionaries that individuals would feel the Spirit, show a willingness to change their lives, and join the church in such a short time period. I felt I was teaching them to set goals they would seldom, if ever, achieve and the failure to achieve these goals would cause future difficulty for them when they were serving in their assigned areas. As I prayed for inspiration, the Spirit taught me the missionary plan set out by the church was what *could* happen but not necessarily what *would* happen. As a result, it was important for me to first teach these missionaries what the model was before allowing them to experience what really occurs.

The Savior did something similar when He declared, "Therefore I would that ye should be perfect even as I, or your Father who is in heaven is perfect."[5] This declarative statement is a high standard and goal for each of us. Why would the Savior give us such a challenge when He knew of our imperfections? My only conclusion is the Savior wants us to achieve our greatest potential and our greatest happiness by becoming a celestial people. He did not say or teach we should live terrestrial lives. To say otherwise would be to justify our own failure to try or to excuse an unwillingness on our part to progress. Yet, I sometimes believe we take this commandment too literally because of our own expectations, perceptions, and timelines. Perhaps a better way to think about this scripture is to change the word "be" to "become" or to add the phrase "in accordance with the principles of the gospel." In that way, we can simultaneously find peace of mind and joy while still accepting our own circumstances and realities, with the realization that work and development is still needed.

For single adults, this idea of perfection can be excruciatingly painful. Our faith teaches (and we believe) marriage and family are the highest goals of salvation. Whether directly or indirectly, the church places an enormous emphasis on single adults entering a marriage relationship. Bishops, mission presidents, and other priesthood leaders actively encourage single adults to find a life partner and to start a family as quickly as possible, the rationale being that single adults need a push or encouragement to take such an important step in our lives, that we are intentionally putting off marriage, or that we are not willing to settle down before meeting personal goals such as finding employment or completing our education.

This perception, coupled with the inability or delay in becoming married, often wears single adults down emotionally. Not only do we face loneliness, but we may also start doubting ourselves, our faith, and even our future because we are temporarily unable to achieve this desired or required outcome. Knowing we are currently imperfect regarding the church's teachings and expectations compounds the pressure and stress we feel about being single.

Additionally, many single adults are separated or divorced, which may amplify our feelings of shame as we have already entered a marriage relationship and been unsuccessful in it. I have often wondered why this is so, as divorce and failed relationships have been around for a long time.[6] I like to believe Heavenly Father gave divorce to us knowing unhealthy relationships destroy rather than lift us. It is a healing mechanism to allow us to move on in our lives.

Despite this, I often see shame manifested in those who are divorcing or who are divorced through a finger-pointing exercise into the faults of their ex-spouse. If we can vilify or demonize our ex-spouse sufficiently enough, we think it will justify or alleviate the shame of divorce in the eyes of the church. However, all this attribution accomplishes is a projection of our own shame onto our ex-spouse. How sad that makes me. The only consequence is a perpetual sense of victimization and rationalization of hurt and pain, irrespective of whether it's justified. This obstructs and hinders our ability to have hope and to find joy in our current situation.

Part of healing from emotional or relational trauma, especially for single adults, is not living for what other people think or even for what we believe we should feel or do. Healing comes from accepting our circumstances and learning to be open and vulnerable with ourselves and with God. It is about accepting, in healthy ways, our weaknesses and our imperfections. Being vulnerable is about recognizing difficult and painful emotions inside of us, not painting them over or discarding them. It's about looking in the mirror and saying, "Right now I feel lonely, hurt, isolated, and that's okay." It's about developing enough inner strength to stand in our greatest pains and be still. It is also about finding and developing workable solutions that are appropriate to our circumstances. For all those times I wished someone else would carry my burdens or wondered why I was tasked with this in my life, I am now learning to carry what I can and to discard the rest. In so doing I am redefining who I am and what I can be.

When Nephi broke his bow while journeying in the wilderness, it created a serious and dangerous circumstance for him and his family. Nephi's bow was special, made of fine and precious steel; it was important and highly prized for its effectiveness in providing for their food and basic needs. Its loss, and thus the inability to acquire food, created need, controversy, and complaint not only from his brothers but also from his father, Lehi, and from everyone else.

Because the scriptures do not say Nephi was negligent in his bow's breaking, it's plausible that it broke in the normal course of use. Irrespective of the cause, it's curious and contradictory that Laman and Lemuel were incensed at Nephi because their own bows had lost their spring and had become equally ineffective. Laman and Lemuel projected their anger onto Nephi, even though the impact from the loss of Nephi's bow was no less than the impact from the losses of theirs. Because of their dire condition, all except Nephi murmured and became victims of their own circumstances.

Nephi's action was not to sulk or lament, but to evaluate the resources he had available to him and to find a workable solution by making a new bow. Maybe that bow was not as impressive or effective as his previous bow, but it was productive enough to sustain him and his family. Nephi had sufficient vulnerability and character to accept the reality of his circumstances and to be in control of his emotions and feelings when others could or would not. It enabled him to find imperfect but practicable solutions to provide for himself and for those around him.[7]

After my divorce, I found myself in the unenviable situation of selling my old home and moving into a new one. Most of the furniture and short-term savings I had available were distributed in the divorce settlement and I had few resources to acquire other furnishings. I had a home, four walls, and a roof over my head, but very little on the inside. I had a great job but an empty bank account that needed time to recover from the adverse financial impact of the divorce.

Each time I came home it reminded me of my loss as well as the emptiness and brokenness of my past. Yet, I determined to improve. I wanted my home to be a place where I could live comfortably while being inviting to others. Rather than become discouraged for what I didn't have, I viewed it as an opportunity to rebuild. I identified my needs and my available resources. Since I had no design skills or abilities, I sought affordable help and advice putting an interior design and plan together. I then went to work. I searched and scoured Craigslist, garage sales, and clearance sales to find the items that fit my plan. I wasn't hurried, and I was particular about what I acquired. If something didn't fit the plan, it was not purchased. If I found an item I needed (in my price range), it was generally damaged and needed to be repaired—which I was happy to do.

This process took over three years to complete. It was a course of discovery, exploration, and effort that became fun for me. I was amazed at what

I could find and what I could accomplish based on what I had available to me. In the end, I was able to create something that was beneficial, useful, and comfortable for me and for those who visited. People who came to my home did not see the damaged items or the repair that was done, nor did they notice the place or manner from where these furnishings came. They saw something worthwhile and marveled at its qualities. They often stated this was not typical for a bachelor pad and wondered how it was done. This always made me smile, not because of pride, but because I knew the necessity and innovation behind it. I also knew the many defects and imperfections that combined to make something greater than it was previously.

Overcoming my relational traumas and rebuilding my life was a lot like my effort to rebuild my house; it didn't happen overnight and it didn't occur randomly, but happened on limited resources through planned and sustained effort over time. It was about taking what I had available, even if it was previously discarded, and making it useful in my life. It was recognizing I was a work in progress, acknowledging I was imperfect, and then continuously doing all I could to improve.

Like my moving into a new home without furniture, we as single adults may appear fine on the outside but feel incomplete or empty on the inside. Alternatively, we may feel like Nephi, existing in or trying to cross a foreign wilderness with inadequate or broken tools that are necessary to provide for ourselves. By maintaining an accurate sense of reality, by accepting our emotions and not allowing ourselves to become victims of circumstance, we too may find imperfect but workable solutions with the resources available to us that will allow us to be successful in our lives. Being happy and finding value with ourselves is about learning we are okay, even when we do not see or feel it, and learning to accept events and circumstances in our lives that are positive and beneficial. It is also about being creative with what we have available to us, no matter the scarcity, and using that in meaningful ways that discover beauty, increase worth, and enhance functionality despite our own brokenness.

EBENEZER #2: I AM WORTH LOVING AND SAVING

During my divorce I received a call from a close friend, a member of the church with whom I was scheduled to play golf. Apologetically, he canceled our plans and told me he could no longer associate with me while my divorce was ongoing. To be frank, this sentiment caught me off guard. I didn't understand his reasoning and I was hurt.

"What does my friendship with him have to do with my divorce?" I asked myself. Becoming divorced was not my choice, so why was I now exposed to this type of perspective? I was already feeling alone from the breakdown of my marriage, and now I learned that at least some in the church viewed me differently—maybe as less than an ideal member of the church— because of my relational situation. There was a stain on me to which I didn't know how to react or how to respond. While this reaction to my divorce was not representative of most people I knew in the church, it significantly impacted me. Part of my personal journey was learning I have worth and value irrespective of the choices, biases, and reasoning of other people. I had to learn I am worth loving and saving.

When Abraham cast Hagar out, he exiled not only her but also their son Ishmael. Abraham, who had great means, provided only bread and a limited amount of water for the two. They were required, without notice or preparation, to leave all they had and all they knew, with nothing. Hagar wandered lost, abandoned, and alone in the wilderness until her scant provisions were exhausted. Devastated, broken, and confused, she placed Ishmael under a bush so she would not have to watch him perish and walked a short distance away where she sat and wept.[8] How truly desolate she must have felt. Fortunately, God sent an angel who spoke to her and who provided lifesaving resources for them. Eventually, they found and established new lives and new opportunities for themselves.

Perhaps we may think Hagar deserved the consequence she received: cast aside and excluded with nothing but her wits. Paul even compared Abraham's casting out of Hagar to the difference between the law of Moses and the gospel. He argued that Abraham chose the superior way because Sariah bore Isaac from the covenant, and Hagar bore Ishmael not from the covenant but from bondage.[9] Paul's meaning was the law of Moses (i.e. Hagar and Ishmael) did not lead to salvation but the benefit of the gospel did (i.e. Sariah and Isaac). In other words, because Hagar did not have the same type of relationship that Abraham had with Sariah, Hagar's exclusion was both acceptable and appropriate.

Whatever the reasoning or justification for Abraham's actions, the individual impact to both Hagar and Ishmael was draconian and life-threatening. For Abraham to banish Hagar and his son Ishmael without substance sufficient to sustain them was not his finest action. God did not condone

Abraham's decision to expel his wife and son, but neither did He prevent it; however, He did provide the means to Hagar to overcome its effects.

Single adults in the church, especially divorced single adults, may feel a lot like Hagar: unfairly cast out from broken relationships or unjustly ostracized from familiar circumstances. Lost in a wilderness of emotion, hardship, and loneliness, we are required to find the means for our own survival and that of our children, oftentimes with few resources or skills at our disposal. Isolated, marooned, and bereft of benefits hoped for or previously enjoyed, we may now feel segregated from the church and its membership. We may see ourselves as second-class members, having access to the church but having separate entrances into it. Additionally, we may feel shamed by others who believe the failure of the relationship is deserved or our fault.

Is it any wonder that, like Hagar, we break down, give up, and walk away? These situations are truly devastating, though the aftermath and consequences are not always immediately seen or understood. They ensue not only in our lives and in the lives of those impacted by the breakdown of the relationship, but they also affect relationships, perceptions, and connections with others. Ultimately, they may diminish the value and worth that we have or see in ourselves both within and outside the church.

Abraham's expulsion of Hagar and his justification for doing so is correlative and provides insight into the complexity, perspective, and bias many single adults may experience or feel in the church, especially as it relates to their perceived value and worth as individuals. Part of the reason for Hagar's expatriation was that Abraham prioritized his relationship with Sariah over his relationship with Hagar. If one accepts Paul's argument that Abraham's marital relationship with Hagar was less valuable because it was not a "covenant" or an ideal type of relationship, do members of the church likewise view single adults differently, thinking we have less worth because we also do not have that type of relationship? Do members of the church legitimize a lack of inclusion, a lack of opportunity, or a lack of connection with single adults based solely on our relational status?

This issue is not one of association with the church but rather one of preference, significance, and merit of the single adults in it. How do members of the church perceive and treat those who are single or those who have broken relationships in their lives? Like Abraham toward Hagar, do members perfunctorily accept single adults when there is need or benefit for our presence but cast us aside without means or assistance when difficulties, misunderstanding, or failure occur? Do members wish single adults well but turn their backs to us when alternative circumstances arise? Do members judge single adults as less than desirable or suppose we are less than worthy or not able to substantively contribute because we are single? Alternatively, do members offer love, acceptance, and support to single adults in meaningful ways? The answers to these questions have a direct bearing on how single adults view and value ourselves within the church.

My favorite part to Hagar's story was not her trial and struggle, but that God loved her enough to reach from the Heavens to save her and Ishmael in their greatest time of need. He did not take sides between Abraham or Hagar, neither did He withhold comfort, love, or blessings from Hagar because of her relational status or divorce. To the contrary, He provided means and deliverance for both her and Ishmael. Even though Hagar and Ishmael's relationship with Abraham was not reconciled, they went forward in their lives. That is what God does for us. He allows us to experience failure but gives us the tools to be successful. Remember, even He cast the children of Israel into the wilderness for forty years because of their rebellion, yet, unlike Abraham, still He fed them, He lead them by day and by night, He healed them, and He made sure their feet never swelled and their raiment never wore out.[10] Is this not true love? Is this not a demonstration of the meaning and value that He has for each of us? He reaches toward us. He does not wait for us to come to Him, nor does He leave us to our own devices. He encourages, extends, and cheers each of us from afar. He allows us to make weak things strong and provides hope where previously none existed.

When we, like Hagar, feel forsaken and lost, or when we face our greatest extremity or adversity, do we have the capacity and courage to turn to God? Can we independently stand and find love and acceptance for ourselves despite previous rejection and despite the adverse actions or unwanted choices of others? After my divorce, these are the questions I repeatedly asked myself. What I was really debating was my value as an individual to the church and to others. Learning to overcome this burden, to accept myself and others even if such acceptance was not reciprocated, was not easy.

Part of the solution for me, whenever I faced these circumstances or feelings, was to strive for self-sufficiency while simultaneously being more open to and reliant upon God. I gained greater hope and faith by doing this. I learned to find strength I did not previously have. When my efforts were insufficient, I learned to rely on God for the strength I lacked. As I grew, it no longer mattered to me what others thought or whether I experienced differences in the church. Of most importance to me was what I thought of myself and what God thought of me. While God did not remove the weight of my burden entirely, He certainly made it lighter to bear. I learned of His awareness of me in my life. I saw His hand moving me, guiding me, and allowing me to find my own sense of value and worth. I learned what the Savior meant when he stated, "Be patient in afflictions, for thou shalt have many; but endure them, for, lo, I am with thee, even unto the end of thy days."[11]

For those of us who are silently struggling, who are in despair, or who feel worthless because of who we are or because of our lack of a relationship, I am truly sorry for the hurt and pain you are experiencing. I wish I could wave a magic wand and fix it for you, but I can't. I believe things will always work out if we stay positive, have hope, and make healthy choices; for there is no hurt, there is no pain, there is no trial the effects of which Heaven cannot remove. Like Hagar, we are each worth loving and saving and we each have value and worth beyond our relationships. Accepting that is important and possible if we allow it. God loves us because of who He is and not because of who we are, what relationships we have, or what we do. That makes all the difference for me in the value, worth, and salvation of my soul.

EBENEZER #3: I WILL ACT FOR MYSELF AND NOT BE ACTED UPON

When I was young, I learned a nursery rhyme about an egg named Humpty Dumpty who was sitting on a wall. Disastrously, Humpty fell from where he sat and tragically broke. Despite good and heroic attempts, all the king's horses and all the king's men were unsuccessful in their efforts to fix and repair Humpty.

I found it curious Humpty was on a wall in the first place and that his fall had caused such a calamitous and traumatic event. I had this odd picture in my mind of all these people frantically trying to superglue pieces of a shattered egg back together. As I grew older, I began to think this nursery rhyme had more meaning. Humpty had suffered a horrific injury; one that was not easily or quickly repaired. Perhaps Humpty was at fault or had behaved recklessly by placing himself in those circumstances. Perhaps he was merely naïve, unaware of the danger. Whatever the cause, many skilled, professional, and noble people tried valiantly to save Humpty but their efforts were in vain.

Sometimes in life we experience great trauma or tragedy and are figuratively knocked off our places of comfort, shattering our reality and causing emotional or spiritual damage. We reach out to friends, family, counselors, church leaders, and other people or resources, saying, "Here I am. I am hurt. Fix me." Yet we are discouraged or disappointed because we do not receive the help we think we need. Part of the reason all the king's horses and all the king's men were unsuccessful in helping Humpty is because Humpty's injury was of the type they could not fix. It was up to Humpty himself to pick up the pieces and move forward.

Each of us struggles with some form of weakness or brokenness in our lives. Sometimes that brokenness comes from nature or our surroundings. Sometimes it is imposed on us from others or is a consequence of the choices we make. The definitive struggle in our lives is not overcoming weakness, it is to find sufficient courage to change ourselves at a base and fundamental level despite those weaknesses. We may say to ourselves, "I have fallen, I am broken, I am down in the mud, and I need to get back to a clean slate." We begin to believe happiness is the proverbial pot of gold at the end of a rainbow, something within sight but ever just out of reach.

Perhaps in this light it is easy to assume we are always halfway to happiness, yet the road to it is littered with potholes and long detours or is continuously under construction. As a result, we may tell ourselves we are not talented or skilled enough to reach our destination. The bigger victory is for each of us to pick ourselves up in whatever circumstance we are in, take control of our own happiness, and move forward. Hope in ourselves and in the Savior is the driving force that allows us to stand, to dust off the dirt and grime, and to exercise faith. The primary purpose of our lives is to live, and we each have tremendous opportunity to choose how we accomplish that. How wonderful it is for us to have charge not only for our direction but also for the way we move forward.

Learning to act for myself meant having sufficient emotional character to control my thought processes, to acknowledge my feelings in stressful situations, and to choose how I respond. It was about becoming mentally and spiritually ready to stand on my own. It was about recognizing what I was afraid of most of in my life, understanding how that fear impacted my perspective and decisions, and developing the inner strength to accept that fear. It also meant having the courage to make my own decisions and choices and not allowing circumstances or others to dictate those to me. As a result, I had to learn and become willing to accept the consequences and outcomes of those choices, whether positive or negative.

The experiences of Abinadi and King Noah contrast the difference between an out-of-control life led from fear and an inability to make choices for oneself and the life that is possible when one chooses and acts for oneself despite one's fears. King Noah was a spoiled despot who lived an entitled life off the work and substance of his people, a man who replaced spiritual leaders with those who were self-minded, and who encouraged his people to live in a manner that was inconsistent with who they were.[12] When the Lamanites began a military campaign against them, King Noah sent his armies against the Lamanites with initial success, but that success was short-lived and over-emphasized as they became overconfident and indolent in their ability to defend the city. They lost perspective as they traded long-term security for short-term victory.

During this time, and at great risk to his life, Abinadi worked with King Noah's people and taught them about the gospel. Eventually, he was imprisoned and brought before King Noah on false charges of sedition. Alone, Abinadi stood before King Noah and his priests to defend the gospel and to witness to them of their wickedness. So great was the power God gave to Abinadi as he spoke that King Noah and his men dared not touch him. Irrespective, several days later, King Noah sentenced Abinadi to death if Abinadi would not recant his words. Abinadi refused, saying he was innocent and, if King Noah carried out this sentence, his words would stand as a witness and testimony against King Noah. Knowing the truth, or at least recognizing the gravity and potential consequences of his decision, King Noah hesitated, almost setting Abinadi free. Briefly, King Noah knew and understood the fear and judgment of God. Still, King Noah was not able to withstand the ridicule and pressure of his priests and executed Abinadi in a vicious and savage manner.[13]

The cowardice of King Noah did not end there as, when faced with annihilation from the Lamanites, he abandoned those whom he was supposed to protect. In an ironic and befitting end, King Noah died at the hands of those who remained with him, in a similar manner to Abinadi. King Noah's life was a tragic and pathetic consequence of his inability to act for himself; a life dominated and controlled by his own fears, choices, lifestyle, and the influence of those around him. King Noah was not able to act for himself despite knowing it was the right thing to do and despite knowing that great consequence would come. How sorrowful and tragic.

Abinadi, on the other hand, stood in the face of overwhelming and unfair judgment. By contrast, despite his own fears, Abinadi could act and choose for himself. Abinadi felt fear, but it did not control him. His actions were not motivated by self-preservation. Rather, he worked for the benefit of others and for something much greater than himself. While Abinadi did not choose the outcome of his actions, his life was far more stable, far more meaningful, and far more impactful than King Noah's life.

Learning to act for ourselves is about developing the courage to engage, the willingness to begin, and the capacity to move and take steps forward. The story of Gideon and his readiness to choose and to act for himself is a useful and illuminating example. Israel was in bondage to Midian for more than seven years when God chose Gideon to raise and lead the Israelite army against the Midianites. When the Israelite army was gathered, God told Gideon this army was too large. As a result, Gideon reduced it to a paltry three hundred men to face the entire might of the Midianite forces. (I have often pondered how these three hundred men felt when Gideon informed them of this decision and of their mission.) God required this troop reduction to demonstrate to the Israelites it was God who freed them and not the strength of their army. At night, Gideon's men surrounded the Midianite army and charged. The noise, fear, and confusion of the charge caused the Midianite army to start fighting amongst and between themselves, leading to their self-destruction. Gideon thus gained a great victory and freed the Israelites from bondage.

After Gideon's triumph, the tribe of Ephraim, who had chosen not to act by denying military support and refusing to participate in the battle, arrived and bitterly complained they were not given an opportunity to fight. They were like a blister that showed up after all the work was done, trying to take credit, without effort or sacrifice. Exhibiting diplomacy and leadership, Gideon resolved a tense situation between Ephraim and the other tribes through soft words and pacification.

Unfortunately, Ephraim did not learn its lesson. Several years later they repeated this same pattern when Jephtah lead the Israelites to victory over the Ammonites. This time, however, when Ephraim arrived after the battle was concluded and complained they were not given an opportunity to fight, Jephtah destroyed the forty-two thousand Ephraimites who arrived.[14] How grievous, how lamentable, and how awful this result and outcome were.

The examples of Gideon and the tribe of Ephraim demonstrate the difference between action and inaction in our lives. Gideon demonstrated a willingness to act even in the face of overwhelming odds. Ephraim failed to act not once but twice, leading first to great consternation within all the tribes and second to great destruction for Ephraim itself. Here, as in the Savior's parable of the ten talents, where those who received and acted were blessed and he who received and acted not was cast out, we learn if we cannot act for ourselves today, we may not be able or willing to bear the burden or to accept the costs later.[15]

By recognizing and learning to overcome our weaknesses, by facing our fears and not letting them have power over us, and by taking beneficial actions, we will be able to face and overcome the challenges and obstacles in our lives. Having self-awareness and courage will be an advantage to us, not a burden, no matter how hard or long the struggle. Learning to act for myself was about having the will to step into the batter's box, grip the bat, and take my swing, knowing that if I didn't, nothing would happen. It was about having the courage to risk failure and to be okay with myself if I missed. For single adults, learning to act for ourselves, to initiate and to do, will help to free us from the terrible feelings of loneliness and despair we may feel.

Initiating and doing is about finding and developing honesty with ourselves. It's an inner quest to discover and reduce those things that hold us back, those things that keep us tied down, and those things that stilt our spirit, conscience, and energy. It's about finding purpose and passion for our lives, in whatever form or manner, and then having the fortitude and determination to go out and do it. It's also about having the capacity to choose for ourselves, to chart the destiny of our souls, and to have the resoluteness to be content with the results. It's not about waiting on an outcome or waiting on a relationship to find fulfillment for our lives. Like Gideon, no matter the difficulty of the task or the size, strength, or capability of our effort, we can find success if we will have the courage to simply stand and to try.

EBENEZER #4: LEAVE THE PAST IN THE PAST

Sometimes those of us who are suffering from emotional and relational trauma react strongly to small or seemingly unimportant things in the present because it reminds us of a past trauma that triggers difficult and unresolved emotions. In a very real sense, we are stuck in an emotional eddy, constantly reliving our traumas. Like an underground geyser, we are on a continual low boil waiting for sufficient buildup or the opportune moment to erupt. Essentially, we are living backwards rather than forwards and are stunted or prevented from seeing progress in ourselves.

How do we remain positive and move forward despite whatever tragedy or difficulty we are asked to endure? Whenever I have moments of self-doubt or regret about things in my life or failures I have experienced, I try to remember what Mormon stated after the horrific and sudden destruction of the Nephite civilization. As Mormon looked over the final battlefield and saw the terrible devastation and loss of life, he stated:

> And *my soul was rent with anguish*, because of the slain of my people, and I cried:
>
> O ye fair ones, *how could ye have departed from the ways of the Lord!* O ye fair ones, how could ye have rejected that Jesus, who stood with open arms to receive you!
>
> Behold, if ye had not done this, ye would not have fallen. *But behold, ye are fallen, and I mourn your loss.*
>
> O ye fair sons and daughters, ye fathers and mothers, ye husbands and wives, ye fair ones, how is it that ye could have fallen!
>
> *But behold, ye are gone, and my sorrows cannot bring your return.*[16]

I used to think Mormon's statement was devoid of all hope. I have come to learn that Mormon, despite the agony he felt, was full of hope and optimism. I love the sentiment he expressed when he stated, "But behold, ye are gone, and my sorrows cannot bring your return." It's a healthy recognition that something bad occurred, that it's in the past, and that no matter how sad it makes you, it can't be changed. The focus is not on lingering on what occurred but rather on preparing for today and being ready for tomorrow.

Sometimes we tell ourselves things would be better if only something had not happened or if someone had done something else. As a result, we allow ourselves to become angry in the present over things that occurred previously. Whenever I find myself in in such moments, I try to follow Mormon's pattern by 1) acknowledging something difficult occurred, 2) recognizing it hurt me, 3) reminding myself it's in the past and it can't be changed, and 4) remembering despite everything I am okay as a person and everything will work out as it should. A quotation from Lewis Carroll's book *Alice's Adventures in Wonderland* hangs on my wall and serves as a reminder: "It's no use going back to yesterday, because I was a different person then."[17] I find this to be true.

After eight long, arduous years in the wilderness, Lehi and his family came to rest in an oasis they named Bountiful. There, God commanded Nephi to build a ship in preparation for traveling to the American continent. Laman and Lemuel vehemently objected and rebelled, complaining that

Nephi's efforts were foolish, based in whimsy and imagination. In dramatic fashion, they proceeded to list their grievances: they had endured tremendous hardship by long-term wandering in the wilderness, their wives had toiled and borne children in conditions that were less than satisfactory, and they had endured everything possible except death itself. They went further by stating it would have been better for them to have died before leaving Jerusalem than to have experienced these afflictions. With much arrogance and contempt, they concluded their complaint by declaring:

> Behold these many years *have we suffered in the wilderness*, which time *we might have enjoyed our possessions* and the land of our inheritance; *yea, we might have been happy*.[18]

What a miserable way to live. How dismal and destructive it is that Laman and Lemuel had spent so much time blaming Nephi for their problems. They believed their happiness was predicated on enjoying the wealth and possessions they left behind in Jerusalem. Laman and Lemuel probably believed money could buy them happiness, and Nephi just didn't know what store to shop in! Like Lot's wife, they looked rearward at what they gave up rather than forward at what they were about to achieve.[19] Filled with regret for things of the past, they failed to prepare and look ahead to a promising future. Laman and Lemuel's lack of contentment for their present state of life created negativity in their perspective, which fostered hostility, resentment, and even hatred for themselves, their family, and for God.

Nephi's experience in the wilderness offers proof that by looking ahead and not behind, we will find happiness and contentment. Nephi wrote he had not previously experienced such joy and he lived "after the manner of happiness."[20] Nephi suffered the same afflictions, walked the same miles under the same conditions, and made the same sacrifices as Laman and Lemuel. One could argue Nephi's suffering was greater than that of his brothers because of the hardheartedness and wickedness of Laman and Lemuel, yet he was happy. What a marvelous principle to learn, that despite experiencing trial and hardship, we may come to know joy, if we but look forward. Nephi's happiness was grounded in his inner satisfaction with who he was and what he had. Recognizing the great gifts God had bestowed upon him, he realized, as should we, happiness is not found in the past, nor with monetary wealth, but in enjoying to the fullest what we have right now. It takes work to be happy and it takes work to be unhappy; the choice is ours as to what work and effort we put in for either.

Ask ourselves: Are we like Laman and Lemuel, so caught up in what we don't have or what we lack that we are unhappy and miss the advantage of life, or are we like Nephi, living in the present while maintaining a steady and positive look to the future? No matter the length, perplexity, or trauma of our journey, the hope or opportunity for our future should never be relinquished. As with Nephi and Mormon, leaving our pasts behind us, having a constant weather view on the horizon, and learning to let go of our prior pain are each important keys for single adults to find happiness. It is the capacity to view our lives not singularly but rather holistically: being the product of our past, present, and future and understanding that while our past may influence us, it does not dictate how we feel or how we react to our opportunities today and in the future.

EBENEZER# 5: I GET MY PERSONAL VALIDATION FROM GOD AND MYSELF—NOT FROM A RELATIONSHIP

Love is something we give without expecting it in return. I learned this lesson the hard way as I struggled to get married and then wrestled with the failure of that relationship. Part of my struggle came from my sole focus on being married—I didn't see what a marriage was supposed to be. I was so willing to give up who I was as a person and as an individual to be in a relationship, even an unhealthy one, that I couldn't fathom happiness without it. One of the hardest truths I had to learn after my divorce was to emotionally let go of what I thought I needed to be happy. I had to find other things and beliefs in my life to validate who I was as a person.

It's an interesting psychological phenomenon that we as human beings seek and pursue connections and relationships that resemble those we had during childhood. Whether it's because those types of relationships are familiar to us or we are subconsciously trying to fix a difficult or traumatic past relationship, we are influenced today by these past relationships in our desire and method for connecting and developing relationships with other people. We also use these past interactions as a prototype for how we act and react in the relationships we have.[21] As a result, we perpetuate the mannerisms and idiosyncrasies of our past relationships in our present and future relationships.

Recognizing this was the first step to finding joy in my life as a single adult. I realized for the first time that I am okay without a romantic relationship and I could base my personal validation on things I choose. I found out there was more to life than just being married. I pushed myself to explore new experiences even if I originally felt they were weird or odd. I searched for new hobbies, new skills, and new applications in my life to fill the void I had previously felt. By way of example, writing this book and developing a series of church-based comics was part of my experiment and my discovery of what I could and could not do as a single adult. No longer was I going to church or to singles activities and feeling disappointed when I didn't meet anyone. No longer was I disappointed that the women I knew were not interested in dating me. I found solace and joy in my own identity. While I haven't abandoned the dream of finding my wife, I realize I am not defined by my relational status. I realize also that I have a lot of good in me and that I can, and do, add positive things to those around me.

Learning to let go of the need for a relationship was probably the most difficult part of my recovery from relational trauma. This lesson was reinforced to me in a dramatic incident involving my beloved bulldog, Tugg. The bond between Tugg and me is extremely tight. I originally bought Tugg as a puppy when the relationship with my ex-wife was deteriorating. I thought if my ex-wife and I could learn to bond together with the dog, maybe we could learn to bond together on other things going forward. Even though my ex-wife and I failed in our relationship, I am glad I have Tugg, because he stood by me with nothing but dedication and friendship. I held onto him when I had nothing else.

Immediately after my divorce, I moved to Minnesota for employment. Minnesota is a wonderful place, yet with temperatures reaching negative forty degrees, the winters can be severe, cold, and long. During my first winter there, on one of the coldest days, the temperatures were so low that work and school were canceled and the government warned us not to be outside for more than a few minutes. These types of days are always tough on Tugg as he is not suited for the cold and he is not able to be outside for any meaningful duration.

On this day, however, I let Tugg out in the backyard, expecting him to come running back to the door within a few minutes. He did return, but for whatever reason he stood by the door and refused to come into the house. Bulldogs can be stubborn over the oddest and smallest things, which is one reason I love them, but in this moment this quality presented a life-threatening challenge. I didn't have a collar on Tugg and each time I tried to reach for him, he ran away. I had no way to catch him or to get him into the house. I tried treats. I tried sneaking up behind him. I tried leaving the door open, hoping he would come in, but he did not. This lasted for almost forty-five minutes. He was shivering so much in the cold and I was becoming distraught and worried that I might lose him. There was nothing that I could do except wait and watch. I was desperate and in tears over this.

Finally, I centered myself and told myself to let go of what I can't control. Fortunately, and to my great relief, Tugg came in on his own a short while later. I have never forgotten this experience and the anxiety I had in letting go of the battle to bring him inside. In some ways, this was a learning moment about relationships for me. If other people can't or won't chose to be in a healthy relationship with me, I can't force to them to do so. I had to be prepared and have sufficient courage to allow them their choice, to be comfortable in who I am despite that choice, and to be prepared if the circumstances changed. I am grateful Tugg eventually came in from the cold and I am grateful for the lesson I learned from this experience. Learning to let go, in a positive manner, of the desire I had for a healthy relationship with my ex-wife is the most arduous and distressing process I have experienced; it is also the greatest lesson I have learned in my life.

The vision of the Tree of Life and the straight and narrow path (discussed previously) is a dynamic and prophetic depiction of our lives.[22] It is a representation of life's journey each must take to come to the Savior and partake in and qualify for eternal life. It is a journey that is started individually in the lone and dreary wilderness and is then walked singularly and progressively through darkness, uncertainty, and difficulty. It is a vivid and powerful representation that the only toll demanded on the road to happiness is not paid in money but rather through vigilance and constant attention by those who journey it. Those who repeatedly reach out to better themselves, who strive to improve, will eventually emerge from the mists of darkness and partake of the fruit of joy and happiness.

The crucial test illustrated for us relates to our individual staying power and our ability to endure. It's a test of our persistence and tenacity in clinging to the iron rod and in overcoming the physical adversities, hardships, and trials of getting to the Tree of Life. It's also a spiritual demonstration of our fortitude and mettle in withstanding the contempt, disparagement, and disdain held by the adversary and those who serve him once we reach and partake of the fruit of the gospel. What we choose to let go of and what we choose to hold onto defines who and what we become.

For those of us trying to recover from past relational traumas, recovery is possible if we know and recognize those things that burden us. The road to relational recovery is not an easy one, but it is worth the struggle and it is better than the alternative. We all have an opportunity in this life to traverse our own path to the Savior, to accept Him in our lives, and to validate ourselves through Him. As we wend and press forward on this path, may we learn to let go of the things that drag us down and to hold on to those things that lift us up.

OVERCOMING FAILURE AND MOVING FORWARD: THE BATTLE OF AI

Shortly after the miraculous crossing of the Israelites over the Jordan River and their extraordinary victory and success at Jericho, the Israelites found themselves in both an extended military campaign and a comprehensive spiritual struggle to regain the Promised Land. This crusade represented not only the reclamation of a land promised to their forefathers but also the individual and collective effort to follow the Savior despite entrenched societal evil and to strive against and surmount worldly challenges and obstacles. It symbolized a spiritual and physical sanctification, not only of the land itself, but of its people as they entered and received the benefit of their covenant and God's intended blessings.

Prior to crossing the Jordan River, the Israelites possessed a land of peace and comfort, a land that could sustain them and with which they were content. Nevertheless, God commanded them forward, to undertake the burden of war and to repossess the Promised Land. Full of faith and certainty, the Israelite army achieved astonishing success at the battle of Jericho as God leveled and razed the city walls and led the Israelites to complete victory.

The news of the Israelites' success had great effect and military advantage as those who remained in the Promised Land feared God's astonishing wonder and mighty miracles. They also feared the sheer strength and presence of the Israelite armies. In other words, the perspective, motivation, and willpower of those who opposed the Israelites was adversely affected. Encouraged and bolstered by their own success at Jericho, the Israelites quickly turned their attention to the smaller but strategically important city of Ai. Having scouted the military strength of the city, the Israelites determined only a small contingent of three thousand men would be required to conquer it and the entire army of the Israelites need not "labor" to achieve this victory.[23] However, when the three thousand Israelite men arrived at Ai, the city's inhabitants provided strong, resolute resistance and soundly defeated the Israelites in battle causing them to flee.

Upon hearing of their defeat at Ai, the "people's hearts melted and became as water."[24] Joshua himself was also upset and discomforted by these events. He prostrated himself before the ark, asking why God had brought this people over the Jordan River to be destroyed by the Canaanites. He lamented, "Would to God we had been content, and dwelt on the other side of Jordan."[25] Joshua further asked God what he should do when the Israelites turn their backs on their enemies, commenting that the Canaanite armies (now believing that the Israelite armies could be defeated) would be emboldened and invigorated by Ai's victory in the battles to come.

God responded to Joshua by stating, "Get thee up; wherefore liest thou thus upon thy face?"[26] God explained that Israel had sinned by taking treasures and spoils at the battle of Jericho that He had forbidden, and they had mixed these things with their own belongings. It was for this cause those engaged in the battle at Ai were not blessed in their endeavor. God also stated He would not support Israel further unless this transgression was remedied. As a result, Joshua conducted an immediate search of the Israelites, resulting in the confession of a man named Achan (who had secretly taken two hundred sheckles of silver, a wedge of gold, and a fine garment after the battle of Jericho and hid them in his tent). Because of his disobedience, Achan and his family were condemned and stoned; furthermore, all his earthly possessions were taken and destroyed. After this incident, Joshua was again commanded to take Ai. This time Joshua did not send a small contingent but brought the entire might of Israel's army to bear, utilizing both overpowering strength and cunning military strategy to completely overcome and destroy the city.

The battle for Ai represented the first real test of the Israelites upon their entry into the Promised Land, not because Ai was as strong as Jericho but because it was the first time the Israelites stumbled and failed in their objective. The battle of Ai presents us with important insight into how we face and respond to disappointment and failure despite previous successes in our efforts to meet worthy goals and objectives (especially those we believe are supported and commanded by God). The Israelites' fundamental issue was their unrealistic expectations, not in the commandments of God, but in the implementation and application of those commandments. Their poor implementation of these is demonstrated by their inadequate scouting report, which wrongly indicated the inferior defensive capability of Ai's inhabitants and their unwillingness to put forward the required effort for the task at hand.

The idea that Israel needed only a token effort to obtain complete victory over Ai left them situationally unaware. They were strategically vulnerable, unprepared for what they encountered, and unable to adapt to their existing circumstances, all of which were contributing factors to their initial defeat. The Israelites overestimated their own strengths and underestimated those of their opponents. Perhaps the Israelites' experiences at the Jordan River and at Jericho promoted a mistaken belief that God would deliver them no matter the circumstances or the odds, that they needed only to perfunctorily attend or show up to behold what miracles would occur. Such expectations belie our responsibilities and the work we must show to receive the benefits of God's blessings. Yes, Ai was not as great an opponent as Jericho, however, that distinction did not excuse a lack of preparation or proper support from the Israelites for future conflicts or issues, no matter their size or scale. Yes, God worked mighty miracles in overcoming Jericho, but God's intervention should not have been taken for granted.

In the face of failure, the response and impulse of the Israelites was not an increase in resolve or faith, but a significant withering and substantial waning of hope as well as a loss of perspective. They became keenly aware of the actuality of their circumstances and the reality that their expectations were not fully aligned with the task at hand. They realized, perhaps for the first time, that they were facing a difficult, long, and potentially costly journey to achieve their desired objectives. Perhaps they also realized the seriousness of their undertaking and were re-evaluating their own resolve to keep going.

Whatever their circumstances, the faith and testimony they had acquired and the fortitude they had previously developed were now insufficient and deteriorating toward their future endeavors. Overall, the defeat at Ai was relatively small in comparison to the previous victory and impending challenges. How can a people who have experienced great initial success universally undermine and overlook those advances through the negative perception of a relatively minor setback? To throw our testimonies and faith away in such a manner and for such a purpose is the proverbial throwing the baby out with the bathwater—to dispose of that which is good (overlooking positive gains) simply because it falls short of our unrealistic or self-imposed expectations.

Joshua himself succumbed to doubt as he distrusted and questioned the commandment to possess the Promised Land. He looked backwards to where the Israelites started, knowing other places and lands existed that were comfortable and available, that did not require the type of sacrifice or effort God was requiring of the Israelites to repossess the Promised Land. How easy it would have been to stay on the other side of Jordan than to face the wrath of the Canaanites and uncertainty of the future. How comfortable and happy could they have been if they were not required to move forward and progress?

In a moment of doubt, Joshua asked how he was to respond and lead a people who lacked courage and who may turn from the battle in the face of invigorated Canaanite armies. I truly love the response God gave to Joshua when he told him to get up and asked him why he was lying down. Sometimes when we are faced with great challenges or trials, we simply need to stand and act: to realize our efforts and motivation are vitally important to our success. How often do we bemoan our failures and allow them to dictate our future decisions or actions? Do we ask ourselves the hard questions such as what must I do or what must I change to be successful? Sometimes we can do everything right and still face failure. In such circumstances, perseverance, not self-loathing, is the required countermeasure.

The severity or harshness of the consequences Achan faced for his individual actions is also difficult to accept. Perhaps it's fair to argue his actions did not require capital punishment for him or his family (i.e. the sentence outweighed the crime committed). We also do not know whether Achan was the only person who retained prohibited bounty from the battle of Jericho. What we do know is Achan represented the collective consequences of transgression or sin. One can reason it was the summative effect, not the individual effect, of his actions that derived this consequence (i.e. the loss of life for those who initially attacked Ai, the depriving of faith from those who should have believed, the withdrawal of God's support, and the emboldening of their enemies, all of which had a direct and material consequence on the Israelites.) Often, we justify our choices by thinking that if our actions do not hurt anyone else—what is wrong with them? As the story of Achan shows, this belief is often misguided; the entire House of Israel shouldered the result and burden of Achan's actions.

The lesson the Savior is trying to teach to the Israelites is one of introspection or self-examination. Are there not important lessons for us as well? How easy it is to blame others, to blame God, or to blame circumstances for the failures or bumps we encounter? Yet, often the most effective solution (and the most difficult) is to first look inwards, at ourselves and our actions or contributions to the problem, before giving up and saying all is lost.

Failure can be our greatest teacher if we allow it. If we succeed easily, we never learn; we are not motivated to change, we never adapt, we never exert, and we never try new things. Failure forces us to re-evaluate, to retry, and to reinvent ourselves. It prepares us for future successes if we embrace it, if we do not fear it, and if we are prepared to meet it. For single adults who face enormous challenge, all is not lost. For those of us who strive to have healthy relationships but are prevented, are unable, or who struggle because of past failure, we still have opportunity. The battle for Ai dramatically demonstrates that when we encounter problems or failure, we should not lose faith, lament our circumstances, or look back to better days. We should not bemoan or repine, but rather look to ourselves for the solutions and strive to bring our best efforts going forward. We must remind ourselves, as God reminded Joshua, to not cry over spilled milk or to agonize over our past failures but to exercise inner strength and self-motivation to pick ourselves up and to move forward.

5

Upon What Do We Base Our Relationships?

> There is no fear in love;
> but perfect love casteth out fear.
> —1 John 4:18

I have spent many years of my life attending church, as both a young-single adult and as a mid-single adult. I have felt and experienced an overarching pressure to become married in the church. For single adults, that pressure occurs in a myriad of forms; however, it usually derives from self-imposed timelines and expectations, encouraged generally by the policies and programs of church, and promoted or specifically applied by church leaders, married members, and family members.

Certainly, this pressure is understandable. Becoming married is an essential part of our growth as individuals; it provides needed opportunities and structure for us to create and to support families. Oftentimes, though, this focus solely on *being* or *becoming* married can have a detrimental impact on the future development of healthy relationships.

I once had a conversation with a dear friend who was struggling through a traumatic and troubling divorce that, sadly, resembled other stories I have heard from many divorced members of the church. She stated her husband was a good man to whom she was initially attracted and they were married after a relatively short courtship. In due course, they had children, but the relationship between them eventually languished and failed. She tearfully stated she had done everything right and didn't understand why she was in this situation. She recounted they went to church regularly, faithfully held callings, attended the temple, held family home evening, read scriptures together, held family prayer, and were even intimate with each other regularly.

Why was she now in a situation where their marriage was broken? I have often thought about this question. My conclusion is the failure of their marriage relationship had very little to do with the expectations and activities in which these two engaged. All these activities are wonderful and helpful from a physical or spiritual perspective, as they bring us closer to each other and to God; however, none of them in and of themselves are the sole basis for a healthy and functioning marital relationship. They facilitate, but they cannot be viewed as a foundational replacement for developing the important attachments and connections within the relationship.

Sometimes in the church, we approach marriage not from the perspective of whether individuals are connecting with each other or whether the relationship is healthy but rather from a check-the-box mentality. This view prioritizes the act of becoming married at the expense, sometimes, of a strong relational bond. Too often, we marry first and plan to work out within the gospel framework the problems and issues that develop later. Because the skills necessary for healthy relationships (to be open and vulnerable with ourselves and with each other) are often undeveloped or altogether lacking, the problem becomes one of relational procrastination or an unwillingness to confront early on difficult relational issues.

While we rejoice at having entered a formal marriage, we are kicking the can down the road on the relationship itself, hoping things will simply work out, or we will subsequently develop the capability to handle the relational challenges as they arise. Yet when these problems arise, the necessary development of essential relational skills may take a back seat to more spiritually based solutions or activities that are highly encouraged and emphasized in the church. In other words, while we readily engage in activities that connect us with God, we struggle with our connections with each other. As a result, we may feel a strong relationship with God but fail to have a healthy relationship with our spouse or with others. When this occurs, we begin to question our worth, our testimonies, and our ability to achieve salvation itself.

Said differently, we often derive our identity, sense of self-worth, or personal validation solely from our dating, family, or marital relationships. This is an unhealthy perspective, especially when taken to extremes, because we feel tremendous inner shame when that relationship struggles, breaks down, or is lost. For single adults this condition is heightened by the shame of a failed past relationship, our discomfort in being currently single, the fear of entering a future relationship, or our inability to do so. Because of the high emphasis on marriage, we find ourselves rushing into or prolonging unhealthy relationships rather than being single in the church or enduring the isolation and stigma of being alone.

Happy relationships and happy marriages are possible between two people who are open and vulnerable with themselves, with each other, and with God. Partners in strong marriages accept each other for who each person is, love each other despite their imperfections, and understand and develop the right skills to support and uphold the relationship. I have often felt that the pressure applied to single adults to get married, without the focus on healthy relationships, leads to poor decision-making or false positives relating to the compatibility and fit of those relationships for each individual involved. This causes tremendous relational, emotional, and spiritual difficulties down the road.

I am not saying the emphasis for spirituality and for following gospel standards in developing and maintaining relationships is not critical. It is. What I am saying is how we connect with each other in our individual relationships is fundamental and essential to the health and longevity of that relationship, and sometimes we ignore or overlook that aspect in favor of physical or individual characteristics, institutional perspectives, or activity within the church.

FIT IN A RELATIONSHIP

While I was married, I wanted to get my wife a designer purse for her birthday. Not knowing how to go about finding an appropriate purse for her, I decided to go to Dillard's, a large department store in Salt Lake City. When I arrived at the store, I was shocked and amazed to discover an entire department dedicated solely to women's purses. *Who knew such a thing existed?* I thought. The choices presented in this department were overwhelming and the task at hand seemed insurmountable.

I spent a long time looking through what appeared to be an endless sea of purses. I looked at large ones, small ones, leather ones, different shapes of purses, purses with multiple pockets and liners, and every color one could possibly imagine. It seemed as if there was a purse for every imaginable purpose and situation. When I finally found a purse I thought was suitable, given my inexperience in this area, I approached the saleswoman and asked her whether this was a good purse and if I should buy it for my wife. Now, I point out this saleswoman's job was to make sales and she most likely received a commission off each sale she made. All she had to do was nod her head and say, "It's a great purse," and she would have made a large sum of money for Dillard's. But she didn't. To my surprise, she looked at me with shock, horror, and bewilderment and stated she couldn't do that. She then told me purses are unique to each individual and she couldn't opine on such an important question as to whether this was a good purse for my wife. She told me my wife would have to come into the store and she would fit her for the right one.

Somewhat embarrassed and disappointed, I thanked her and left without buying anything. I felt shame at my inability to even accomplish a small task that I had hoped would bring some joy to my wife and a benefit to our relationship. I have thought for a long time about this experience and the response I received. The more I think about it, the more grateful I am for this saleswoman's frank response and for the lesson I learned from it. You see, I was focusing on the characteristics of the purse itself and not on whether it was the right purse for my wife.

I tell you this story because I notice single adults in the church often discuss and approach relationships in a way that centers on an analysis and discussion of the characteristics and behaviors of individuals in relationships rather than the characteristics of the relationship itself. In some respects, this is like my effort to find the right purse: we search through a wide array of people, wanting to find the perfect person with just the right characteristics in the hopes that we can be happy. We look at the individual, size them up, and make judgments based upon our personal likes, experiences, and desires. If we aren't sure about the choice we make, we go and ask other people what they think, hoping to validate any insecurity we may have.

Relationships, however, aren't built by a list of individual characteristics, what other people think, or our perceptions of the other person. Relationships work when they are a good fit for the involved individuals and when each person has the capability to be open and vulnerable to one another so that healthy attachments, connections, and bonds may grow.

Sometimes we speculate about what we would do if someone were unfaithful or was not a member of the church. We question whether wanting more kids is a good or bad thing, or what level of intimacy is appropriate at given time periods. These questions are valid and, in the right context, important to understand, because the answers and our reactions thereto affect our ability to be open and vulnerable to those we date or with whom we pursue long-term relationships. The danger in asking these types of questions generally, especially if we use the answers to disregard relationships, is to foreclose not only ourselves, but also others from being open to potential relationships that may be healthy and viable for us in the future. Additionally, our strong opinions in these areas may make someone who we perceive as lacking to feel isolated or unable to have needed attachments in their lives.

When I lived and worked in Wyoming, my boss once urgently called me into her office, where she asked me to close the door and sit down. Thinking I was in trouble, I was anxious to hear what she had to say. After a moment's pause, she looked at me and said, "Kevin, we are going to set you up on a date. What do you like?"

Relieved I was not in trouble, and half joking, I smiled and replied, "Well, I have two, and only two requirements: she can't be named Beulah and she has to have all her teeth." Laughing, my boss looked at me for a moment and said I was being too exclusive for Wyoming. I have often thought about that interaction and asked myself whether my desires and expectations are too high or too restrictive when evaluating and deciding whether to pursue or engage in a potential relationship.

Every so often, I have conversations with various single adults about lists of characteristics, talents, or attributes they have developed to guide them in their search for an eternal spouse. I have even been asked to review these lists and provide feedback as to whether their lists are deficient in any way. Most times the desired characteristics are listed from a positive point of view (i.e. this person must have this attribute); however, sometimes the desired characteristics may be listed from a negative point of view (i.e. this person must *not* have this attribute).

Whether express or intrinsic, we all have characteristic lists of our own that combine both positive and negative requirements forming what our ideal match should be. Yet whenever this occurs, especially if such characteristic requirements are extensive or unreasonably high, we restrict the scope of partners available to us and we take the chance that future dating or relational opportunities will be limited or reduced. Additionally, if we chose to engage or enter a relationship with an individual who does not closely match our desired criteria, we may develop a negative perspective of that relationship because we feel we are settling for somebody who is less than the ideal and there may be someone better we could find. Both situations are problematic for our ability to develop and be in healthy relationships. As well, even if we find the perfect person who conforms to everything on our list, there is no guarantee they will reciprocate a similar desire to be in a relationship with us.

One of the more common characteristics I have observed single members of the church use when evaluating relationship potential is the requirement of righteousness in the other person. This evaluation in and of itself is not bad, especially if a temple marriage is the end goal; however, it will have little bearing on whether two individuals may have a functioning and healthy relationship. Sometimes the beliefs, perspectives, and practices of the gospel for individuals can be so varied, even within the same faith, as to cause relational difficulties and complications.

In the same vein, I sometimes hear parents say it doesn't matter who their child marries as long as they have a temple recommend. Likewise, I have heard individuals express that their reason for dating someone is that the person in whom they are interested is the son or daughter of a bishop, stake president, or general authority, as if the righteousness or church service of their parents qualifies them for a good relationship partner. What is it about those characteristics that would lead to a healthy relationship with the involved individuals? I worry members of the church assume they are marrying a Nephi when they are in fact marrying a Laman.

I often laugh at the absurd thought of going to a single-adult activity, pulling out my temple recommend, holding it up high, and saying, "I have a temple recommend. Who wants to date?" I am certain if I did that, I would foreclose whatever hope or opportunity I may have to date among that group in the future. The truth is righteousness is a very important characteristic, but it is still a characteristic. Righteousness in terms of relational fit is more nuanced and refined than the short shrift we may give it. Like my attempt to buy a purse by looking solely at characteristics, the query isn't whether an individual is righteous but whether their beliefs and actions are a good fit for us as individuals.

Occasionally, a concerned member will look favorably on me and try to set me up on a blind date with someone they know. I am always appreciative when someone thinks highly enough of me to want to introduce me to someone else. Generally, the first question they ask me is whether I have a valid temple recommend. I have often wondered why my worthiness to enter the temple is the defining criteria for whether I may even be considered for a relationship. Whenever this line of questioning begins, I have learned to start asking questions back as to why they think this person is a good relational fit for me. What about this person makes this member think we could have a good and healthy relationship together? I ask these questions not from a meanness or sardonic perspective but to genuinely understand why someone would want to set me up.

It's always interesting to see the look of shock on their faces because it's a question they did not anticipate and a topic they likely had not considered. If their only answer is we are both single members of the church and two righteous people should be able to co-exist, I begin to worry their intentions, while good, are misplaced.

I also often hear people tell me they pray about the suitability of individuals they date and the Spirit tells them whether they should enter or continue in a relationship. The Holy Ghost does watch over us and does guide us in the relationships we want or choose to have; however, I am often cautious of the conclusions we draw about the sustainability of a potential relationship because of received personal revelation, especially if those conclusions are quick and without effort or work.

There is a physical, biological, and chemical component to human attraction. I like to believe God gives this to each of us as a natural incentive for us to pursue and enter long-term relationships with each other. These elements often evoke powerful emotions and feelings within ourselves toward individuals to whom we are attracted. I have asked myself how I distinguish between what the Spirit wants and what I want when it comes to choosing potential dating partners or a future spouse. Sometimes the intensity of the inner debate with ourselves on this question can create uncertainty that stymies or delays us from decisive action toward developing potential relationships. On the other hand, our own biases or needs may mislead us in our judgments of the relational suitability of someone who is a romantic interest.

Think for a moment about Mormon's communication with Pahoran, the Nephite chief judge, during a serious and difficult conflict with the Lamanites. Despite both Helaman and Mormon's marvelous military victories on two different fronts, the Nephite government neglected to provide needed support to these two armies, which weakened and endangered them. As a result, Mormon wrote a scathing letter to Pahoran, condemning him personally as well as the Nephite government. In that letter, Mormon states God told him if the appointed governors did not repent and provide the required support for the cause of freedom, Mormon should go up to battle against the Nephites themselves.[1] Unbeknownst to Mormon, Pahoran had been true to the cause but had been ousted from power in an internal coup d'état that treasonous individuals planned and executed.

After this occurrence was revealed, Pahoran and Mormon joined forces to recapture Zarahemela, to reinstate Pahoran to the judgment seat, and to put down the civic rebellion.

In this instance, God gave Mormon a personal revelation, yet Mormon initially imposed on that revelation his own bias and (incorrect) assumptions toward Pahoran. The revelation itself was correct, but Mormon's application of it toward Pahoran was not. As a result, I have often wondered how much personal bias, emotion, and desire we place or impose on the whisperings of the Spirit in our lives. That is not to say the revelations we receive are incorrect or should be doubted, yet I often ask myself whether the manner in which we apply those revelations is correct or right, especially as it pertains to relationships. Said differently, are we more open ourselves to the whisperings of the Spirit as it pertains to entering relationships, when an individual possesses the physical, emotional, and spiritual characteristics we hope for and desire? Do we foreclose it altogether if that individual does not have such characteristics? These are the questions we should ask and objectively answer as we seek after healthy relationships in our lives.

Many times, when I ask single adults about their spiritual promptings relating to individuals and relationships, I will hear a response like this: "I prayed about it and the Spirit told me they were not the right person for me." Rarely, if ever, have I heard single adults say, "I prayed about it, and the Spirit told me I was not the right individual for the other person." Think about the difference between these statements and the perspective each represents. Have you ever thought the reason the Spirit told you, "No," was that you were not open or vulnerable to the other person in that relationship? If we haven't in good faith tried, been willing to work, exercised forgiveness, or given trust an opportunity, what other message would the Spirit give to us?

Does this mean we need to date every person we encounter to determine whether someone is a good fit? Heavens no! It does mean we should base our relational needs and decisions on criteria that will lead to the long-term success of that relationship. In this way, we can evaluate our emotions in the proper context of the spiritual promptings we receive. Part of balancing our emotional and spiritual feelings in our relational decisions requires us to fairly and dispassionately view ourselves in light of that potential relationship. Ask ourselves: *Can we be happy over the long-term? Does the relationship grow or stagnate? Are both individuals benefited through the relationship?* These are all questions that are answered through the practice and application of the relationship between each person in it. If we can accomplish this over a reasonable time period, we have a greater likelihood of having a long-term healthy relationship as well as having a greater surety of the spiritual promptings we receive.

Another common piece of advice I hear people in the church give single adults is that we need to be (or become) the type of individual we want to attract and marry. For example, if we want to marry a charitable person, we need to be charitable ourselves; if we want to marry a social person, we must also be social, etc. On its face, this advice seems sound and wholesome, yet I find this advice misses a crucial aspect. Relationships depend far more on how we successfully navigate the connections and interactions of the relationship and how we manage and cope with its problems than how similar the couple is. Additionally, such advice can lead single adults to feel further shame and disappointment, especially if we are trying to develop a certain characteristic only to realize there are no others who have that characteristic or if we are unable to develop a desired relationship with those we perceive to have that characteristic. It can further lead to the incorrect assumption or belief that we are not good enough.

Consider an individual who sought after and married someone because they were a kind person. The desire to be in a relationship with a kind person is absolutely a wonderful thing. The problem in healthy relationships isn't that the individuals are not kind people, but that at some point an event will occur where one or both people in the relationship will not be kind to the other.

In other words, no one and no relationship is faultless; eventually we will stumble. At that moment, the other spouse will look around and say, "Hey, I thought you were a kind person. It's why I married you." Frustration, failed expectations, and hurt will always be the result. It is in these moments where perception meets reality that we must decide whether to accept and love our significant other for who they are, imperfections, warts, and all. The measure of any healthy relationship isn't in the achievement of entering a relationship; rather, it's in our ability to overcome the reality of each person's weaknesses within that relationship when such weaknesses are exposed.

The advice I give to single adults when entering a relationship is to ask whether the relationship is likely to be healthy and positive rather than asking about the characteristics of the individual person. We should ask ourselves: *Can I be open and vulnerable in the relationship? Does the other person receive and reciprocate my vulnerability? Does attachment grow equally between both individuals because of the bonds that are built? Am I a better person because of the relationship?*

If the answer to those questions is yes, then it is a relationship worth pursuing and developing. If the answer is no, then further analysis should be given. For example, look for things we can fix or change with ourselves either in our giving or our receiving of love that will facilitate a healthier relationship. If a relationship needs to end because it is not healthy, that is okay too—just keep the focus on the relationship not being the right fit for us rather than on the characteristics of the other person.

Part of the reason why we date before marriage and why we should date multiple and various people is so we can experience different types of relationships and evaluate how we react within the bounds of those relationships. As I mentioned earlier, there are no perfect people and no perfect relationships. Healthy and positive relationships form between two people who are open and vulnerable enough with themselves and with each other to allow trust and growth. If we focus too much on individual characteristics, we may very well end up buying a fancy and expensive purse that everyone gushes about, but we find out, to our dismay, that on the inside, there are a lot of complications making it a far less satisfying fit than the one for which we are looking and hoping.

THE RELATIONSHIP BETWEEN RUTH AND BOAZ

Whenever I think about relational fit, I like to contemplate the story of Ruth and Boaz and the basis for their courtship. After leaving Moab and arriving in Bethlehem, Ruth and Naomi had a problem: they had little money and few, if any, means of supporting themselves aside from some family property from Naomi's deceased husband. Both widows were reliant on the charity of others and on their extended family for support. To help support herself and Naomi, Ruth took it upon herself to glean food from the local barley fields during the annual harvest. By happenstance, Ruth found herself in Boaz's field.

Boaz was a wealthy and important man who was a distant relative of Naomi. Boaz took notice of Ruth working and was aware of Ruth's acts of service in forsaking her homeland to care for Naomi. Touched by this selfless act, Boaz allowed Ruth to work daily in his fields and made sure, while she worked, she had access to the same food and water provided to his servants. He even instructed his servants to leave behind some of the harvest on purpose for Ruth to collect to ensure her and Naomi's well-being. Ruth was grateful for this charity and worked diligently to collect the needed food for herself and Naomi.

At some point during the harvest, Naomi undertook an independent matchmaking effort to encourage Ruth to seek after a relationship with Boaz and to interest Boaz in taking Ruth to wife. Naomi was concerned about Ruth's emotional and relational welfare, as well as her future and personal happiness. Additionally, Boaz was a relative and it was traditional for the next of kin to marry the widow of those family members who had passed on and to raise up posterity in their name.

As part of Naomi's plan, Naomi asked Ruth to conceal her identity while she was working with Boaz and his servants who were processing the harvested barley. Naomi instructed Ruth to wait until Boaz had finished working, had eaten, and had lay down to sleep. Once Boaz was asleep, Naomi charged Ruth to uncover his feet and lie down. (I like to think of this as one of the few successful blind dates in the Old Testament.) Ruth did as Naomi instructed and fell asleep at the feet of Boaz. During the night, Boaz awoke and was startled. Upon asking who was there, Ruth identified herself and asked Boaz to marry her, for Boaz was a near kinsman.[2]

I love Boaz's response to Ruth's request:

> Blessed be thou of the Lord, my daughter, for thou hast shewed more kindness in the latter end than at the beginning, inasmuch as *thou followedest not young men, whether poor or rich.*
>
> And now, my daughter, fear not; I will do to thee all that thou requires: *for all the city of my people doth know thou art a virtuous woman.*[3]

Boaz understood the nature and meaning of Ruth's request. Ruth showed both respect and courage by following Naomi's advice, and vulnerability to Boaz in what must have been a tender but awkward moment between them. Boaz validated both Ruth's request as well as Ruth herself with his response. Boaz's recognition that Ruth had not chased after frivolous relationships with less-respected men is important and shows that Ruth was not seeking after a relationship that was not a good fit for her. Despite her impoverished circumstances, Ruth was not willing to compromise on what she needed for a good relationship going forward.

Boaz reassured Ruth he would fulfill his promise to marry her and requested she allow him to work out the details as there was another relative who had legal priority. Ruth was mindful of the relationship with Boaz by remaining at his side the remainder of the night and leaving without fanfare or notice of the other servants. This showed sensitivity to the early stage of the relationship by not publicizing something that was still forming. It was also a recognition that Boaz might be disadvantaged or compromised in his negotiation for marriage if his promise to her were publicly known.

The interaction between Boaz and Ruth contains valuable lessons for us in entering, and maintaining, a relationship, especially in its early stages. Unlike Ruth, we are sometimes too quick to publicly announce a new relationship or change our relationship status in social media profiles. Whenever this occurs, I wonder whether that relationship is prepared for the weight and responsibility of such unrestricted public declarations and scrutiny. Moreover, Ruth and Boaz's relationship was unconventional in its development and culmination as Ruth—not Boaz—instigated and requested the marriage. Sometimes we can be so rigid in the societal formalities of courtship, we forget the most important aspect of any relationship is for two people to be vulnerable to each other in such a way that trust is developed.

I am not suggesting a deviation or abandonment from time-honored traditions or that women should now be the ones to propose marriage to their significant others. However, strict adherence to perceived or self-imposed beliefs of gender roles, age, or other elements in our instigation and development of our relationships may inhibit, delay, or altogether prevent our ability and opportunity to enter into and have them. Again, the analysis regarding any relationship should first be about its fit for the involved individuals and less about the personal characteristics of those individuals or the manner and customs for how the relationship is formed.

The day after Ruth's proposal, Boaz approached the city elders and Naomi's near kinsman to discuss and resolve the family matter. Boaz initiated the discussion by stating Naomi had an inherited parcel of land for sale. Because this kinsman had a right of priority to the purchase of this property, Boaz requested his kinsman decide whether he would redeem the property: if he would not, Boaz would. The kinsman, knowing the value of the property, immediately agreed to purchase the property. Boaz further pointed out to him that he would also have to not only care for Naomi but also marry Ruth because of the transaction and be responsible to raise up posterity in the name of Ruth's deceased husband.

The kinsman then responded as follows: "I cannot redeem it for myself *lest I mar mine own inheritance*: redeem thou my right to thyself; for I cannot redeem it."[4] The reason the kinsman was not willing to enter the relationship or to purchase the property was because it did not meet his current needs or life situation. In other words, it was not a good fit. Even though he initially deemed the transaction worthwhile, upon further investigation and consideration, he determined such a relationship would negatively affect his current family situation and responsibilities. Boaz understood this point.

Unlike Naomi's near kinsman, we often enthusiastically jump into a relationship based solely upon perceived benefits but take no heed of the burden or negative effects of such a relationship on our lives or the lives of others for whom we are responsible. This is not to say that the relationship was bad or undesirable, but the relationship itself may create unintended consequences or uninformed circumstances for either or both individuals.

Often the puzzle of piecing together the logistical needs and external requirements for individuals within a relationship, no matter how healthy, is difficult and complex. Think about a divorced mother who is required to remain in a specific geographic area so her children may have access to their father. Should she seek a new relationship that necessitates relocation outside this area, such relationship may not be possible without serious discussion and certain compromise. Or think about a divorced man who has significant debt or other financial obligations that would materially burden the relationship. What happens if children from prior marriages are not able to adjust to the new familial relationship?

There are no easy answers to these types of situations. Such situations should not foreclose any potential relationship, but how these and other relevant factors impact the quality and the fit for each person in the relationship is an important and necessary consideration for us in deciding whether we chose to pursue or continue a relationship. It's okay to conclude that a relationship is not a good fit. All this conclusion means is we have experienced that relationship and recognize there are other relationships better suited to meet everyone's needs.

Lastly, I have several female friends who are sealed in the temple and who are widows. Sometimes part of the difficulties these sisters encounter is maintaining their sealing to their deceased spouse while pursuing a church marriage with someone else who may also want to be sealed. Such a predicament profoundly impacts the fit of any relationship for individuals seeking a temple marriage. I have seen good single women seek marriage and healthy relationships outside the church because of this dilemma. Perhaps this too is a healthy outcome as it pertains to the relational fit; however, such a situation will require an acceptance and understanding of their temporary partner and the possibility they may not want to live the same standards as those found in the church.

I do not purport to have any answers to this dilemma except to say I understand this struggle and have great empathy for it. In some cases, this circumstance will mean the relationship is not a good fit for someone wanting to be sealed in the temple, and that is okay. However, as Boaz demonstrated, there are some individuals for whom a relationship of this type will be a good fit. Remember, Boaz took on not only the benefit of the relationship but also the burden and deemed it good. The result of this relationship was a lineage from which the Savior himself was born. What a wonderful and noble outcome.

HEALTHY VERSUS UNHEALTHY RELATIONSHIPS

I have learned most relationships have problems in some form or another and those problems are found either in the giving or the receiving side of the relationship. Sometimes relationships fail because one person (or both) has difficulties being open and vulnerable to the other and struggles in providing the needed nourishment required in a loving relationship. Other relationships fail because one person (or both) has problems recognizing and receiving the love they are given.

A helpful and useful example of giving and receiving in a relationship occurred when a woman anointed the Savior just before His crucifixion. This woman brought an alabaster box of precious and costly ointment with which she anointed the Savior's head.[5] I often think about the sacrifice, effort, humility, and love this woman showed to the Savior in that instance. Shocked at the Savior's acceptance of this act, several of the disciples were upset and angry, arguing the gift should have been sold to help the poor. Perhaps the indignation of these disciples is understandable as they had spent years by the Savior's side, and at His teaching, sacrificed all they had for others.

I have often wondered myself why the Savior would allow such an act to be done. Alternatively, I have asked myself what would have occurred or how this woman would have felt if the Savior had redirected or rejected her efforts altogether. Considering both viewpoints, it is my belief the Savior was not accepting this woman's gift to benefit Himself but rather to accept, receive, and confirm the love that she had for Him. By so doing, the Savior appropriately recognized this woman's charity, not only validating the bond between them but also enhancing it. Healthy bonds are formed, beneficial attachments made, and trusting relationships built in those tender moments where we give sufficient love and then appropriately receive it. The failure of either party in a relationship to both *give* and *receive* will have negative consequences on any relationship.

Whenever I face a difficult relationship or problem, I try to ask myself these questions: Have I shown enough love to this person and have I done so in a manner in which they are able to receive it? Do I need to change the way I approach or think about things, or is there something I can do for them so that they may recognize and accept the love that I am giving? I also ask myself whether I have recognized and validated the love in whatever form that they have shown to me. For what it's worth, I think that the relationship success we have in dating and marriage, and with our kids and those around us is based off our ability and capacity to both show and to receive love.

SAMSON'S FOLLY

The account of Samson is one of great tragedy, selfishness, and heartbreak, that teaches us several important lessons about relationships.[6] Heralded by an angel, his birth occurred at a time of oppression and captivity for the Israelites at the hands of the Philistines. He was raised as a Nazarite, meaning his life was consecrated to God, to the service of others, and to the salvation of those around him. Sadly, Samson did not realize the potential and opportunity that God gave to him, primarily due to his own inadequate sense of self-worth, his lack of self-control, and the unhealthy relationships he chose in life. Blessed with tremendous strength, Samson was destined to lead the people of Israel from bondage, but was unable, falling victim to the betrayal of those who were supposed to love and care for him.

Early in Samson's life, he sought an opportunity to engage the Philistines. His first attempt to accomplish this was through marriage to a Philistine woman whom he had previously seen but not met. Samson did not have any contact or interaction with this woman and based his decision for marriage solely off his physical attraction to her. His parents initially objected to the marriage because she was not of their faith; however, Samson did not relent, stating this woman pleased him.

At the wedding ceremony, Samson proposed a large wager to thirty of the Philistine guests in attendance, challenging them to answer a riddle within seven days. After the Philistines accepted the wager, Samson told the riddle, one of his own making, and they could not answer it. As a result, the Philistines approached Samson's new wife demanding she entice

Samson to reveal the riddle's answer. They threatened to burn her and her father if she was unsuccessful. For seven days, his wife wept before Samson, saying, "Thou dost but hate me, and lovest me not: thou hast put forth a riddle unto the children of my people and hast not told me it."[7] Samson responded he had not even told the riddle or its answer to his parents; why would he tell it to her? Still, his wife did not cease her pleading, and Samson on the last day of the wedding relented and told her the riddle's answer. She then told the answer to those who had made the wager.

When the Philistines gave Samson the correct answer to the riddle, he was publicly embarrassed and enraged. Knowing his wife had betrayed his trust, he insulted her and accused the Philistines of wrongful doing, stating, "If ye had not plowed with my heifer, ye had not found out my riddle."[8] In order to pay the owed wager, he went to a neighboring city where he killed thirty men and took their clothes and belongings. After this, he left his wife and, without explanation, returned home in anger. After Samson left, whether for spite or for cause, his father-in law gave Samson's wife to another in marriage.

After some time, Samson returned unannounced with a token and trifling gift (a goat), expecting to be reunited with his wife. His father-in-law, however, refused. He indicated he thought Samson hated his daughter and for this reason he gave her to another in marriage. Infuriated, Samson stated, "Now I shall be more blameless than the Philistines, though I do them displeasure."[9] Samson then set fire to the Philistines' cornfields.

After learning Samson had done this and why, the Philistines cruelly murdered Samson's father-in-law and Samson's wife. In retribution, Samson slaughtered many of the Philistines who were responsible, inspiring the armies of the Philistines to rise and fight against the House of Israel. When confronted with the enormity and scourge of war, the Israelites sent three thousand men to bind Samson and deliver him to the Philistines to satisfy their anger and to alleviate the conflict. Yet upon deliverance of Samson to the Philistines, he burst his bonds and slew over one thousand men with only the jawbone of an ass. Thirsty, he then demanded water from God, rather than find it himself. He complained that if God was going to preserve him in this victory, why would He let him perish afterwards?

Samson's motivation to get married was based on something other than the desire to develop a healthy relationship. [10] Perhaps he thought engaging the Philistines was a noble and worthy cause—given the captivity of the Israelites—and whatever means he chose to confront them justified the ends. Think about that mentality for a moment in terms of the goals we have in our relationships. Sometimes, single adults develop the same mentality when searching for a temple marriage, because we believe a temple marriage the key to salvation and marital bliss. In other words, because it's viewed as necessary to our faith and our own eternal progression, the type and location of the marriage takes precedence over the actual health of the underlying relationship.

While getting married in the temple is an important and wonderful event, individuals seeking after a temple marriage without the basis for a healthy and functioning relationship will have tremendous difficulty, no matter how laudable the goal. Newlywed members are often shocked when they discover the reality and difficulty of their relationship after the temple marriage occurs, especially if they have had short engagements or bypassed needed dating and courtship periods prior to the marriage. These dating and courtship periods are intended for and allow us to gauge the health and fit of the relationship. Without them, we may leave the fate and success of the relationship to chance, or at least increase our future level of effort in it.

The priority of any single adult seeking a relationship should be the vitality and health of the relationship so that when a temple marriage is entered, it has the best opportunity to achieve the hoped-for and desired outcomes. Stated differently, for healthy relationships to occur, both individuals must always be motivated by the needs of the relationship itself, not the desire to check a box for religious or personal achievements. We should not be caught in the trap of believing marriage in the temple will be a solution to relational problems or will automatically and consequentially improve the health of the relationship. A temple marriage will enhance, augment, and help the relationship, and it will also give opportunity to perpetuate that relationship in the eternities; however, it is up to us to develop the necessary skills to have and maintain the health of that relationship. Samson's marriage is a prime example of someone trying to achieve a desired and beneficial outcome through a relationship, while ignoring the basis and purpose for entering that relationship.

Temple marriages ask two things of us: we accept the individual choices and agency of each person in the relationship and we receive each other in a capacity that may be blessed of God. It's an acknowledgement of our own choices and responsibility for the relationship and the acceptance of the other into our lives. What does it mean for us to receive each other? The concept of receiving is one of personal and spiritual vulnerability. It is the concept of taking something into you and making a part of who you are. It is the process of becoming one with each other and with God. If we are not able to receive each other or are not able to be vulnerable with each other, our ability to achieve relational happiness in this life and in the life to come will be restricted. It will also diminish the purpose for having the marriage itself. Disappointment and heartache will be the result.

Samson's choice in whom to marry was based solely on who pleased him the most visually. Even when his parents expressed concerns about whether the relationship was a good fit, he singularly focused on his own desire, quickly disregarding those concerns. He had an entitlement mentality, believing he was deserving of what delighted or entertained him. How unhealthy is that expectation and practice in our lives, in particular for the relationships we pursue? How often do we as single adults undertake the same type of behavior when choosing those we date? When we disregard relationships that may be a good fit for those that are not, based solely on personal desires, it is a recipe for disaster.

While Samson's parents' concern about religion may or may not have been justified, Samson's blatant disregard for whether the relationship was a good fit impacted the health and well-being of that relationship and prevented short- and long-term trust from occurring. Such narcissistic tendencies from both men and women show a callous disregard for the relationship and the other person involved. When this occurs, the relationship becomes solely for and about that individual; relational problems and issues will most certainly arise later.

The events surrounding Samson's wedding epitomized both selfishness and drama. I suppose if they ever made a TV show of weddings gone bad, this would be the premier episode. Samson's making a public wager took emphasis away from the wedding festivities, showed apathy about the purpose of the wedding, and centered the attention solely upon him and the conclusion of the wager. Samson also manipulated the situation by wagering large sums of money with individuals and tried to control the outcome through an answer only he knew. Such a wager was not fair and created the circumstance under which his wife and her family faced threats to their lives.

The interaction with Samson and his wife regarding his wager was also hugely problematic. Still, Samson's wife seemed more concerned about herself and her family's welfare than Samson's welfare.

This does not mean she had to support or agree with Samson's choices, but she did not need to deceive him to benefit others. Samson had the ability to protect her and her father from any physical harm, if the spouses had only been willing to trust each other. Instead, Samson showed a serious lack of consideration for his wife when he compared his relationship with her to the relationship he had with his parents. He deprioritized the relationship between himself and his wife for his relationship with his parents. What an unhealthy and unhappy situation. This raises another issue we can learn from: what emphasis or priority do we place on our relationships? If there are other relationships that take priority, whether family, friends, or otherwise, is there little wonder the lower priority relationship will suffer or be unhealthy?

Additionally, Samson showed great selfishness by not paying for his debt himself but rather seeking the payment from those with whom he sought conflict. This also makes his anger upon his payment of the debt curious, as he did not pay the bounty with his own possessions. His abandonment of his wife to return to his parents was pathetic and showed a high level of immaturity. In a sense, he punished his wife through denying her access to the relationship. Is it any surprise their marriage was short and his father-in-law gave his daughter away to someone else? Our ability to resolve conflict, to be sensitive to the needs of others, and to be accepting of our spouse's needs plays a critical part in the success and duration of any relationship.

Samson's unexpected return after an extended leave with no contact, bearing only a perfunctory gift, showed no concern toward his wife. It was almost as if he believed his nominal gift, which had little or no thought behind it, would make up for his behavior and allow the couple to move forward as if nothing had occurred. His expectations did not reflect reality and only considered his own wants and needs. When presented with the consequences of his actions, he neither accepted them nor acted appropriately. His justification for burning the Philistines' crops after his rejection placed the blame solely on the Philistines without any recognition on his actions. He projected his own anger and shame onto those from whom he would seek retribution for his public humiliation.

The Israelites' willingness to deliver Samson to the Philistines when faced with the retaliation of the Philistines' military campaign demonstrates that Samson did not have the Israelites' support for his actions. Having acted independently, he had now brought the two nations to the brink of war. These actions speak to the ability of Samson to be open and vulnerable with himself and those with whom he was in a relationship. Samson was incapable of recognizing his own actions, their consequences, and the solutions thereto. He cared solely for his own interests, ignoring the consequence for those for whom he was supposed to have responsibility. The aftermath of which cost the lives of his wife, her family, and many others. Additionally, his demand on God for water after his victory over the Philistines shows no remorse for the consequences of his actions and demonstrates his incapacity to become vulnerable with himself and with God. How regrettable and unfortunate.

Based primarily on the outcome of Samson's extraordinary victory, the House of Israel tasked Samson to lead and judge them for twenty years. Samson did not live up to his high responsibility and station, and he sought escape through an empty and desultory relationship with a prostitute in Gaza. Samson subsequently fell in love with another Philistine woman, named Delilah. Seizing the opportunity, the Philistine leaders approached Delilah and offered her a large sum of money to lure and seduce Samson into revealing the secret of his immense strength. Delilah asked Samson directly what his secret was, upon which he told her a lie, stating if he were bound with seven green withs he would become weak as any other man.

The Philistines then brought the withs to Delilah, who tied Samson therewith. The Philistines hid in Delilah's chamber, hoping the tactic would work; however, when Delilah called out that the Philistines were coming, Samson broke the bands as if it were a game. Undeterred, Delilah told Samson he mocked her and again requested Samson to tell her his secret. Samson lied once more, stating that if he were bound with new ropes, he would lose his strength. Delilah then bound Samson, this time using new ropes, and repeated the process with the same result. Again, Delilah pressed Samson for his secret, upon which Samson told her if she weaved his hair into a web he would lose his strength. Once again Delilah tried and failed to take away Samson's strength.

Delilah then approached Samson, stating, "How canst thou say I love thee, when thine heart is not with me? Thou hast mocked me these three times, and not told me wherein thy great strength lieth."[11] Delilah repeated this sentiment to Samson daily until he told her the secret of his strength: that he was a Nazerite and that if his hair were cut his strength would depart. Once Delilah was satisfied Samson had told her the truth, she called the leaders of the Philistines and received payment of the promised sum. At an opportune time, Delilah caused Samson to sleep whereon she had his head sheared. Delilah called out to Samson the Philistines were upon him. He arose not realizing his strength was gone. As a result, the Philistines captured, tortured, and blinded him. They then enslaved him in a grinding mill as a trophy for their sport and amusement.

After some time, Samson was brought before the Philistines, who were celebrating and gloating over his capture. Overconfident, the Philistines placed Samson, whose hair had regrown, between the pillars of the house. Samson cried unto God saying:

> "O Lord God, remember me, I pray thee, and strengthen me, I pray thee, only this once, O God, *that I may be at once avenged* of the Philistines *for my two eyes*."[12]

Samson then took hold of the house pillars and caused them to fall, killing himself and more than three thousand people.

What a sorry and tragic story. Often people in the church rightly point to Samson's sin (that he visited a prostitute, married outside the faith, etc.) as the true reason he lost his strength. His hair is seen as the outward manifestation of a covenant Samson neglected and abandoned. Samson's story, though, is much more than a lesson on the effects of sin in our lives. It is also a lesson on the effects of healthy and unhealthy relationships in our lives. Above all else, it was Samson's unhealthy relationship with Delilah and the choices he made in that relationship that led to his own downfall and destruction. Samson and Delilah's relationship exposes and exhibits to us the impacts of unhealthy relationships in our lives and the repercussions from our responses to the intense feelings and emotions that occur at the failure of those relationships.

Delilah was a siren-harpy whose only thought was of herself. She had no connection, emotion, or feelings toward Samson and was beguiled by the fame, notoriety, and monetary wealth she would receive for her relationship with him. Her betrayal of Samson is epic for its depravity and has stood unchallenged throughout history. That any woman would take advantage of any man in this manner for personal gain and satisfaction is terrible. Delilah was more concerned about worldly things than the health, welfare, and success of her relationship with Samson. Not only did she seek to deceive Samson for his capture and destruction, but she also repeatedly and intentionally applied the mechanism for his downfall herself. This makes me sad not only for Samson, who endured the fallout, but also for Delilah, as she was incapable of having healthy connections and relationships in her life. In a very real sense she is exactly like Samson: unhealthy and selfish.

Both Samson and Delilah typify individuals who enter a relationship for ulterior motives. Similarly, I have seen many single adults seek relationships not based on a desire for a healthy relationship but based upon the need for security, finances, or other tangible benefits. It is my observation that when such motivations are the basis for a relationship, the involved individuals are at risk of having similar outcomes as that of the relationship between Samson and Delilah—maybe not as impactful as the loss of life, but certainly as destructive in the consequences and to the emotions and well-being of all involved.

Perhaps Samson and Delilah deserved each other. They were two people so incapable of dealing with their own internal issues that they could not reach past themselves to work for the betterment and welfare of the other. Why would Samson, the Judge of Israel, engage in such a meaningless and destructive relationship? Why would he trade away the secret to his success and strength for nothing more than a verbal validation from someone who intended him harm? Was it the pressure of his office, the inability to cope with his tremendous power, or the trauma, lack of confidence, and shame of his previous relationships? We will never really know.

The real tragedy with Samson was his inability to learn from his experiences with his first marriage. As a result, almost the exact same pattern was repeated, with one unhealthy relationship after another, leaving a trail of emotional and physical destruction in Samson's life. It was a never-ending cycle of drama, pain, and a lack of real and meaningful connection that led to greater pain and self-inflicted misery. Even in the very end, Samson's last actions were motivated by selfishness and revenge on the Philistines for the cruelty and viciousness they inflicted upon him. The truth is, Samson was blinded long before the Philistines captured him, through his inability to see and to discern the basis for a healthy relationship.

Samson's tragedy is echoed in the plight of many single adults in the church. Not that single adults are bad or selfish, yet we may enter relationships with good intent but for the wrong purpose, and then struggle later with the application and reality of that relationship. As a result, we find ourselves in a never-ending cycle of unhealthy relationships leading to disappointment, loneliness, and despair.

Maybe there are holes in our lives that prevent appropriate giving and receiving of connection and love. Maybe there are attributes or qualities that are not apparent but negatively manifest themselves in our relationship later. Perhaps we choose individuals for less-than-perfect motives or pass by healthy relationships based upon a prioritized need for attraction. Perhaps we are unwilling or unable to risk being open and vulnerable to another individual after the hurt and trauma of a past failed marriage or relationship. Whatever the reason, it's the failure or inability to have healthy relationships that causes much of the pain, loneliness, and heartache in our lives. The tragedy of Samson is preventable and its root is something that, if recognized and addressed, may be a strength to each of us in our lives as we try to enter, maintain, and most importantly be vulnerable to healthy relationships.

HOW DO WE RECOGNIZE AND THEN MAINTAIN A HEALTHY RELATIONSHIP?

I don't believe single adults enter any relationship with the expectation that it will be unhealthy; however, accomplishing a healthy relationship is often more difficult than anticipated and is contingent upon both individuals' ability to work, forgive, and accept each person for who they are. Love itself has very little to with the feelings and emotions associated with entering a relationship; rather, it is the outcome or product of a healthy and trusting relationship.

Many divorced people truly love and are attracted to each other, yet they lack the ability to facilitate a functioning and healthy relationship. Why is that? Part of the problem is most initial connections occur based upon a natural and mutual attraction between individuals. When we find ourselves attracted to someone else, our own biology releases chemicals into our brains that may cloud or impair our initial judgment as it pertains to the fit and the health of a relationship. Many times, the euphoria of this condition will sustain and perpetuate a relationship, even an unhealthy one, in the near term.

At some future point these chemicals will abate, leaving only our own ability and skills to resolve relational problems and issues. Many times, when this emotional euphoria wears off, we find ourselves looking around and saying, "I don't like this relationship. It's not what I signed up for." Adversity then occurs in the relationship as deficiencies that were originally mitigated or, better said, overlooked are no longer resolved. On top of that, the emotional exhilaration originally experienced is no longer as easy to retain. If we are not willing to put in the work necessary to sustain and move a relationship forward, often the relationship is at risk to struggle and fail.

At this point we repeat the process with new and different people; however, when we go back to or enter new relationships, we are again put into the same attraction process whereby our judgment is influenced by biological factors. In other words, if we haven't developed the skills and abilities to maintain a healthy relationship, we will recycle current relationships, continuously going back to the euphoria of new relationships but never developing the long-term connections and attachments that have true meaning in our lives. It is a relational regurgitation where we discard old relationships and enter new ones hoping for improved or different outcomes but base our choices on similar criteria as the previous relationship. Being single then becomes an unending relational merry-go-round of superficial relationships. It's easy to get on but very difficult to get off. Frustration and loneliness, even if we are actively engaged in dating, will eventually result.

The following is one of my favorite experiences from the Savior's ministry:

> And he cometh to Bethsaida; and they bring a blind man unto him, and besought him to touch him. And he took the blind man by the hand, and led him out of the town; and when he had spit on his eyes, and put his hands upon him, he asked him if he saw ought.
>
> And he looked up, and said, I see men as trees, walking. After that he put his hands again upon his eyes, and made him look up: and he was restored, and saw every man clearly.[13]

Here is a man who was without sight who came to the Savior seeking and asking to be touched. Rather than directly heal this man, the Savior took him by the hand, walked with him, spit upon him, and then blessed him not once but twice. Why did the Savior do this? What did He hope to teach this man by His actions? What can we learn from what occurred?

The Savior had the demonstrated ability to immediately provide this blind man the sight he so desperately wanted, yet the Savior showed infinite patience, love, and charity by taking him by the hand and walking and talking with him. By spitting on him, the Savior touched this man in a unique and personal way, not as we would define it, but as the circumstances dictated and as this individual needed and required to develop and have sufficient faith for the Savior to heal him. Additionally, the Savior applied the requested blessing in a progressive and adapted manner, allowing the blind man to grow, recognize, and receive that blessing in accordance with the blind man's own individual capability and spiritual capacity. He also lifted this man's eyes and expanded his perspective so that he could clearly see.

In many of the relationships we initiate, we and our significant other are like the blind man. We start not knowing and not seeing what the outcome will be but have a desire to be touched or connect in a meaningful way. Yet, are we sufficiently receptive and open to each other and to a relationship? Are we individually ready to develop the necessary skills and to work towards the relational outcome we so desperately desire? Do we take the time and make the effort to know and understand the relationship and our significant other? Like the Savior, do we take our significant other by the hand and walk with them in their troubles and tribulations or stand with them in their times of greatest need? Do we reach out and touch them personally in significant and meaningful ways as circumstances allow and as they will accept so they may find comfort in their infirmities, obtain healing from their traumas and pains, and achieve peace in their lives? Do we constantly and continuously work with them in such a way and at such a level that they are enabled to connect with themselves and with us? Do we broaden their perspective and elevate their vision so they may recognize the Spirit? Do we assist them in such a manner as to allow them (and ourselves), like the blind man, to look up and with their own eyes to behold the Savior and to be healed?

Too often we assume relationships will be fine, that little or no effort or work is required. All relationships need help and support to come to the Savior. Even then these relationships need connection and attachment to allow those within it to grow and develop in healthy and productive ways.

If unhealthy relationships lead to or cause emotional trauma and difficulty, healthy relationships can heal and repair the holes, weaknesses, and disabilities in our lives. When we are truly open and vulnerable with each other and with God, there is a relational and spiritual edification that occurs. Love enables, facilitates, and is the result of that edification process as we strive to connect and build healthy relationships. Love is the critical building block upon which we base our faith and testimonies, that provides to us shelter and respite from the terrible darkness and loneliness of our lives, and enriches and enhances the bonds and relationships that we have with ourselves, our families, and those we interact with in the gospel. It is also the best and most effective way to lift our vision above the mundane, to clearly see with the right perspective, and to come to the Savior.

THE RELATIONSHIP BETWEEN JACOB, RACHEL, AND LEAH

Jacob is a polarizing figure in the Old Testament.[14] He was the younger twin to Esau and he was a righteous man who is exalted with God.[15] Esau was a hunter and was favored by their father, Isaac. Jacob was a plain man and was favored by their mother, Rebekah.[16] Difficulties occurred between the two brothers causing a sibling rivalry impacting everyone around them.

Jacob's purchase of Esau's birthright for a meager meal and the method and way in which Jacob received his patriarchal blessing caused friction with Esau to such an extent that Esau began to seek Jacob's life. As a result, Jacob left his parents and lived with his uncle, Laban, for decades. Fortunately, after almost twenty years, Jacob returned to his homeland, where he and Esau reconciled their relationship. Jacob later traveled to and died in Egypt because of a great famine and because of his son Joseph's, miraculous preservation with Pharaoh. Before dying, Jacob requested his body be returned to his homeland to be buried with his first wife Leah and his forefathers, which is where he is buried today.

Most of us know and understand that the twelve tribes of Israel derive from the twelve sons Jacob had with his four wives, Leah, Rachel, Bilhah, Zilpah. Leah and Rachel were sisters and the daughters of Laban. Leah was the oldest and is described as tendered-eyed (meaning plain or homely). Rachel was the younger sister, whose beauty was revered and well-favored.[17] Bilhah and Zilpah were the servants to Leah and Rachel and were later given to Jacob in marriage in the hopes of acquiring a greater posterity.

The relationship between Jacob and Rachel is one of story and legend. After leaving his homeland, Jacob first met Rachel on his arrival in Haran, where Laban lived. Rachel was in the process of watering her father's flocks when Jacob met and assisted her with her work. Jacob both kissed her and wept at this initial meeting, showing he was immediately attracted to and was interested in a relationship with Rachel.[18] The courtship for Rachel was very short, for within a month Laban and Jacob agreed that, in exchange for Jacob serving Laban for seven years, Rachel would become Jacob's wife. I love the affection expressed in this scripture: "And Jacob served seven years for Rachel; and they seemed unto him but a few days for the love he had to her."[19] What a beautiful and heartfelt expression regarding two people starting and developing a long-term relationship.

After the seven years of service were completed, Jacob approached Laban and demanded the right to marry Rachel. Laban agreed, but on the wedding night, and unbeknownst to Jacob, Laban switched the intended bride to Leah. This switching was most likely an indication of Laban's character and deception as opposed to any malfeasance by Leah. The next day, when Jacob realized the deception, he protested to Laban. Laban's unconvincing explanation was that Leah was the eldest daughter and he could not allow Rachel to be married before Leah.[20] This was a selfish explanation as Laban had seven years to either correct this oversight or to explain the situation to Jacob. Laban's objective was most likely intended to benefit himself by keeping Jacob in his service for an additional amount of time, rather than for the benefit of Leah. Irrespective, Jacob did not demand an annulment or request a divorce and accepted the marriage to Leah. In return, Laban allowed Jacob to marry Rachel one week later but required an additional seven years of service, to which Jacob agreed.

After Jacob's marriage to both Leah and Rachel, Jacob preferred, loved, and dwelt with Rachel. Perhaps this preference is understandable given the circumstances of Jacob's marriage to Leah and his feelings for Rachel. Yet the scriptures state God, seeing Jacob's preference, gave children to Leah; Rachel, on the other hand, was not able to bear children until much later in life.[21] Fortunately, Rachel was eventually able to bear two children; however, she tragically died during her second childbirth and was buried near Bethlehem.

We do not know the timing of Leah's death; however, it is believed she died after Rachel but prior to Jacob and is buried in the Cave of the Patriarchs in Hebron. This cave is also the burial place of Abraham, Sariah, Isaac, and Rebekah. We have little insight into Jacob's reasoning and decision to bury Leah in the Cave of the Patriarchs or his basis for burying Rachel elsewhere. Certainly, it bothered Jacob this situation occurred, yet he did not change or alter Rachel's burying place.[22] Upon Jacob's passing he requested he be returned to the Cave of the Patriarchs to be buried with Leah and his forefathers, not with Rachel.[23]

The quality of the marital and family relationship created among Jacob, Leah, and Rachel is fascinating to review. How can Jacob, a man who sacrificed fourteen years of his life for Rachel, who loved and preferred Rachel over all others, in the end request he be buried with Leah? Jacob had the means and capability to have Rachel's remains moved to the Cave of the Patriarchs or to choose to be buried with her. The finality of Jacob's choice raises several philosophical and fundamental relational discussion points: *Upon what traits and attributes do we base our initial desire to enter a relationship? How do those traits and attributes translate into the health and success of the relationship? How does that relationship affect and change our perspective on life and on the decisions and choices we make?*

Jacob, Rachel, and Leah's relationship illustrate valuable lessons to us today for recognizing healthy and unhealthy behaviors in our own relationships. Our ability to recognize these qualities will assist us in making informed choices that are more likely to lead to successful and healthy relationships, to recognize and accept the beneficial relationships *we need*, as opposed to seeking out and tolerating the less-than-beneficial relationships *we think we want or desire*.

The scriptures record the following events:

1. After twenty years of service to Laban, Laban intended to cheat and deprive Jacob of the remuneration Jacob had rightfully earned. Jacob, Leah, and Rachel decided to discretely escape from Laban and travel back to Jacob's homeland with all their possessions. After three days, Laban discovered their absence and pursued them. Unbeknownst to Jacob, Rachel had wrongfully removed and taken two valuable objects from her father. When Laban caught up with Jacob, a heated exchange occurred between them regarding the missing objects. Jacob declared a search should occur and whoever was found with those objects would be put to death. Rachel hid the objects by sitting on them while the search was ongoing and lied about having them to her father and to Jacob.[24]

2. Desiring to have children, and envious of Leah, Rachel approached Jacob and demanded he give children to her or else she die; Jacob became upset and angry at Rachel's demand.[25]

3. Rachel approached Leah and demanded Leah's son Reuben give her certain medicinal plants (mandrakes) that he had collected, believing these plants would assist her ability to conceive children. Leah responded to this request by stating that Rachel had already taken her husband; why did she now want to take Leah's one connection to Jacob (i.e. her children) as well? As a result, Rachel agreed to allow Jacob to spend time with Leah in exchange for the medicinal remedies. Ironically, Leah conceived her sixth child because of this bargain, yet the medicinal remedies had no effect on Rachel's ability to conceive.[26]

These examples give us a glimpse or insight into the type and quality of relationship Rachel had with Jacob and how Rachel approached and viewed that relationship in her life. The purpose of pointing out these events is not to criticize, harshly judge, or cast doubt into the character and worthiness of

Rachel. Just because we have difficulties with or are unable to have a healthy relationship with someone does not mean we or they are bad people—it just means there were impediments to the health of the relationship that were not resolved. The relational aspects these events demonstrate are: 1) Rachel exhibited selfishness, poor judgment, and failure to communicate with Jacob; 2) she projected fault and gave unrealistic and unattainable demands to Jacob; and 3) she devalued and deprioritized the marital relationship in favor of other wants or personal needs. Each one of these situations exhibits behaviors or traits that are harmful or negative to any healthy relationship.

By removing the items from her father, Rachel behaved selfishly, thinking solely about her own needs and wants. Perhaps she felt she deserved these items, perhaps she was sentimental toward or unwilling to let go of her past. Whatever the reason, her theft placed not only her but her entire family at extreme risk. Additionally, she hid the truth when confronted with the actuality of what she had done. Rachel's actions demonstrate an individual immaturity regarding real-time circumstances as well as an unwillingness or failure to communicate with Jacob on important and critical issues. Rachel's actions placed Jacob's own credibility in question and gave Laban a legitimate grievance in addition to his illegitimate and unfounded desires. This complicated an already tense and dangerous situation.

I often wonder what Jacob would have said to Laban if he knew Rachel was the culprit—would he still have allowed a search of the family's possessions and decreed the culprit would be put to death? It probably did not even enter Jacob's thought process that Rachel was the one who had done this act. Rachel's actions impacted the trust between her and Jacob, hampering the health of their relationship. On the other hand, Leah was similarly situated to Rachel, yet she seemed content to be with Jacob and her family.

From a relational perspective, the importance of communication and trust cannot be understated. Individual selfishness often hinders the ability to engender a trusting relationship as we hold onto material things or other relationships in our lives to which we give a higher priority or significance than our spouse or partner. Such traits may overtake the relationship as they prevent individuals in the relationship from being or becoming open and vulnerable with themselves and may lead to dishonesty, manipulation, and other unhealthy or controlling behaviors.

Rachel's demand on Jacob for children is also telling. The basis for Rachel's desire was envy of her sister's ability to bear children.[27] Rachel's primary desire for children was founded less upon her opportunity of being and becoming a mother and more on her concerns regarding her individual station and how other people viewed her. Perhaps this reason is the cause for Rachel's melodramatic and heavy-handed demands on Jacob that he give her children or else she would die, something Jacob could neither control nor fix had he so wanted.

Rachel knew Jacob could have children as Leah already had several. Rachel's demand on Jacob seems to be more of a projection of her concern onto Jacob as an alternative to accepting her own condition in life. Like Sariah, Rachel's inability to bear children was through no fault of her own, yet unlike Sariah, Rachel was more willing to project her problem or cast responsibility for this onto Jacob. By placing an ultimatum he could never meet onto Jacob, Rachel burdened not only Jacob but also her relationship with him.

Sometimes we have expectations of our spouses that they can neither meet nor accomplish. A refusal to adjust such expectations demonstrates a failure on our part to accept and love them for who they are in life. Projecting or casting fault onto our spouses or significant others covers up our own faults and conditions and demonstrates an unwillingness to be open and vulnerable with ourselves. It prohibits our ability to be self-aware, to see that a problem exists, and to recognize our role or part in that problem. Perhaps in this context it's understandable why Jacob became upset at Rachel's demand.

Finally, the interaction between Leah and Rachel regarding Reuben's medicinal remedies is also noteworthy. As discussed above, Rachel saw the many children Jacob and Leah had together and wanted the same. Rachel assumed that the mandrakes Reuben collected were the basis for Leah's fertility and demanded them from Leah. I love Leah's response to Rachel: "... is it a small matter that thou hast taken my husband? And wouldest thou take away my son's mandrakes also?"[28] While Leah probably did not want her sister to go childless, she was at least outwardly concerned that if Rachel were to have children, then Jacob's attention would be entirely directed to Rachel's children, abandoning Leah altogether. Leah was concerned about her relationship with Jacob, while Rachel was concerned about her inability to have children. I am sure Leah felt alone in her relationship with Jacob, especially because Jacob prioritized his relationship with Rachel. I also believe Leah must have loved Jacob dearly, for why else would she long for Jacob's presence and attention?

Rachel's bargain for these mandrakes is complicated not because of what she wanted, but because of what she was willing to trade to receive it. Rachel was willing to trade Jacob for her supposed opportunity to have children. Just as Esau sold his birthright to Jacob for a mess of pottage, Rachel was now bargaining for perceived needed remedies. But the price was not food; rather, it was what she valued the least: the relationship itself. Should not Rachel have been concerned about the relationship between Leah and Jacob as well? Should she not have encouraged Jacob to spend time with Leah without cost to alleviate the lonely and abandoned feelings of Leah, who was equally married to him? Rachel's devaluing of her relationship with Jacob and her willingness to barter it for things of no worth demonstrate just how low a priority she gave the relationship. When evaluating the outcome of the bargain Rachel struck with Leah, Leah got what she valued the most—a relationship with Jacob—and Rachel was left, by her own actions, with nothing at all.

Is there not a lesson for all of us about the quality and health of the relationships we have with those we date and those we marry? Jacob initially pursued a relationship with Rachel based solely upon her beauty, not the qualities she brought into the relationship. He was so enamored with her, he was willing to sacrifice his time and talents just to be with her. He overlooked the time and opportunity to develop a lasting relationship and to analyze and see whether a relationship was in fact a good fit for him and for Rachel.

So often in the church we rush into permanent relationships before knowing or understanding the relational qualities of each person and whether such qualities will bring the desired healthy relationship. We often operate under the misleading idea that Christian people of good character who practice their faith should be able to overcome all relationship difficulties. Because of this assumption, we justify searching for what pleases us the most, cursorily basing our relational decisions on how a person looks, what family they come from, or our perceived notions of worthiness within the church. Each of these things is important, but none serves to create or maintain viable and healthy relationships on a long-term basis. Marriages all too often struggle not because of the faith or testimonies of the involved individuals but because one or both individuals lack the skills necessary to develop and maintain a healthy relationship. As a result, we may become trapped in unhealthy relationships trying to hold on to our own testimonies and wondering what we have done to get to this point in our life. Hurt, pain, and discouragement are the result.

On the other hand, some of us, like Leah, have the skills necessary to maintain loving and healthy relationships but struggle to find the attention or opportunity to enter those types of relationships. Even when we do, we may be forced into relational situations that are not ideal and that do not reciprocate the type of love we give. Leah endured a tremendous amount of loneliness in her marriage to Jacob. Despite Jacob's preference of Rachel, Leah found happiness in her children and her family situation. She also continuously maintained her love for Jacob and accepted him for who he was.

Jacob's decision to be buried with Leah is arguably a realization or acknowledgement that the relationship he had with Leah was healthier than the relationship he had with Rachel. This realization has nothing to do with Jacob's love for Rachel or the number of children Leah had compared to Rachel, but rather with the capability of each to coexist in the context of a relationship. Perhaps the fact Laban switched Leah with Rachel on Jacob's wedding night was a great blessing to Jacob despite Laban's intentions—but one Jacob appreciated only many years later.

We should ask ourselves whether we are pursuing relationships with individuals who are like Leah or who are like Rachel and what are our expected results and outcomes of those endeavors. There is nothing wrong with attraction. In fact, attraction is one of the feelings that Heavenly Father gives to us to encourage us to enter and develop relationships with the opposite sex; however, He also expects us to evaluate the choices we make in the relationships we enter. When we prioritize attraction over all else, and without consideration of other possible relationships, we may end up struggling later.

6

Relational Expectations

*And Jacob kissed Rachel, and lifted up
his voice, and wept.*
—Genesis 29:11

Relational expectations are similar to and closely linked with the fit of the relationship. While relational fit deals with the direct circumstances and immediate impacts of the relationship, relational expectations deal with the obstacles or opportunities that either keep us from or allow us to be open and vulnerable with each other. They are the hopes and anticipations that open doors and initiate connection or the self-imposed walls that foreclose it. The combination of these either facilitates or restricts our thinking, emotions, and ability to be open and vulnerable to other people. Relational expectations take many and varied forms as we each individually measure and weigh differently those things we want in a relationship. In my observation, there are three principal and primary relational expectations commonly found or recurring among single adults: chemistry, sex, and finances.

CHEMISTRY, LOOKS, AND THE SPICE OF LIFE

Allure, seduction, attraction, endearment, and charm are all related to chemistry, yet chemistry itself is very difficult to define in the context of a relationship. Chemistry is an amalgamation of multiple factors, including proper timing, individual respect, admiration, desirability, personal habits and hygiene, spiritual and emotional connection, and self-assurance, to name only a few. Just as no two snowflakes are the same, no two individuals have the same likes or dislikes; thus, chemistry is highly subjective to the individual and to the circumstances in which they find themselves. Chemistry is the great "it" factor that is pieced together from many different elements, rather than a well-defined checklist of ideals or preferences. It's more like a fine gumbo: something delicious in and of itself, but to those of us without the recipe, the ingredients and steps to cook it are a complete mystery. Often, we don't know in advance what chemistry is for ourselves but we know when we see or encounter it. Chemistry is thus something we are more likely to experience, rather than characterize or delineate.

What then lies behind our choice to date someone or not? How do we determine what we want and what we hope to have in developing and entering a relationship? These are the subjects and topics that fill online chat rooms, on which we spend hours pontificating, and about which poets write. To be honest, I don't know. Despite this continuous sea of opportunity and choice, it's my experience that many if not most single adults place a disproportionate amount of emphasis on the looks and appearance of those we date or hope to date.

As a result, chemistry is in large measure influenced by, centered on, or based on the physical attributes of the individuals to whom we give opportunity and with whom we pursue relationships. It's the endless chase of the quintessential person and the outward manifestation of an inward desire to achieve and to have others view us as achieving perfection. It's the idea there is someone special, someone perfect for each of us (i.e. a Cinderella or a Prince Charming) and it's just a matter of time and effort for us to find the right shoe that fits. The problem is, you can't simultaneously wear a flip flop on one foot and a glass slipper on the other. Said differently, it's tough to be who we really are as an individual when we are chasing the ideal or are ourselves trying to become it. To partner with anyone other than who we define as the perfect or optimal match (particularly as it relates to appearance) is to live below our means in terms of relationships. When dealing with the eternal nature of marriage, this concept takes on a deeper and more complex scope because no one wants to settle or to marry down, especially when it's forever.

The progression of online dating seems to mirror this phenomenon and to intensify our desire for physical attraction in those we date. Today we look at a picture of someone online and instantaneously swipe right or left based solely on our initial impressions of the attractiveness of the person in the picture. The speed and thought about these decisions on individuals leaves little or no time to focus on or consider any other attributes that may be associated with or linked to chemistry. It is relational window-shopping and our only criteria is what we see.

I once read a blog entry from a single sister in the church where she posed a group query about dating and chemistry.[1] This sister indicated that the man she was dating was an excellent person, they got along well, they had similar tastes and likes, and she was generally happy with everything in the relationship with one exception: he had very small lips and it was hard for her to kiss him. This post seemed to touch a nerve with many people on the blog as a tremendous amount of discussion occurred about whether this sister should continue to date this man. I do not judge or decry this good sister's concern. At a minimum, this point was important to her and there were many people who responded both for and against a relationship. Still, there are instances when all of us choose to accept or reject individuals or relationships based not on the merits of the relationship but on the merits of our own subjective determination of what chemistry is or should be.

There is an old saying: Not every dog likes every other dog in the dog park. I have always taken this saying to mean that a lot of different variables exist in the people with whom we interact; some we meet and don't get along with and some we meet and find it's just the opposite. The same is true in dating, and that's a good thing. We should ask ourselves, though, how many times we have recommended to a friend someone we think they should consider dating, only to have them say, "I'm just not attracted to them." This answer is easy for us to say and slips off our tongue as an elegant but unsupported justification for not wanting to get to know someone or to be vulnerable in a dating context.

I have learned that someone's appearance is just as important to us in starting a relationship as the goal of having the relationship itself. It motivates, encourages, and prompts action. I view this as a blessing from God as it incentivizes us to enter healthy relationships with others. It is the start of the procreative and biological process for interaction and connection between men and women. The caution I always give, though, is while I have often seen chemistry be the basis and source for commencing many relationships, I have rarely, if ever, seen chemistry be the long-term fuel that sustains them.

Single adults will often debate the importance of chemistry as opposed to the importance and health of the relationship. One of my favorite scenes in the film *Fiddler on the Roof* occurs when Tevye asks his wife if she loves him. Tevye's question surprises her as they had been in an arranged marriage for decades. Their marriage wasn't founded in chemistry or choice but need and circumstance. Their efforts and experiences over a long period of time had brought them together in such a manner that true and enduring love had grown between them.

Today's relationships take a different track in their development and purpose. I used to kick and scream, arguing looks do not make a healthy relationship. Perhaps this argument was based in my own bias and feeling I was on the short end of the stick when it came to the beauty department. I found, though, when making this argument, I was always beating my head against a wall with individuals, for they either disagreed entirely or agreed but acted in a manner that was inconsistent.

Today, I accept that looks and appearance are a primary and essential basis for chemistry among single adults. Having said that, I do ask whether our increased dependence on this criteria and our individual ideas about chemistry force us to become too narrow or selective in our definition and expectation of chemistry. This narrowness can constrain our relational opportunities, giving us misplaced or miscalculated confidence in our choices that unintentionally diminishes our ability to effectively decide whether a healthy relationship may occur. What happens when circumstances change and alter the physical characteristics that created the initial attraction? What happens when the emotional and chemical highs found at the initial stages of the relationship shift into plateaus and valleys? The more we base our relational decisions on looks and appearance, the more our relationship becomes self-centric and self-focused as we fixate more on our own relational needs and requirements rather than the other person's needs.

Does this mean we should stop basing our relational decisions on looks and appearance? No, it does not. But we should recognize its impacts and effects on the relationship itself as we strive to have long-term, healthy relationships. When taken to the extreme, these criteria may negatively affect our ability for attachment and connection in the relationship should the physical characteristics change from what the relationship was originally based upon. We may become less motivated or lose interest in the current relationship or seek fulfillment or connection outside the current relationship, either through other relationships, work, hobbies, etc. Additionally, the constant potential for a loss or change of the chemistry in the relationship (if based solely on appearance) may cause long-term self-worth and trust issues in ourselves or in our significant others as we constantly worry whether we are attractive enough to hold on to our significant other or we are ourselves out there looking for the next eye-catching opportunity.

Can chemistry change overtime? Absolutely, and it should. We are not static individuals. We age, we grow, we have children, our tastes change, we obtain different perspectives about life and alter our priorities. The person we are in a relationship with today or with whom we hope to be in a future relationship will be a different person tomorrow than they are today. As a result, how we interact with each other and how we relate to each other determines the breadth, scope, and basis for the chemistry that occurs. My hope is that if we enter a relationship based organically or naturally on physical appearance, the resulting attachments and connections we develop will evolve and expand outside that single parameter, that the range or amplitude of the relationship will develop in sufficient levels and in sufficient time to accommodate healthy changes in the chemistry of the relationship without disrupting the purpose for the relationship. This takes a lot of work, effort, and understanding by everyone in the relationship.

OUR BASIS FOR RELATIONSHIP CHOICES: SAUL'S STORY

After their exodus from Egypt, the House of Israel was governed both civilly and religiously by prophets. Desiring to have a central and constant leadership to perform civic and governmental functions, like other nations, the House of Israel approached the prophet Samuel and requested he anoint a king to rule over them.[2] This request displeased both Samuel and the Savior because it was tantamount to a rejection of the Savior as their true king and the implementation of another in His stead.[3] Still, Samuel relented and anointed Saul to be the first king of Israel.

The initial description of Saul is interesting:

> Now there was a man of Benjamin, whose name was Kish . . . And he had a son, whose name was Saul, *a choice young man . . .* and there was not among the children of Israel *a goodlier person* than he: *from his shoulders and upward he was higher than any of the people.*[4]

It is fascinating to note the House of Israel based its acceptance of Saul as their king not upon his civic qualifications but rather upon his heritage and more importantly on his appearance. In other words, he came from a good family and he was taller than everyone else. There is no doubt God sent Saul to Samuel to become the king and there is no doubt Saul was a decent person; however, his reign was a failure and was fraught with difficulty, turmoil, and selfishness. This difficulty was mostly due to Saul's leadership inexperience and his unwillingness to grow to meet the significant responsibility and the circumstances he faced. Perhaps the Savior chose Saul because He wanted to demonstrate to the House of Israel the consequences of making essential decisions based upon exterior and less-relevant factors such as outward appearance. Saul was the prototypical person the House of Israel desired to have in the role of king. Sadly, Saul's reign was short-lived and ended without fanfare in great tragedy with the deaths of himself and his son Jonathan.

Contrast Saul's anointing to that of David. As Saul struggled in the role of king, the Savior sent Samuel to the house of Jesse to anoint a new successor to the throne. The interaction between Samuel and the sons of Jesse is interesting and instructive. When Samuel met with them, he looked at Jesse's eldest son, Eliab, and was originally struck by how good he looked and at how tall he was. He even exclaimed that Eliab was surely the chosen one of God. The Savior counseled Samuel, saying:

> But the Lord said unto Samuel, *Look not on his countenance*, or on *the height of his stature*; because I have refused him: for the Lord seeth not as man seeth; *for man looketh on the outward appearance, but the Lord looketh on the heart.* [5]

Samuel then proceeded to look at each of Jesse's seven sons to see whether he should anoint them king. When none were accepted, Samuel inquired if Jesse had any additional sons. Jesse responded that David, the youngest, was out tending the sheep. When David arrived, he was "ruddy" and he was without a beautiful countenance or physical appearance. In other words, he was unattractive and did not have the type of physical characteristics of a person we would normally consider for a relationship or for public responsibility. Nevertheless, the Savior chose David to succeed Saul as the king of Israel.[6]

Despite Saul's failure as the king of Israel, Samuel continued to evaluate potential successors for Saul based solely on physical characteristics (i.e. appearance and height). The Savior instructed Samuel to look to David, the least of Jesse's children, not because David was tall or good-looking but because his heart was right.

Think for a moment about Samuel's initial decision-making process and whether we seek after similar characteristics or use the same process when pursuing relationships. Do we constantly seek after the model or the perceived ideal because we want it, feel more comfortable with it, or think others will look favorably at us because of it? Do we say, "I didn't get the relationship I wanted the first time, so I will make certain I get what I want the second time," yet base our future choices on the same physical characteristics or previous relationship expectations, thinking things will be different this time around? These are the questions only we can answer for ourselves.

Even though Samuel relied on non-physical characteristics in choosing David as Saul's successor, it did not guarantee David would be a more improved king to the House of Israel. In fact, David's reign was no less problematic than Saul's reign. Despite the difficulty of David's reign, it lasted much longer and was perpetuated after his death, where Saul's was not. Many eternal blessings also came about as result of David's time in power that lastingly benefited the House of Israel, including the liberation and defense of Israel, the preparation for the construction of the temple, and later the birth of the Savior.

Think for a moment what this means for the ability of each of us to have meaningful and lasting relationships. All relationships struggle, no matter their origin or basis; however, those relationships based entirely on chemistry, solely on individual wants, or exclusively on physical appearance or other extrinsic factors will be more susceptible to risk and failure. Likely, those relationships will be less durable, less healthy, and of shorter duration than those relationships based upon intrinsic characteristics or those that are able to evolve and expand beyond their initial basis for chemistry. Like Samuel's example and benchmark in choosing David, if we base our relational choices upon criteria that is more likely to lead to healthy relationship outcomes, we will have a greater likelihood of positive connections and attachments. And while there is no guarantee of success or happiness, these relationships are more likely to have positive results and long-term blessings for each despite the relational problems and impediments that arise.

I believe in the potential of all relationships. I also believe we must all expand our individual definition of what chemistry is, whether in the forming of relationships or in the maintaining of them, so when changes, complications, or trying times come, we may in the long-term find benefit and lasting security, allowing light to come from difficulty and advantage from trial. By so doing, we will all find the opportunity and capacity to develop enduring connections and healthy relationships in our lives.

SEX, SEX, SEX

YES—I said it. The concept of intimacy and sex, especially as it relates to singe adults, is complex. One of my primary concerns about addressing it directly and openly is that its discussion may offend some or cause others to raise internal walls on the topic. Yet the issue of intimacy and sex is such an underlying and foundational issue for single adults, I felt it a disservice to write about single adults without including at least some discussion of it. As a disclaimer, I am a lawyer, not a therapist or a general authority. These are my thoughts and observations about how single adults view and deal with intimacy as it pertains to the application of pre-marital abstinence and living the law of chastity in a modern-day world.

Several years ago, I attended a mid-singles conference in Washington, D.C. As part of this conference, the mid-singles were split into groups to identify, discuss, and address the issues and concerns collectively of single adults in the church. Afterwards, several individuals were selected and asked to present their findings to the entire group. One of the presenters stood up and audaciously stated worthiness was a prime factor for inactivity of single adults and the church should re-evaluate (i.e. lower) its worthiness standards as it pertains to single adults. To be honest, the brazenness of the concept caught me off guard as I had never disputed or opposed the legitimacy of the standard itself. I have found, though, worthiness standards pertaining to sex and other related issues, such as pornography, illicit very strong feelings for and against. The emotions created are often so pronounced, they hinder or altogether obstruct important discussions about these topics.

Sometimes, when I try to engage in these topics from an unbiased or fact-based perspective, I feel shamed by others in the church who are not open to the perspective or I alternatively think they view me as advocating for or defending a position I do not personally believe or support. Sometimes members of the church may treat the discussion of sex as taboo or sacrosanct: only to be discussed in the most sacred of places and then only with local priesthood leaders (who themselves may or may not have a complete understanding of the topic). My intent of this discussion is neither to campaign for a different worthiness standard in the church, nor is it to say the church has a sex problem. What is intended is an unemotional and experienced-based perspective allowing us to make good decisions in our lives regarding intimacy and basic human needs that lead to the betterment of those in the church and the opportunity for all, single and married, to be part of the gospel family. I fully expect people to disagree, yet I hope it will lead to greater discussion, increased understanding, and more empathy for all involved.

I once had a bishop for a single-adult ward tell me his job was to keep the single adults out of bed before marriage and to get them in bed after marriage. This statement articulated to me not only the problem of dealing with the issue of pre-marital sex but also its implication and impact after marriage. Even though sex is an important matter for single adults, my observation and experience are that sex is generally addressed and discussed in an orthodox, black-and-white manner leading to false assumptions or incorrect understandings that may result in serious complications later. I find it sad that something designed to be a positive stimulus and influence in our lives can have such profound negative impacts on our emotional, physical, and spiritual well-being both before and after marriage. How we deal with intimacy and sex is a reflection on our understanding of who we are as human beings and a model for how we relate and develop connections with members of the opposite gender.

In January 2007, Public Health Reports released a study of the sexual activity of individuals in the United States. Data from that study showed, in the year 2002, by the age of twenty, over seventy-seven percent (77%) of the responding individuals had engaged in sex, with seventy-five percent (75%) of those having had pre-marital sex. The study further indicated that ninety-five percent (95%) of responding individuals had engaged in pre-marital sex by the age of forty-four. Not much difference occurred in the rate of sexual activity for people engaging in sexual activity when compared to statistics between 1952 and 1963. Statistics from these earlier years show eighty-two percent (82%) of individuals had engaged in premarital sex by age thirty and eighty-eight percent (88%) had done so by the age of forty-four. The study noted individuals were today delaying marriage into their late-twenties and thirties as the correlative reason for these statistics. The study concluded that within the United States pre-marital sexual behavior is "nearly universal" by age thirty and very common at much younger ages.[7]

These statistics and the inferences they draw are staggering. Granted they are based on statisitical sample sizes, but even with a large margin of error, the conclusion is essentially the same: for at least the past seventy years, marriage has not been the demarcation point when sexual behavior occurs for most people. Said differently, it's not a matter of if pre-marital sex occurs, but at what age and under what circumstances. As a result, it is incredibly difficult for a faithful single adult in the church to diligently abstain from pre-marital sex and if they do, he or she will be viewed in society as abnormal.

Even without seeing these statistics, most single adults implicitly understand the impacts of this behavioral trend in their dating lives. The challenge for maintaining abstinence before marriage is a monumental undertaking, especially for those single adults who are not able to marry or remarry for prolonged periods, who are geographically isolated, or whose lack of dating opportunity in the church may require dating outside it. Sadly, even within the church, views and pressures regarding pre-marital sex exist among single adults, creating a counterculture of individuals who may believe one thing but act in a different manner based upon their needs, wants, and circumstances. Because today's societal conditions relating to how sex is perceived and practiced are at odds with the church's views and standards on it, a single adult who engages in pre-marital sex is likely to feel shame. This shame leads to decreased activity in the church, difficulties in making and keeping healthy relationships, and a diminished capacity to feel the Spirit.

Each week I invite local missionaries over to my house to work on and practice their teaching skills, something I truly love and to which I look forward. Once, I hosted a pair of elders who were struggling to teach people about the law of chastity. Admittedly, this is a very difficult concept for the missionaries to teach given the universal acceptance and perspective of pre-marital sex. I suppose teaching individuals today about living the law of chastity is as awkward and difficult as requiring circumcision for admission to the church in olden times. Perhaps the difficulty of the topic relates to the church's minority perspective and the sacrifice required for those who accept the gospel in their lives.

When I asked these elders to teach me the principle, they could not. Each time they would say the word "sex," they would look at the ground and nervously laugh. It was if they were ashamed of the concept of sex itself. In coaching these elders on how to teach the principle of the law of chastity, I needed them to understand and accept sex was not bad. The first step, though, was to get them to be comfortable with just using the word "sex," for how can you teach someone the doctrine or principle if you are ashamed of saying the word itself? My homework assignment to them was to go home and each day to look each other in the eyes and repeat the phrase "sex, sex,

sex." Once they had socialized themselves to the concept, we were able to get to the heart of what the law of chastity is and why it matters for members of the church.

What is it about sex that causes so many problems in the church? Personally, I believe it's based on our treatment of the principle out a sense of fear. In other words, the fear of having sex (or at least the spiritual and physical consequences of it) paralyzes or stymies the opportunity to acquire real-time relationship skills or to develop meaningful attachments with the opposite gender in our lives. We are so conditioned to look at sex as sinful, we become uncomfortable or embarrassed at the mere thought of it. Alternatively, we may see it as positive but only when strictly regulated in its timing and implementation, thus we focus more on its controls than its purpose. By way of illustration, if you ask church parents today what are their greatest fears about their teenage kids, they would probably be their kids having sex and doing drugs (most likely in that order).

This discomfort with sex can be seen or manifest in uneasy or embarrassing interactions among our families, cursory teachings on the subject in the church, or odd interpretations or assumptions of what sex is. A common example of this may occur when parents first educate their children about sex. Without a valid context and firm understanding about sex, the important and educational conversations we have about it with our kids can be unproductive and negative. My first and only discussion with my parents about intimacy was undertaken in an uncomfortable manner for everyone involved and was focused on providing information without much concern for how much of that information was understood or received.

Additionally, parents sometimes hand out the harshest and most swift childhood punishments to children who err or experiment with sex (or variations of it) as part of their natural development into adults. I have wondered why this reaction may occur and whether it is based in a desire for corrective action in the child or an outgrowth of the shame and fear the parents have relating to sex. Irrespective of the motive, by doing so, we teach our kids to fear sex through imposed punishments and penalties that are not always fair, explained, or understood.

We also teach our children to fear sex through over-emphasized and fear-based consequences of sex: *You will get a disease, you will get pregnant, you won't be able to go on a mission, or to attend BYU*. These things, irrespective of their truth, lead to the belief sex is bad and shouldn't be engaged in for any reason at any time under any circumstance. The result is a developed negative view and perspective about sex, its purposes and reasons, and about ourselves. This negative view does not end when we are married either; it is as malignant after marriage and affects our ability to engage in healthy sexual activity. In its most pernicious form, it leaves us feeling unworthy after sex even if we are married in the temple.

In terms of sexual activity, the day an individual is married in the temple may be a literal shock to the system, for what we viewed the day before as sinful behavior is now a licensed, sanctioned, and holy activity. We are left wondering what changed once the marriage ceremony is over. Additionally, sex itself is a learned behavior between ourselves and our partners. Think about this verse from the Old Testament:

> When a man hath taken a new wife, *he shall not go out to war*, neither shall he be charged with any business: but he shall be free at home *one year, and shall cheer up his wife which he hath taken.*[8]

Even under the Law of Moses, there was a recognition of the need for intimacy in developing healthy relationships and the delicacy and timing needed for it in those relationships after marriage occurs. It takes time, patience, and practice from a relational and a physical perspective to develop a working framework and the healthy attachments necessary for individuals to feel safe in the relationship and for vulnerability to flourish. For this reason, I tell people temple marriage is not a quick fix or cure-all, especially as it relates to relationships and sex: it is an important initial step that assists and allows the real work of building meaningful and eternal relationships in our lives.

Sometimes, for those who have practiced abstinence, expectations of sex can be so artificially high at the beginning of a marriage as to impose incorrect assumptions about what sex really is like and what is beneficial for each involved party. When difficulties arise, and they frequently do, feelings of shame and rejection may accompany them, causing problems not only from a faith perspective but also from a relational perspective. In extreme cases, such feelings and perspectives affect our ability to be vulnerable, striking at the heart and viability of the marriage.

I am not aware of anyone physically dying from not having sex. However, I do know many marriages have died because the individuals in those relationships could not or would not have sex or could not cope in a healthy manner with the ramifications of intimacy in their relationships, especially in context of the gospel. Sex is such an important and foundational part of marriage relationship, not just for procreative or recreational purposes but also to validate the relationship, to foster vulnerability, and to grow trust in personal and edifying ways. If one may not be vulnerable in the context of a marriage, what then is the purpose of the marriage itself?

The use of sex, without suitable connection, vulnerability, and validation, has caused innumerable relational and other problems throughout history. Some prominent examples in the scriptures of the use and result of sex without connection, vulnerability, and validation include: Reuben's affair with one of Jacob's wives and the resulting loss of his birthright; David's affair with Bathsheba and his murder of Uriah; Amnon and Tamar; Samson and Delilah; Corianton's pursuit of Isabel; and the daughter of Jared's influencing of Akish. Even today, the use of sex without a correlative level of attachment and validation leads to the diminished ability to connect with ourselves and individuals.

Given God's intended natural drive for human beings to have sex, why does God care so much about its use and implementation? At times in my life, I felt an inherent unfairness in the strength of these desires as compared to the unyielding and unbending redline from the church regarding abstinence both before marriage and after divorce. I have wrestled with the loneliness and despair of abstinence for long periods of time prior to marriage, as well as the feelings of being emotionally stuck, not desired, and not accepted. I have also wrestled with living the law of chastity after divorce where expectations, feelings, and maturity pushed the desire for intimacy to higher levels than previously experienced. Yet these tugs and pulls have caused me to think about the purpose and meaning of sex in my life and my hopes and desires pertaining to a successful relationship in the future.

It is my belief that God's interest in our sexual behavior is related to its purpose and function in developing and maintaining the relationship between men and women. Sex has an integral role in procreation, in self-worth, and in entertainment for individuals, yet its primary function is an indispensable and vital demonstration of vulnerability between two people. It is an acceptance of each person individually for who they are in their natural and human condition.

Just as Adam and Eve were naked in front of God, sex is at its core the act of becoming naked to each other, not only physically, but also in our feelings, thoughts, actions, and emotions. It is the ability to unconditionally receive each other and to validate our spouse's vulnerability. When that vulnerability is accepted and reciprocated, especially at the intensity that occurs with sex, lasting and meaningful relational bonds are created.

It is the greatest and most powerful demonstration of the relationship. Whenever sex is engaged in without the requisite validation of both partners, loss, loneliness, and frustration will inevitably result. Sex without a strong connection and continued vulnerability will in the long-term be negative, limiting, or destructive to any relationship.

God cares a great deal about our ability to be open and vulnerable, for when we are not able to be open or vulnerable, deception occurs, whether to others or to ourselves. Because sex is the utmost form of intimacy and acceptance of another, it heightens the level of emotional risk individuals take with someone else. The risk we take during sex in allowing our partner to see us for who we are is what allows us to be truly open. If we have internal fears relating to personal rejection or feelings of low self-worth, we may raise emotional barriers that inhibit our ability to become sufficiently vulnerable during sex. This impacts the purpose for sex itself as it affects the degree and capacity for relational connection and bonding. On the other hand, if our partner does not accept and validate this openness and vulnerability, the negative impacts may be magnified as compared to other less committed (or less risky) forms of intimacy.

Part of the problem with sex today is this concept of openness and vulnerability within the relationship has been lost or devalued. People engage in sexual behavior so rapidly and so early, it prohibits or stunts the meaningful connections that are supposed to occur. Sex then becomes something that does not enhance or support the relationship but something that solely stimulates or entertains. People care more about the act of sex itself than the relational outcome. In this context, sex has entropic benefits and temporary effects that over time lose their meaning between individuals. It is like eating an entire bag of marshmallows: the first few are sweet and delicious, but the remainder are less and less satisfactory.

Consider ballroom dance as an illustration. Ballroom dance has played a major role in my life, and I found solace and joy in learning it. Dance is an outward expression and representation of our relationships. It is two people working in tandem, each having responsibility for the beauty of the dance itself. Each must lead and follow, each must give and take, and each must respect the role of the other. When done correctly, it is an incredibly powerful, elegant, and sophisticated connection. I think this reason is why we traditionally dance at weddings, not only because it's fun but because it symbolizes and embodies the relationship between the two people.

The problem today is, social dance has evolved away from what was once a partnership exercise to that which is individualized. As a result, social dancing has become highly titillating and stimulating. All we must do is go to a dance club, high school dance, or other dance activity to see the effects of the loss of this partnership component. What is lost today in dance are the skills and capacity necessary for us to connect, move, and interact with each other for a common purpose as well as an enjoyment of the beauty created from the synergy of working together. I think the same has occurred today regarding sex. Sex has evolved to a point that is more individual in nature and less about the relational connections and the opportunity for vulnerability and validation. While sex still serves a primary function for relationships, its purpose and meaning have evolved and changed in terms of its role in developing needed and healthy connections.

Sex and touch are basic human needs. They are like air and water, and depriving them over extended periods of time is detrimental to human development and existence. Given this, when and at what level should we engage in intimate behavior? My answer to that debate is, it depends on the people involved and the timing and level of commitment in their relationship. Occasionally, we will be in a relationship where one person is more committed than the other. One person may know for sure they want to marry the other while their partner is unsure or wavering. Sometimes one may want to be in an exclusive relationship while the other is not ready to date exclusively.

I have watched people postpone or deny other relational opportunities while they are focused solely on one individual who does not reciprocate their level of commitment. Hurt, disappointment, and failure are usually the result. My advice to people is to make sure the timing and level of intimacy we engage in is supported by the commitment level of both parties within the relationship. To some, holding hands means one thing, a hug another. To some, a kiss is a sign of affection and to others it's a demonstration of love.

Single adults will ask me whether kissing on the first date is appropriate. I always respond by saying whether it occurs on the first, second, or tenth date is less important; what matters most is whether the relationship between them has progressed far enough to adequately support the degree of intimacy in which we engage so vulnerability and trust can grow. Jumping in too fast and at too high a level of intimacy is like constantly opening the oven door to check on a soufflé. Too much too soon, and the soufflé will fall. On the flip side, I often hear of single adults who delay even the smallest acts of intimacy (i.e. holding hands, hugging, or kissing) until they are sealed in the temple. While on the outside, such actions may be laudable, I often wonder if these couples have built sufficient relational bonds and connections for the type of intimacy in which they are about to engage after marriage occurs.

Outside the church, in today's dating environment, sex is something that oftentimes occurs within the first few dates. Many times, the reasons given are to judge whether they are compatible sexually, to see whether the individual will remain in a relationship once sex has occurred, or to keep from feeling lonely. I believe many of our relational problems result from the failure to lay the appropriate groundwork prior to engaging in intimate sexual behaviors. Obviously, for members of the church, the highest level of commitment, marriage, is required for sex to occur. Personally, I believe this is an appropriate and meaningful standard as it is an outward manifestation and legally binding assurance that the involved individuals share the highest level of commitment. Such commitment should enhance and deepen the connection and vulnerability of the couple, thus allowing greater benefits from sexual activity within the relationship than are possible outside a marriage.

For me, keeping the law of chastity is less about being pure, less about what is right and wrong, and more about a personal choice about the type of relationship I hope to have in my life. It's about making sure I have every opportunity to be open and vulnerable with my future wife in such a way and in such a manner that removes barriers and will uplift our souls with the hope of building an enduring love that may be perpetuated in eternity.

My final thought about sex has been shaped by my experience and an observation. When I was a young single adult, I wrestled with the notion of dating someone who was divorced or who had not remained abstinent prior to marriage. Because I had never had sex myself, I believed the only type of person I should consider dating was also someone who had never had sex. Within the church, I was taught this notion from an early age: the purity of the individual and the sanctity of having sex only with one another was the most important part of the relationship. As a result, dating someone who was divorced was a foreign and almost repugnant concept for me in my early twenties. It was almost as if accepting such a relationship would constitute a failure on my part. As I progressed into my late-thirties, my ideals had to shift to face the reality that most single adults in my age range had been previously married. I was forced to re-evaluate what was most important to me when it came to marriage and relationships.

I do not belittle or minimize the doctrine the church teaches about the importance of virtue between two people in marriage. Neither do I rationalize or justify individuals' choices not to follow gospel standards as it relates to sex. What concerns me is how single adults apply this concept of purity when evaluating dating and marriage opportunities, especially given today's trends in sexuality and marriage. I am concerned we may, based on our belief or concept of purity, eliminate viable opportunities for healthy marriages and relationships in the church because we exclude or negatively judge those who are divorced or who have not practiced abstinence.

Sometimes I will hear faithful single adults say, "I am saving myself for my future spouse," as if their purity is an honorarium bestowed upon their future spouse, like two people exchanging engagement gifts. Abstinence before marriage should not be practiced out of consideration for the other person but for ourselves, to allow ourselves greater opportunity to be vulnerable in the relationship. Vulnerability is not something we give to someone else; it's a state we inhabit with ourselves and our spouses. Sex is about taking the emotional and spiritual risk and saying to the other person, "I am here and I accept you."

Anyone who is divorced, or who has failed with their sexuality in their lives, can become sufficiently vulnerable again in a future relationship. We all have the capacity to love and to love again, especially in the context of new or different relationships. For this reason, dating someone who is divorced or who has had previous abstinence problems may be okay, because a strong marriage is not about two people who have never had sex before; rather, it's about how you as an individual may be and become vulnerable. It isn't about their past but rather about their capacity and capability to be in a healthy relationship today and going forward. The reasons for a divorce, and the propensity of individuals to live gospel standards, is an important consideration in determining fit for the relationship; however, the act of having sex in and of itself should not be the conclusive or deciding factor in our decision-making processes.

Additionally, those who have practiced abstinence prior to marriage may in fact find an increased ability to be vulnerable to themselves and with their spouse in ways that may enhance and allow their spouse to grow and reciprocate in like manner. I believe we should view our individual choice for abstinence as an opportunity for ourselves and for the potential growth of our future relationships rather than as a non-negotiable prerequisite for those we date and marry.

SEX AND PORNOGRAPHY

A few brief thoughts about sex and pornography. I had a real internal debate with myself about whether to write about pornography. Of all the topics among single adults in the church, pornography is the most frictional and difficult to discuss. I think the topic of pornography is discordant not only because of its influence on those who utilize it but also because of the personal perspectives and its impacts on those affected by it. There are both institutional and individual perceptions that clash in a rancorous contest of wills, leaving in its wake inactivity, heartache, and pain for all involved. As a result, I decided to treat this subject in the same manner as Moroni when he sealed up two thirds of the gold plates: written, but only available on an as-permitted or as-needed basis.

Having said that, and without wishing ill or offense to anyone, I will briefly say the following about the use and treatment of pornography in the church. Whenever I hear a talk on pornography or see someone post an article online about it, it is usually based on the *impacts* or *effects* of pornography on individuals and relationships. Such discussions or posts are often followed by a testimonial of sorts that these things were the causal factors for the breakdown of marital relationships. This emphasis on effects rather than causes leads us to become afraid, and we address the topic based upon our personal fear or individual insecurity. The problem is, whenever we address issues based on fear, shame is the result.

I truly believe this approach is why we are not having as much success against the use of pornography among the members of the church. It's because we as an institution and a society end up shaming those who need healthy connection and acceptance as a remedy. It's a lot like handing a drowning individual a glass of water, as these individuals are often isolated and stigmatized in ways that only push them further into the use of pornography rather than receiving the healing benefits offered through the church and the gospel. Additionally, whenever the individual involved is single, this approach increases and magnifies these impacts. It's a very sad thing when people who need help are not able to receive it for these reasons.

I do not believe in pornography or its use; however, I do understand the reasons and needs of those who do. The use of pornography is an inappropriate coping mechanism that in varying degrees restricts healthy thinking and healthy relationships from occurring. Some may view it as an inexcusable breach of trust or an emotional betrayal in a relationship, greater in scope and degree than if an extra-marital affair itself had occurred. I do not challenge or diminish these feelings; however, I believe the solution to the use and practice of pornography in society lies in a seachange in the way we all understand, view, and address it.

For those interested in learning about and understanding sexual addiction (of which pornography is a type), I recommend reading the book

Don't Call it Love by Dr. Patrick Carnes. Dr. Carnes is one of the preeminent researchers and scholars on the topic. Shame fuels pornography in all its varied forms. The antidote to shame is the ability to overcome negative perspectives and the ability to have healthy and meaningful connections. The truth is, most relationships and marriages are capable of healing from the effects of pornography if both individuals are open and honest about all problems with themselves and the issues in the relationship.

For those interested in developing better, healthier attachments and connections, I recommend the book *Hold Me Tight* by Dr. Sue Johnson. This book is about how we develop normal and healthy bonds and attachments in our lives. The key is, we all are open and willing to be vulnerable with ourselves, rather than to point at the other's problems or issues.

My hope is that we begin to understand the causes of pornography and deal with those directly to have a legitimate impact on its use and its effects in our lives and in our relationships. In this way, we can accept those who struggle, embrace those who have been impacted, and allow healing and acceptance to occur for everyone in a way that repairs and saves relationships, allowing healthy connections to go forward.

IMPACT OF SEX ON INDIVIDUALS: DAVID AND BATHSHEBA

David is another amazingly complex and revered individual in the Old Testament.[9] The son of Jesse, he was anointed as a young boy to be a king over Israel. One of his first and defining acts was the miraculous defeat of the Philistine giant in hand-to-hand combat, allowing the Israelite army to gain an important military victory over the Philistines. Invited into Saul's court, David grew in fame and stature, which provoked and angered Saul. As a result, Saul cast David out. Expelled from Israel, David was a refugee for many years, struggling for survival in hiding from a king and a government that would, without cause, destroy him. Eventually, both Saul and his son Jonathan were killed in battle and David was crowned king over Israel. David's reign, however, was fraught with difficulty and turmoil, much of which was his own making.

God blessed David with many wives and with many children. Despite this blessing, David found himself in a multifaceted and precarious predicament after he sought after and engaged in an extra-marital affair with Bathsheba, the wife of Uriah the Hittite. Shirking his duty to be with the

Israelite army, David remained in Jerusalem when his army campaigned against the Ammonites. One evening David was out walking when he viewed Bathsheba bathing. Perhaps this was an innocent encounter, yet David was highly attracted to Bathsheba and, in an abuse of his power, summoned her to him.

As a result, Bathsheba became pregnant with David's child. Attempting to hide this consequence, David recalled Uriah from the battlefield. Over a two-day period, David tried, surreptitiously, to get Uriah to go home to Bathsheba in the hopes of covering David's sin; however, Uriah would not go in unto Bathsheba. Uriah's reasoning was the Israelite army was fighting in the fields and living in tents, and he could not partake of the comforts of home when others were suffering under the auspices of war.

Frustrated, hindered, and stymied, David sent Uriah back to the battlefront carrying a message to Joab, the general, with instructions for Uriah's own demise. The appalling irony of David's action is grim and difficult to fathom. David's instruction commanded Joab to place Uriah at the battlefront and to withdraw, exposing Uriah in such a lethal manner that he would be killed. This was done, and Uriah was cruelly and unmercifully killed.

When Joab sent a messenger back to David to report on the progress of the battle, Joab was concerned David would be angry at the precarious position in which Joab had placed the troops. Joab instructed the messenger to state that Uriah was killed in the military effort if David questioned Joab's strategic decisions, reminding David publicly, but without acknowledgement of the actual cause, why Joab did this. When the messenger reported to David, including the death of Uriah, David concealed and camouflaged his actions with his response:

> Thus shalt thou say unto Joab, *Let not this thing displease thee*, for the *sword devoureth one as well as another*: make thy battle more strong against the city, and overthrow it: *and encourage thou him*.[10]

After this exchange and report, David brought Bathsheba into his household and made her his wife.

Subsequently, the prophet Nathan confronted David with a parable of a rich man who refused to take of the plenty he had and instead took that which belonged to the poor man for his own gratification. David, who was hiding his sin, was caught and forced to confess what he had done. Because David had killed Uriah and because he had taken Bathsheba to wife, Nathan decreed: God would bring constant conflict to David's house, the source of that conflict would arise internally (i.e. from within David's own house), and David would lose the wives God gave to him. Nathan also told David he would not die, but Bathsheba's child would.[11]

Attempting to assuage God's judgment against the child, David lay for days vexed and penitent before God in fasting and prayer in hopes the child could be saved. Sadly, the child died seven days later. Incongruously, David, who had been so grieved while the child was alive, became emotionally disassociated the moment the child passed away, surprising even his servants.

> Then said his servants unto him, *What thing is this that thou hast done*? thou didst *fast and weep* for the child, while it was alive; but when the child was dead, thou *didst rise and eat bread*.
>
> And he said, While the child was yet alive, I fasted and wept: for I said, Who can tell whether God will be gracious to me, that the child may live?
>
> *But now he is dead, wherefore should I fast*? Can I bring him back again? *I shall go to him, but he shall not return to me.*

David's actions with Bathsheba are often discussed and used by many, both in and out of the church, as an important example of the impacts of sexual sin. David's affair was the result of his failure to follow his civic duty by remaining in Jerusalem, his failure to remove himself from viewing Bathsheba when he came upon her, his acting upon his desires in bringing Bathsheba to him, and the improper use of his position to influence her. The appropriate use of self-governance or self-control in any one of these matters may have prevented the tragedy that followed.

In any case, the larger sin was not David's affair or its cause, but his subsequent actions to cover it up. David's attempt to hide the effects of his affair by recalling Uriah from the battlefront is challenging and problematic. When Uriah was committed and steadfast to his charge and did not spend the night with his wife, David's strategy was frustrated. Rather than acknowledge his wrongdoing, David took the even more extreme and detrimental step of having Uriah, an innocent and loyal man, killed. Joab's report to David and David's response showed David's willingness to excuse any action to hide his sins.

Essentially, David told Joab that Joab's actions and the placing of his troops in harm's way was not a major concern, that people die in warfare, and that he should move forward without concern in the work to which he was charged. David's action represented a secret combination at the highest level of government to carry out and hide serious individual sin that had tremendous and wide-reaching aftereffects. Thinking he had sidestepped or sufficiently whitewashed the consequences of his affair, David began to lead a dual life: representing to those around him an outward appearance of propriety while internally and in secret living a lie. How sad.

Nathan's indictment of David is significant, and the consequence to David was dire indeed. David did not lose his life or his kingdom; rather, he lost the opportunity for peace in his life. He lost in part his posterity, and in due course, he lost his wives (his personal relationships.) Additionally, the cause of this calamity was not external but internal.

Think about that for a moment. What David really lost was his ability to have healthy associations with those around him. That inability led to conflict, despair, and heartache, not only for David but for the entire House of Israel. Is this not the culmination or result of the inappropriate use of sex or its derivatives in our lives? Is it not the loss of vulnerability and the ability to accept those around us that diminishes or causes us to lose important and valued connections with spouses, children, friends, and other loved ones? Surely the extent and scope of these impacts were different for David, yet are not the results, at least in part, the same for us and for society?

David's response to the loss of his child is also telling. While he mourned during the child's short life, his complete lack of remorse once the child died shows David's lack of connection not only with himself but with those for whom he naturally should have affection. The curse from the improper use of sexuality, as spoken of in the scriptures, is not something that comes or is imposed on us from the outside; rather, it impacts us from the inside and results in the diminished ability to have healthy connections in our lives. These impacts are not static: they perpetually recur from unhealthy relationship to unhealthy relationship, leading to individuals who are disassociated from themselves and from others.

As prophesied by Nathan, David's troubles did not end after the death of his illegitimate child. Shortly after David's affair, a disturbing incident happened, setting into motion a complex and sordid series of events that instigated the fracturing of David's family and thrust the House of Israel into a civil war. Amnon, David's eldest son, coveted and lusted after Tamar, his half-sister. Through pretense, he entrapped and raped her. Having satisfied his own lust, he discarded her as if she were chattel, refusing even to accept her into his household. As a result, she was by law left desolate and not allowed future opportunity for marriage or family.

David, while angry at Amnon, refused to act or to provide judgment against his son or to relieve Tamar's pain. Absolom, Tamar's brother, was angry at both Amnon for his action and his father, David, for his failure to provide the requisite justice. Several years later, Absolom took matters into his own hands and murdered Amnon. David again did nothing and eventually invited Absolom back into court. Absolom used this opportunity and his position to conspire against David and planned sedition with those who would overthrow him. Because of this conspiracy, David, who had never fled before the face of an enemy, abandoned the safety and security of Jerusalem and left the throne to Absolom. To solidify his authority in front of all of Israel, Absolom profanely took David's wives to himself.

The conflict between David and Absolom escalated quickly into a large-scale war that resulted in the loss of more than twenty thousand men. The result of this conflict was the death of Absolom and reinstatement of David to the throne. Yet after Absolom's death, David was distraught over his son's death and he mourned exceedingly. His mourning was so excessive it offended those who fought for David against Absolom. David almost lost his kingdom a second time because of his failure to recognize the sacrifices made by those on his behalf.

What a tragedy, all derived from David's inability to connect with his family. David was not responsible for Amnon's sin, but his inability to exercise judgment or to rectify the consequences led to ill will and the destruction of both his sons and thousands of others. His failure to see current and present dangers led to a long and lengthy downward spiral that metastasized throughout the entire kingdom. Additionally, David's unhealthy and co-dependent attachment to Absolom, even after Absolom sought after his destruction and usurpation, is difficult.

On one hand David could not appropriately attach to his illegitimate son, and on the other he focused so intensely on his relationship with Absolom that he could not let go of an unhealthy situation. How truly dissociated and dysfunctional David had become. David's ability to have healthy and meaningful relationships was gone, as was his ability to make correct and needed decisions. All of this was a byproduct of his affair with Bathsheba and his inappropriate use of sex. Significantly, the tragedy of David's story is not about the *external giants* he confronted and overcame but rather the *internal giants* and problems that plagued his life that he did not or could not rise above or address. This failure led to great heartbreak and misfortune for him and those around him.

The caution I give to single adults as it pertains to the desire for sexual activity, or the actual engagement in its use, is not about being worthy or about being a virtuous member of the church. It is also not about whether we are a good person or a bad person. What we need to consider is how that activity will affect us without the necessary connection and validation that is required for the type of vulnerability in which we are engaging. Without commitment, without vulnerability, and without validation, we run the risk of constantly having a depthless or one-dimensional relationship that meets temporary and biological needs but never achieves the meaningful and desired connections in our lives. The long-term outcome of this is hardship, loneliness, and despair.

DEFINING THE NET PRESENT VALUE OF RELATIONSHIPS

Imagine you are asked out on a first date. You are excited, nervous, and anxious as you get together for the planned activity. Shortly into the conversation, your date directly asks you how much money you make and what your credit score is. Shocked, bewildered, and unsure what to do, you have no answer. The date quickly ends, and you go on your way wondering what happened and frustrated by the encounter. You speculate on whether that person is interested in you or in your earning potential. Are they looking for a relationship or future financial support? Such situations are difficult and can lead to a lack of trust and problematic relational situations.

After chemistry and sex, the most influential relational expectation I see today with single adults is the earning capacity and debt obligations of those we date. Many of us both in and out of the church today decide whether we enter healthy relationships or exit unhealthy relationships based entirely, or in part, upon a financial analysis of the current net present value of that relationship.

According to a recent survey, approximately forty-two percent (42%) of people in the U.S. admit that knowing someone's credit score factors into their decision making about dating. The same survey indicated approximately fifty percent (50%) of women and thirty-five percent (35%) of men use this metric to determine if someone is appealing.[12] Interestingly, both genders place some value on the financial wherewithal of the individuals they consider for relationships. Financial security is thus the new rating system or measuring stick, separating the haves and the have-nots in evaluating potential partners for dating and marriage. It is no longer chocolate and roses, but a computer-generated algorithm of our financial capacity that is the preferred aphrodisiac. Simply put, those who make money or possess low debt ratios have a leg up in the dating pool.

But why are money issues so important so early in a relationship? What is it about money that makes it one of the top priorities for those we date? Undoubtedly, dating or marrying someone with a large debt may impact the ability of that relationship to finance daily needs. It may also affect the couple's ability to acquire housing loans or other long-term capital requirements normal in functioning and healthy relationships. In short, what we earn and what we individually spend has a direct bearing on the future well-being and opportunities in any relationship.

I think this phenomenon derives in part from a growing realization that there is a minimum earning standard in the U.S. that assists the happiness and health of individuals. Recently, researchers from Purdue University published a study indicating the optimal amount of annual income required for our personal and individual happiness in North America is $105,000. I assume earning this amount means we will have sufficient access to wanted and needed life necessities at a practical level; free from worries about daily needs or wants, we are reasonably able to enjoy life. The researchers also found emotional well-being or satisfaction for us can occur at lower income amounts ($65,000–$95,000), meaning happiness is not always in the amount we earn but in how we manage the resources available to us.

Curiously, people who earned more than $105,000 were not necessarily happier as individuals. As a result, how we spend our money, or better said, our prudence and frugality in our spending choices are important to our happiness.[13] I think today we are less willing to start a relationship with someone earning below what we perceive to be a minimum financial threshold. We look at life and define our relationships not just by whom we enter the relationship with but also whether that relationship can sustain us at a comfortable level without compromise.

Consumer debt is becoming a problem for all of us in the U.S., not just those looking for relational opportunities. Approximately forty-three percent (43%) of Americans have carried a credit card balance for the past two-plus years. The average credit card balance for an individual American is $6,375 and the American household maintains an average balance of $16,883. Additionally, the typical American household pays an average of $1,292 in credit card interest each year. Surprisingly, the total amount of credit card debt in the U.S. has increased, surpassing over one trillion dollars.[14]

What does this mean? It means those we date or those with whom we pursue relationships are highly likely to carry some form or degree of debt. As a result, how we deal with that actuality and how we view those with debt as it pertains to our relationships is important. It means we must have a proper understanding of how these obligations will impact the relationship not only today but also in the future.

What happens or what do we do when we have large amounts of debt and want to date? When do we discuss these issues with those we are dating? How do we manage the impacts of these debts? Some may be tempted to hide large debt from those they date, hoping the strength of the relationship will overcome the dismay and disappointment that will surely come later at its revelation. How do we react when someone has not been as fiscally sound in the past but is slowly making improvement? These are all topics requiring objective thought and perspective.

Not all debt is bad. Some debt is used to acquire important skills and education or for assets that may appreciate, such as housing. These are investments and we should not look at these with contempt or skepticism. Still, the amount and duration of any such debt should be a consideration. Consumer debt on the other hand is likely not to appreciate or to have a return. When evaluating debt, it is important to consider not only the existence of that debt, but its purpose, role, and how it is managed in the lives of those we hope to date. A good place to start the discussion with ourselves and those with whom we want to have a relationship is asking whether the debt is for an investment that will appreciate or depreciate.

Even if a relationship can meet the minimum financial thresholds for happiness, it does not ensure the relationship will be healthy. During the Savior's ministry, a man approached and asked Him to adjudicate a complicated and sharp family disagreement having to do with money. "Master, speak to my brother . . . that he divide the inheritance with me," requested that man. The Savior declined to settle the financial dispute, cautioning instead about an important and fundamental principle: "Beware of covetousness . . . for a man's life consisteth not in the abundance of the things he possesseth."

Irrespective of whether this man was justified in his request, the inability to resolve existing money and financial issues had a dramatic influence on the capability of these two brothers to maintain a functioning and healthy relationship. True prosperity lies not in the pursuit and acquisition of fortune and wealth but in the connections, relationships, and attachments we develop in our lives.

When discussing the concept of money among individuals in the church, Brigham Young once famously stated that wealth would be the greatest trial the saints would endure:

> The worst fear that I have about [members of this Church] is that they will get rich in this country, forget God and his people, wax fat, and kick themselves out of the Church and go to hell. This people will stand mobbing, robbing, poverty, and all manner of persecution, and be true. But my greater fear for them is that they cannot stand wealth; and yet they have to be tried with riches. [15]

The acquisition of money and wealth is often regarded in the church solely as a debate between the spiritual and temporal needs of its members: the doctrine being, if we prioritize the pursuit of worldly or monetary things in this life, we deprioritize the pursuit of spiritual blessings. The church is also quick to point out that the pursuit of wealth is not in itself wrong, so long as its acquisition is used to facilitate charitable ends and to support the building-up of the kingdom of God. Despite this doctrine, I have rarely heard individuals in the church discuss or view money as a relational issue. In fact, many singles in the church, especially young singles, are taught that monetary issues should not be a consideration when making decisions about entering a relationship or deciding whether to get married.

Today, the financing of relationships is one of the most complicated and difficult problems both single adults and married couples face. The inability to resolve money issues is a key driver of failure in many relationships and is by far one of the primary causes for divorce. How can this be? What is it about money that reduces relationships into a hissing pool of acid so caustic it dissolves love and ruins the connections we so desperately want and need? Is it the relentless pursuit of wealth, the lack or inability to acquire it, or the complexity of managing it? These questions and their resolution are important for us whether we are currently in relationships or we are hoping to enter them.

Naively, money wasn't a concern for me when I first married. I wasn't wealthy, but I had established myself in a stable career, I had paid off my student loans and my house, I had no consumer debt, and I had both short- and long-term savings. With two degrees in finance, I felt I had the skills necessary to be financially responsible, especially in the context of a family relationship. I thought if there was anything that would go right in the marriage, it would be the financial stability I provided. It was the mistaken belief the amount of money I earned would reduce the stress of its role, function, and management in the relationship.

I quickly learned money has significant impacts in the relationship, especially if individuals within that relationship have different ideas about its acquisition, its purpose, and its use. Where I had relative freedom and control over decision-making on financial matters prior to my marriage, after the marriage I had to account for the thoughts, desires, and wishes of my wife. I realize today the problems I experienced with finances generally weren't about money itself, rather about significantly deeper relationship issues such as individual identity, trust, relational control, social status, and equality. Many times, these differences were so distinct we were not able to even discuss appropriate financial resolutions, which caused relational drama and unresolved conflict.

Relational failures relating to money are less about the lack of agreement on the allocation of resources and more about the inability of individuals to adequately discuss, agree, and resolve the underlying relational concerns. That is not to say that we should not be concerned about the actual finances of the relationship. We should. What it means, though, is we need to focus on understanding both the individual needs of each person and the collective needs of the relationship. We must also look for viable and fair solutions to the financial and underlying relational issues that meets both these needs. Those relationships that can balance the needs of each individual while meeting the collective needs of the relationship, especially over time, are those that have the best opportunity for establishing a healthy financial base that supports and enhances the relationship.

A couple that budgets and plans together has a greater likelihood of remaining together. Too many of us spend without a plan; we simply hope the required money will be there when bills are due. Relationships are strained and pushed to extremes when differing financial priorities occur between significant others, where one person spends what the other is trying to save. The ability to effectively communicate financial needs and wants to each other and the capacity to develop a mutual and reliable plan allows all to participate in the spending process and feel empowered in the relationship.

Financial planning requires a firm understanding of how much monthly items cost and how much disposable cash is available to spend. Financial planning also allows us to search for cheaper and more cost-effective methods of living. Finding inexpensive ways to live and relate to each other can be a fun challenge for everyone. Limiting our exposure to easy credit or to multiple credit cards will also help alleviate the temptation to overspend on the planned amounts. Financial planning is also about finding a balance of our own needs and those of our significant other. It is the ability to communicate about, implement, and be held accountable for the appropriate use of the relationship's resources. For those looking to improve their budgeting skills, I recommend reading *One for the Money*, by Marvin J. Ashton. There are also many resources both in and out of the church that are beneficial on this topic.

Oftentimes, I hear single adults debate who should pay for dates, especially in the early stages of the relationship. I find it interesting one of the initial experiences couples generally have together with finances is the first date they go on. As gender roles have evolved over time, the earning potential and employment opportunities for both men and women in the relationship have increased. As a result, the subject of finances at a very early stage of a relationship is a chance for individuals to evaluate how they respond to financial issues in context of that relationship. Who finances the relationship activities is less important than making sure both individuals feel empowered, validated, and loved in the relationship. The truth is both individuals are equally responsible for this environment and for these feelings in the relationship. The more quickly we can discuss and resolve financial issues and participate in a mutually beneficial financial plan, the greater the chance that relationship will be healthy for all involved.

Finally, and on a humorous note, I recently took a personal vacation on a cruise for single adults. As part of this cruise, I was asked to participate in a group activity called Singled Out. I was required to sit blindfolded in a chair with my back to all the single women on the cruise. The moderator would ask probing and informative questions such as, "Do you like skiing or snowboarding?" The women would split into groups of what they liked or thought I liked.

After I answered the question, the group whose answer did not align with mine would sit down. This question and answer process continued, whittling the group of women down until a final match was selected. I suppose this is every man's dream, to have a competition from a myriad of beautiful women to see with whom you best match up. To be honest it was great, and I loved it.

Still, I was nervous about participating in this activity, while grateful they asked me to do so, and I felt sheepish about accepting the invitation.

I have great friends in these groups, but I am usually quiet about myself and what I do for a living. I thought this would be an appropriate way and a constructive opportunity for me to let others know more about who I am. I figured if I didn't have high marks in the chemistry or sex-appeal departments, the fact I had a decent job and a modicum of financial stability might be the linchpin for me.

The moderator asked me to provide in advance a detailed biography, which I did; however, when the time came for her to introduce me, she was hurried and simply stated that I was a cartoonist. The comical result to this story is, for the rest of the cruise most of the women thought I was an out-of-work artist with no earning potential, rather than a senior executive for an international company. It was strike one, two, and three all at once. Sigh, lesson learned. I think next time my strategy should not be to provide a detailed biography about myself or my employment but rather to bring a certified copy of my credit score.

I suppose such events and outcomes are the funny and entertaining things that make life worth watching! I am still laughing and smiling today at how things turned out and how expectations and hopes don't always go as planned. In the end, I don't think anyone really wants to be loved only for the money or wealth they bring to the table, but I also know its importance in fostering and maintaining trust in a relationship. By defining appropriate safeguards and balance in our relationships regarding finances and by having early and regular discussions about it, we can develop the tools and means to manage relational assets in ways that uplift ourselves and our relationships.

7

Considering the Needs of Single Adults

Therefore they did watch over their people, and did
nourish them with things pertaining to righteousness.
—Mosiah 23:18

Immediately after my divorce, I found a new job and moved to Minneapolis, Minnesota. It was a fresh start and a new opportunity. Despite its large and robust population, living there had many challenges that were like my many years living in Gillette, Wyoming. I had no friends or acquaintances in Minnesota, and although I attended a family ward, I had no real contact with anyone in the church. I did find there was a group of mid-singles, totaling about thirty individuals, who would get together each month for a break-the-fast dinner. While limited, I was grateful for the opportunity to meet and associate with other single adults.

This group was supported by eight different stakes, and the geographic area it covered was large—many of us drove several hours each way just to participate in these activities. At some point, the individual stakes decided it would be in the best interests of the mid-singles program if each stake undertook its own mid-singles activities rather than trying to collectively support a larger, more regional program. A significant part of their reasoning was logistical: the distance and burden the regional gatherings imposed on single adults and the time commitment and difficulty of coordinating among the various stakes. However, this decision had the complete opposite effect, as the single adult attendance at these activities drastically declined, and in some cases, the activities stopped altogether. The primary cause of this failure was simple: the local stakes lacked a critical mass of active single adults, and the changes did not generate additional activity as desired. This result left many local leaders puzzled and concerned.

Several years later, I was asked to meet with my stake president regarding steps our stake could take to improve the program. Like other stakes, our stake mid-singles program was languishing. While there were many stake activities designed for single adults over the age of thirty-one, people were disenchanted, unwilling to participate, or feeling lost. The first question the stake president asked me was, "What type of events or activities could the stake arrange to encourage more participation for mid-singles?"

I told him he was asking the wrong question. Participation or engagement for any single adult in the church is not merely a matter of the existence of a series of church-sponsored activities; the church and its single-adult programs must meet each single adult's personal, relational, and spiritual needs. Too many times I have sat in church council meetings where the discussion centered on what types of activities the church should sponsor. Alternatively, they centered on lengthy debates over generating lists of assigned speaking topics and which individuals would be best to give them. The thought process for both discussions is, if we can sufficiently energize, interest, or entertain single adults through church activities or events, our desire to attend will increase.

This is not to argue or imply that church-sponsored activities are not important for single adults; they are our lifeblood. But a focus solely on church activities without addressing or understanding the basic underlying issues for single adults will often cause such activities to be less inviting or provide less opportunity for connection and attachment for us. This condition will leave us wanting and disappointed if we choose to participate. Rarely has the conversation within church councils I have attended centered on the problems, issues, or needs of single adults, and whether the church can help to alleviate them. Granted, this is a much more difficult topic, for which there may be few if any solutions. Still, an increased understanding of the needs for single adults may lead to increased ideas and solutions for us, both locally and generally, within the programs of the church. This heightened and expanded understanding will help facilitate a broader base of single-adult activities and functions that have increased reach and applicability for single adults.

While there are many different needs relating to single adults, I believe the opportunity and availability to become married, the impacts of loneliness, and the exposure to poverty are principal and guiding issues that should be considered.

THE MARRIAGE CRISIS

In February 2017, right around Valentine's Day, the U.S. Department of Commerce published the following news graphic titled "Stats for Stories: Singles Awareness Day":[1]

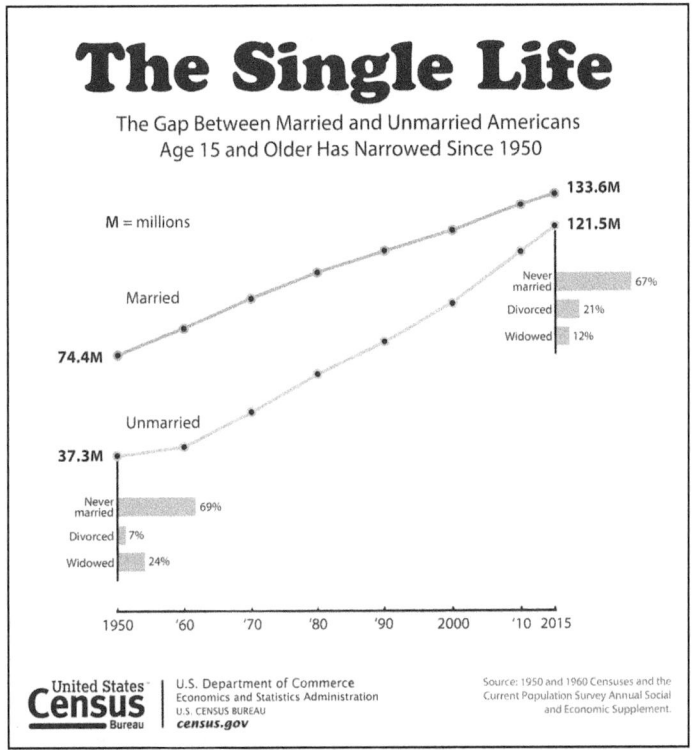

My first reaction to the title of this news graphic was to laugh; the U.S. Department of Commerce is known more for its dry statistics than for its humor. I realized, though, despite the witticism, the issue the agency is discussing is no laughing matter: As of 2015, almost fifty percent (50%) of people in the United States are single, whether by choice, divorce, or circumstance. Additionally, over the past sixty years, the rate of those who are single has increased more sharply than the rate of those marrying. If trends continue, the ranks of those who are married will be smaller than those who are single and for the first time, marriage as an institution will only be practiced by the minority.

What does that mean for individuals in the church and society at large? What are the causes, trends, and patterns that lead individuals to marry, not to marry, or to remarry? As society progresses, how will this trend impact population sustainability and growth or social issues like poverty, family values, resource allocation, and government? Only time will tell; however, the current and future impacts of the decline in marriages are a major issue and concern for all of us.

MARRIAGE IN THE UNITED STATES

According to the U.S. Department of Health and Human Services, marriage is one of the principal events that facilitate the transition into adulthood.[2] Despite this, many people in the United States today are choosing not to marry or to postpone marriage until later in life, electing instead to cohabitate or to have other alternative family arraignments. Financial instability, not having found the right person, and an unwillingness to settle down are often given as reasons for this trend.[3]

Today the median age for an individual's first marriage in the United States is 25.8 years for women and 28.3 years for men. The probability of women marrying by age twenty-five is trending downwards: in 2010 forty-four percent (44%) of women married by age twenty-five; however, in 2002 fifty-two percent (52%) of women married by that age. That is an astounding eight percent (8%) decrease in only eight years, representing a substantial decline in the marriage rate for women in this age group in just a relatively short time.

Because men generally marry at an older age, the probability for marriage in these time frames for them is less affected by age range; still, it is likewise trending down. In 2010, fifty-six percent (56%) of men were married by age thirty, whereas in 2002, sixty percent (60%) of men by that age were married. That represents a four percent (4%) decrease in the marriage rate for men during that time frame. Both statistics for men and women show a postponement of marriage over time until later in life. Curiously, the statistics also show, no matter the year studied, approximately eighty percent (80%) of both men and women have married by the age of forty, leading to the belief that while single adults in the United States are delaying or postponing marriage, they are not altogether forsaking it.[4] Marriage thus remains an important life pursuit and achievement for most people in the United States.

This collective postponement of marriage, however, has many social impacts and implications, including the number of children couples will have, the economic potential and well-being of individuals, and the exposure and risk to poverty, to name just a few. Additionally, the postponement of marriage affects the health of the marriage itself as more and more people choose to cohabitate rather than to marry. Statistics show cohabitation prior to marriage negatively impacts the likelihood, especially for women, that the marriage will remain intact after twenty years.[5] As a result, the rise in cohabitation does not just delay marriage, but it affects the longevity or durability of that relationship should marriage later occur. The irony of this fact is, many people cohabitate to see if they are a good fit for marriage, to try things out if you will, yet statistically, this endeavor is detrimental on the long-term outcome.

The following chart shows the probability in the United States a marriage will remain intact over a twenty-year period. These statistics show most marriages last for at least five years but by year twenty, nearly fifty percent (50%) of all marriages have ended. These statistics do not track whether those marriages that remained intact after twenty years will endure for the life of the individuals; thus, it is unknown whether this trend continues or flattens after the twenty-year mark. These statistics also do not track or measure the health of the marriage relationship, merely its length and durability.[6]

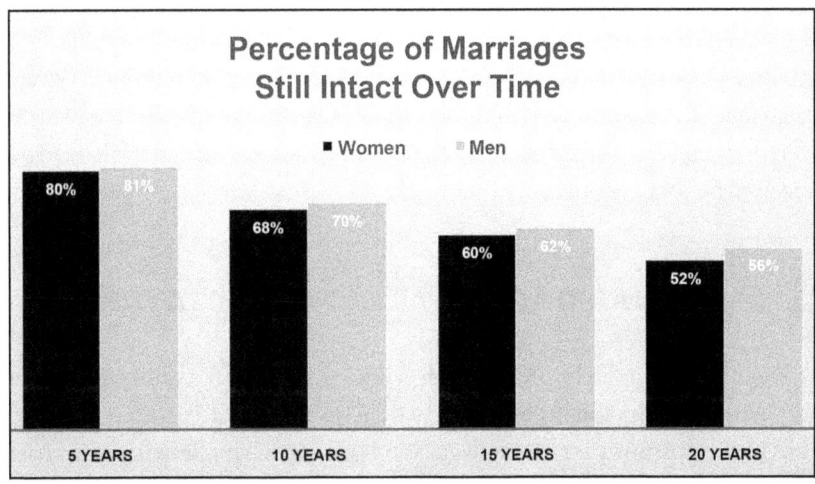

This chart does not reflect the statistical impact to marriage longevity due to cohabitation. For those who chose to cohabitate rather than marry, statistics show a substantial decrease in marriage longevity by year twenty. For women who cohabitate prior to marriage, the likelihood of still being married at year twenty is forty-five percent (45%). For men who cohabitate, the probability of still being married after twenty years is forty-nine percent (49%) if they were not engaged and is marginally better at fifty-seven percent (57%) if they were engaged.[7]

What does this all mean for single adults? Certainly, it sets up a societal dichotomy that is difficult to reconcile, as the church advocates and teaches early marriage is beneficial. *Get married, do it fast, do it quick, and things will work out*, is generally the church's message. Statistical support exists for the church's counsel, as marriages occurring prior to the age of twenty-four have a higher likelihood of lasting at least twenty years than those occurring after that age.[8] It also has the added benefit of helping church retention and activity because inactivity for single adults increases over time. Each of these consequences of an early marriage is positive and, given the statistics for remarriage discussed below, represents sage counsel.

Still, the trends in the United States for dating, meeting, and marrying individuals go counter to this counsel as more people are single for longer periods, as the age distribution for marriage continues to rise, as cohabitation is increasingly utilized as an alternative to marriage, as the permanency of marriage itself decreases, and as pecuniary as well as other duties and functions within family units continue to shift and evolve. As these trends continue, single adults will have fewer opportunities to date, fewer opportunities to marry, and fewer opportunities for raising families of our own.

On the flip side, we will be faced with increased pressure to live lifestyles that may not be conducive to church teachings or church doctrines. We will also face the real prospect that the marriage we enter will be more likely to fail than not. It is the proverbial coin flip on whether marriage will have the desired benefits or outcome.

REMARRIAGE IN THE UNITED STATES

Given the likelihood for marriage dissolution shown above, any discussion about marriage in the United States would be incomplete without considering the opportunity for remarriage. Most American singles will get married in their lifetime, but the reality is, we don't always stay married. For American singles today, it's not necessarily whether we participate in marriage but how many times we choose to engage in it. The problem American singles face is remarriage is often not a solution to the marriage crisis. In fact, statistically, it is a riskier endeavor than first marriages, as the probability of divorce increases significantly among second and third marriages.

Some statistics place the likelihood of divorce in a second marriage at sixty-seven percent (67%) and for third marriages at seventy-three percent (73%).[9] These statistics paint a bleak picture not only for American singles hoping for their first marriage but more so for those who hope to try it again after their first marriage has failed. It reminds me of professional baseball batting averages where a batting average of .300 will earn you great achievement, fame, and fortune, yet the failure rate for this average means you are successful less than one out of every three attempts. Is it any wonder why we either give up on marriage altogether or recycle one bad relationship after another?

The following chart shows the longevity and median duration of marriages in the United States.[10]

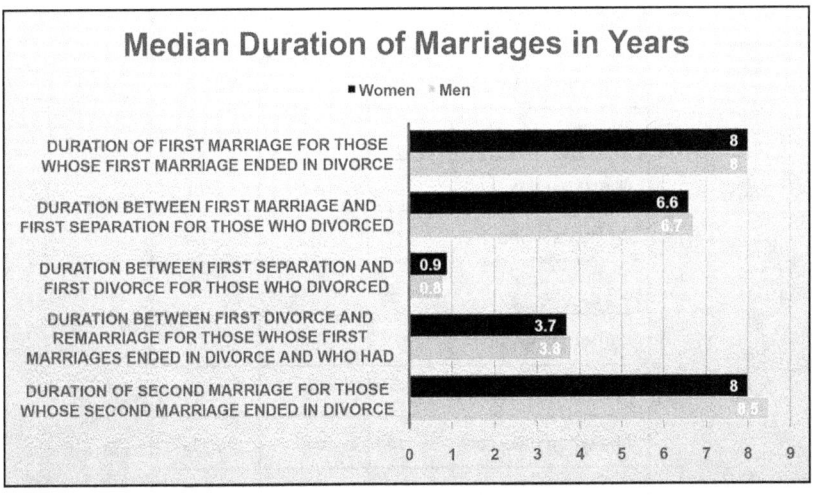

According to the U.S. Department of Commerce, the median duration of marriage for men and women in the United States is eight years. Interestingly, this timing holds true for the duration of second marriages as well. Statistically, couples in first marriages who divorce generally separate around year seven and live separated for nearly one year prior to divorce. Approximately fifty percent (50%) of singles who remarry did so within four years of their first divorce and in their early to mid-thirties. The median age for American singles entering second marriages is thirty-three for women and thirty-six for men.[11] Statistics also show marriages entered prior to

1975 tend to last longer, the establishment of new divorce laws and changing societal trends being some of the primary reasons for a shorter marriage duration today.[12]

The following table shows the median age at a marital event for men and women in the United States. These statistics are from 2009, the latest report the U.S. Department of Commerce has released; however, in 2015 the agency did update its statistics on the median age of first marriages (25.8 for women and 28.3 for men). This update is not reflected in this table, but as the age of people marrying has increased since 2009, it is reasonable to assume the other categories and their respective numbers and time frames will likewise shift. The 2015 update also demonstrates how quickly these statistics are changing.

Median Age for Marital Events

	Men	Women
First Marriage		
Age when married	24.5	22.3
Age when separated	30.8	28.8
Age when divorced	32	30.1
Age when widowed	61.1	59.4
Second Marriage		
Age when married	35.8	33.3
Age when separated	39	36.4
Age when divorced	42	39.3
Age when widowed	61.4	60.3

According to the U.S. Department of Commerce, approximately half of all men and women have married only once; however, this percentage is decreasing. Additionally, the percentage of individuals marrying three or more times is increasing, particularly for women over age fifty and for men over age sixty.[13] Although some unmarried people marry a spouse who has been previously married, approximately sixty-seven percent (67%) of all marriages occurring in the United States are between people who are both entering marriage for the first time. The remaining thirty-three percent (33%) involve marriages where one or both spouses had been previously married.[14]

These demographics are fascinating given the higher rates of divorce for second and third marriages. One can assume as a result that almost one in every three marriages is at a higher risk for divorce today in the United States because at least one spouse has been previously married. From a personal perspective, I found this statistic applicable as I married someone who had been previously married. Because this was my first marriage, it is personally interesting to see in the United States, 7.4 percent of marriages are between a man who was married one time and a woman for whom this was a second marriage. The following table is provided for you to consider how your relationships or future relationships compare to the makeup of other marriages within the United States.

Percentage of Times Married by Gender

		Total	Men		
			Married 1 Time	Married 2 Times	Married 3 or More Times
	Total	100	75.8	19.3	5.0
Women	Married 1 Time	76.8	67.4	8.2	1.2
	Married 2 Times	18.7	7.4	9.0	2.4
	Married 3 or More Times	4.5	1.0	2.2	1.4

What do all these statistics mean? The statistics are not favorable for someone looking to marry (or remarry) and stay married. If you thought the statistics were bad for first marriages, they are significantly worse for second and third marriages. That is a dreary outlook and demotivating reality for single adults who want to marry or remarry.

Why is it so much more difficult for individuals to marry after divorce and to remain married? There are many factors leading to the failure rate of second and third marriages. Often, it's easier to go through another divorce once we have already experienced its impacts. The fears, unknowns, and consequences generally seem less insurmountable in these dissolutions; we are also more comfortable with or knowledgeable of the laws and regulatory requirements when divorcing. In general, those who have already lived through a divorce are more willing to go through it, especially if a relationship is struggling or not working.

Another difficult factor for second and third marriages is the complexity of blending new and different families, specifically when children are involved. While the marital relationship may be beneficial, the family relationship may not. Sometimes, we may prioritize the relationship with our direct children over the relationship with our spouse's children. Sometimes that priority will diminish the importance of the marital relationship, causing difficulty and problems. Parental roles and discipline issues vis-à-vis the children are also complicated and not easily solved. Similarly, dealing with contentious ex-spouses and long-term custodial issues can affect the relationship.

Another factor is, many times we aren't ourselves prepared for a healthy relationship when we remarry. Maybe we have not sufficiently healed from our previous relationship, we have not changed unhealthy behaviors, or we have pursued relationships with individuals who have similar unhealthy behaviors to those of our ex-spouse. Second and third marriages also have unique financial complications. Sometimes there are added financial encumbrances like alimony and child support, as well as other obligations that continue into the new marriage and cause additional burden and strain.[15]

All divorces, whether it's the first, second, or third, occur, in part, due to unfulfilled, unmet, or unrealistic relational expectations. We expect marriage to enrich and enhance our lives, but the reality is all relationships require hard work, relational skill sets, and effort. When entering a second or third marriage, we may have the expectation we are going to get the relationship we did not have in our previous marriage and are shocked to find out the new relationship is similar or worse than our previous relationship.

Having said that, and despite these statistics, I believe in the goodness and opportunity for everyone—married, divorced, single, widowed, or otherwise—to have healthy and happy relationships. We should not give up our hopes and dreams for these because statistics or societal values are negatively trending, neither should we compromise who we are, our morals and ideals, to be in a relationship. However, we should understand and accept the circumstances and realities we face in the relationships we choose so we can make wise decisions and take appropriate actions to support and maintain them. The hope and opportunity for healthy relationships and connections comes from within, from knowing who we are, relying on our capability to take appropriate relational risk, and our being open and vulnerable to other people.

AVAILABILITY AND OPPORTUNITY

The disproportionate gender imbalance between men and women; a reluctance to engage in or to commit in relationships; a lack of priority or no sense of urgency for marriage; a fear of missing out on, or incessantly searching for, the perfect person; a lack of communication and relational skills; and an increasing unwillingness to be active in the church or to follow church standards: these and countless other explanations are often cited as the reasons why single adults are not marrying or are at least delaying marriage in the church. Yet the core of each of these relates to one (or both) of two intrinsic issues for single adults in the church: *availability* and *opportunity*.

These two issues, the availability of single adults to enter relationships and the existing opportunity to accomplish it, are the fundamental obstacles underlying the relationship dilemma for the church regarding its single-adult programs. These issues represent the two most challenging and unrelenting problems single adults face for developing connection and the potential for creating meaningful and lasting relationships. They also impact our ongoing willingness and desire to worship and to be active in the church.

Availability refers to the geographic location and demographics of single adults that direct and influence our willingness and capability to attend or participate in the church's single-adult programs. Opportunity deals with the activity rate for single adults in the church as well as the proportion or ratio of men to women in the church's single-adult programs. Together, availability and opportunity create significant and real impediments both for the church in its support and implementation of single adult-programs and for single adults to attend and find meaningful connection and attachment through participation in them.

Availability

The church is an expansive, worldwide institution comprised of over sixteen million people.[16] The problem for single adults isn't the size of the church, rather the varying concentration of single adults over large geographic areas. In the United States, geographic areas that have a high concentration of church membership will likely have more developed programs for single adults, which are generally well-attended. These areas often have the bandwidth and capacity to support single-adult wards, initiate formal and informal activities, organize single-adult conferences, etc. These undertakings provide, at least on a macro level, for the prospect of single adults to regularly meet and interact with each other, all with a relatively low constraint on the time and cost for us to travel and to participate.

Places like California, Utah, and Washington, D.C., are often focal points, especially for mid-singles who arguably have sufficient or adequate mass to form and support robust single-adult programs. As a result, the draw for single adults to relocate to these areas for relational opportunities is high. Yet single adults may be unable to move to these locations due to employment, educational or legal obligations, family responsibilities, or otherwise. As a result, we can be torn between our hopes and faith while balancing the reality of our circumstances.

That said, regional areas with high concentrations of single adults are not immune to problems either. The single-adult programs supported in these areas can be inundated with such a plethora of people, it becomes difficult for us to develop meaningful connections. Some single adults prefer to meet in large groups of other single adults, thinking the more people around, the greater the chance we may have to meet friends, date, and build relationships. This approach is a lot like playing the lottery: the more tickets you acquire, the greater your odds, even if the overall odds of winning are slim.

Still, congregation size is not a definitive solution, and too large of a ward may lead to other issues. Take for example some of the Utah mid-singles wards, which may have memberships of over eight hundred single adults. These wards are wonderful and great vehicles to meet the spiritual needs of many single adults, yet the number of people in attendance within one ward can be overwhelming. A regular family ward may have two to four hundred people with multiple people constituting one family unit; thus with fewer collective units, the ward's administrative and support mechanisms are better able to manage the individual and familial needs therein. The coordination and administrative support for the mid-singles wards (with each person representing their own unit) is a whole different animal, particularly when there is only one bishop. Think about how long we might have to wait just to get an appointment, let alone attention to and support for the issues and concerns we may have.

Ironically, the greatest strength for these congregations may also be the greatest weakness. Attending these wards can feel like showing up to our first class in college and realizing we are anonymous in an auditorium full of hundreds of students with the professor lecturing without any acknowledgement or class interaction. *Do people even know I am there? Will they notice if I am gone? Is it even worth the time and effort to go?* As a result, single adults who attend these large wards may lack the opportunity to connect, to make lasting friends, or to even feel accepted because of the daunting size of the congregation and low available support from leadership. We are like individual grains of sand on the beach, imperceptible and lost in the magnitude of the whole.

Large single-adult wards are not bad. The church should not seek to mitigate any adverse impacts of these large congregations by unilaterally emphasizing smaller, more localized wards or branches. On the contrary, the more decentralized the programs become, the less capacity these programs will have to meet the needs of single adults and the more incentivized we will become to flip back and forth from family wards, or to hop between various single-adult wards, never really connecting, never really serving, never really having any accountability within the church.

Even though the challenges are different for smaller wards and branches, these can face the same difficulties as the larger single-adult wards in serving their adult single members, because the condition for us to develop connections and attachments is either limited or altogether not feasible. The church must carefully balance and orchestrate the size and parameters of the single-adult wards and branches to allow connection and attachment to occur: too little availability and the programs fail; too much availability and the numbers may defeat the purpose altogether.

Sometimes, the inclination of local leaders in areas of low single-adult concentration is to look at and try to emulate the programs that are successful in areas of high single-adult concentration. Yet they struggle with the attempt because there is not enough bench strength to support them. I have heard leaders of the church state that if the church were to provide single adults with more service opportunity (i.e. callings) in the church, more single adults would participate. This is in part why the church tries to create more wards and branches, believing a more local and direct focus will increase single adult involvement. It's the, "If you build it, they will come" rationality where allowing more leadership roles, more callings, and more participation in the implementation of programs of the single-adult ward or branch will promote and encourage greater activity.

This rationale is also part of the reason why stakes with low activity rates or with low concentrations of single adults, like those in my area, may want or choose to decentralize single-adult programs. While this thinking may be appropriate in areas with a high concentration of single adults, it burdens areas with a low concentration of single adults because there is not a critical or sufficient mass of single adults from which to support or grow these programs. In my opinion, it is also why the various single-adult programs in these areas struggle.

Sometimes, single adults will attend the church's single-adult programs out of a sense of duty while wrestling internally because there are no eligible people for us to meet or with whom to socialize. If this condition continues for long periods of time, we may become discouraged and look outside the church to build meaningful connection. Not only will we not participate in these programs, but also we may leave the church altogether, telling ourselves that we will return to church activity when we find a viable and permanent relationship.

The problem is, after we leave the church, the motivation for us to return is low. To put it bluntly: once we are gone—we are gone. Additionally, those with whom we subsequently develop relationships may not share our desire to participate in or become part of the church. This negatively impacts our ability to come back to the church even if we so desire. Thus, the church and single adults are in a constant, never-ending struggle to maintain activity and faithfulness. For this reason, church leaders must look closely at and consider the needs of single adults, not just through the lens of church activity but also through the lens of attachment and connection. Spiritual connection is incredibly important, but if that is all the church provides its members, the church single-adult programs will face a complicated and never-ending struggle for our activity and for our very souls.

An additional obstacle in the church's single-adult programs that affects availability is the age demographics within its various singles programs. We start in the young-single-adult program. This program is designed for individuals ages eighteen to thirty-one and is generally situated around colleges and universities or satellite institute programs. When I attended these wards—and I attended many—I found them filled with people eagerly engaged in life's pursuits, whether education, work, or otherwise. These individuals were filled with vigor, optimism, and hope for life and the search for their eternal companion. Many activities grew organically from either the institute or the young-single-adult ward. They had regularity to them, buy-in and support from those who participated, and people for the most part came and enjoyed themselves. While the program wasn't perfect, generally, it provided a good deal of the social and spiritual interaction needed for single adults. As a result, I felt it was successful.

Around my twenty-fifth birthday, I began to realize I was aging out of the program. I was welcome and part of all the young-single-adult activities, yet as I grew older most of the individuals in the ward were becoming much younger than me. Stated differently, while I was changing, it seemed the people in the young-single-adult ward always stayed the same. Most of the people I knew in the ward were getting married between the ages of twenty and twenty-five. They were moving on with their lives, starting families and careers. The remainder of people with whom I could interact were typically between the age of eighteen and twenty years old. As a result, the older I became, the less connection and opportunity the young-single-adult ward seemed to provide. This concerned me; for the first time, I didn't feel like I fit anymore. I was no longer in an undergraduate program, and it seemed I had no or limited prospects to socialize with those participating in the young-single-adult ward or its activities. Put simply, I was a graduate student trying to relate with the life experiences of college freshman.

Even though I didn't feel I belonged in the young-single-adult program anymore, I wasn't old enough to participate in the church's mid-singles or over-thirty-one programs. Additionally, at that time, my own biases relating to older single adults and divorced members of the church impeded my desire to participate had I been able. I continued to experience this quandary for many years.

When I turned thirty-one, I found myself in Wyoming, where there was only a small young-single-adult branch, consisting of fewer than twenty people, who attended the local community college. There was also no program for those single adults over thirty-one. As a result, I stayed in the single-adult branch to assist them as best I could, but the same issues existed. At the recommendation of my church leaders, I tried to attend the mid-singles activities in Denver, Colorado, but the experience was poor as I was significantly younger than those in attendance. I found I didn't belong in that age demographic either.

The reality for me after the age of twenty-five was that a solid decade went by where I didn't fit in either of the church's single-adult programs. I was either too old to relate with the young-single adults or too young to relate with the older single adults. I felt like I was in limbo—a man without a country. It was as if I were sitting at a playground on a teeter-totter hoping and waiting for someone to sit on the other side to balance it out, yet no one came.

The church loses many single adults in this time frame because we don't fit within the defined age parameters that have been set within its single-adult programs. The truth is, there are many twenty-six-year-olds who may have happy and healthy associations with those who are just a few years older but are prevented because they are on the wrong side of the age limit and have little or no opportunity to meet or to interact.

The reasoning for maintaining these age demographics for single-adult programs usually centers on two aspects: 1) single adults who are over thirty-one have different needs, different wants, and different circumstances that warrant their own group, and 2) it can create difficulty, awkwardness, or undue influence to have people who are significantly older pursue after or show interest in younger people for dating and relational opportunities. Both these reasons are legitimate for having separate programs in the church, yet the existence of these demographics is also the genesis of the problem.

I have often felt that understanding the nuances and complexities of these demographics will lead to better decision-making for church leaders who want to help or increase the activity of single adults. Rigorous adherence to age requirements for the church single-adult programs, especially as we become older, may not always be the best policy on an individual basis. Single adults understand their needs better than most. By working with local leaders to provide individuals with specific and tailored opportunities, whether through the young-single, mid-single, or the over-thirty-one programs, or a combination of all three, solutions may present themselves that will benefit all involved.

Additionally, the differences in age demographics sometimes create unique and somewhat quirky complications to the prospects for single adults to interact, as single adults today seem to be more concerned about age differences in those they date than previous generations. I have often observed that single adults tend to look for individuals who are relatively close to their own age or, alternatively, they are looking for excessively younger people to date. Even though the reasons for this are based in individual preferences, this idiosyncrasy can also create problems as the balance of eligible people to date within each age demographic is different.

While there may be many people in total who are single and available, there are not enough single adults within the desired or relevant age demographics to support or facilitate any meaningful interaction with other eligible people. This has the effect of further constraining availability even though there may be many people who are single but are excluded as a dating prospect due to individual age preferences.

Opportunity

"Where are all the good single men in the church???" This lamentation and protestation booms, echoes, and reverberates throughout the church and its single-adult programs. It is neither a still nor a small cry for many single sisters. The side effects and fallout from this disparity are a major part of the problem the church faces in its activity rate for single adults.

The biggest and most important issue for single adults is not necessarily the strengths (or weaknesses) of the church's single-adult programs, but whether single adults themselves take interest or participate in these programs. This interest is based primarily in the amount of opportunity we have within these programs to develop relevant and purposeful relationships, connections, and attachments irrespective of whether these relationships lead to marriage.

For both genders, the church is losing ground in the battle for the activity rate of single adults; this loss is, however, more particularly pronounced for men than for women. Recently, while I was attending a mid-singles conference, the key note speaker related some eye-opening church statistics. He stated that single adults constitute a large portion of the church and for those who are from ages nineteen to thirty, the activity rate for women is forty-five percent (45%) and for men it's twenty-two percent (22%). For single adults older than thirty, the activity rate decreases respectively for women to thirty-two percent (32%) and for men to eight percent (8%).[17]

That is a remarkable statistic for single adults in the church, particularly for older single adults, where only one out of every three single women and one out of every ten single men participate in some manner with the church. Think about that for a minute: the longer an individual is single, the less likely they are to participate in the church or its single-adult programs. Based on these statistics, we may assume both the church and single adults are failing each other at unsustainable levels. It also means for those single adults who remain active, there are fewer dating and relationship opportunities, as there are significantly fewer available men than women. That is a serious problem for all of us because it is incredibly difficult for both genders, especially older singles, to find and marry eligible people within the church.

In 2015, *Time* magazine published an article by Jon Birger titled, "Mormons and Jews: What 2 Religions Say About the Modern Dating Crisis."[18] According to Mr. Birger, whenever you have a skewed gender ratio of women to men, it has a dramatic influence on how people behave, as the culture and its values are less likely to favor monogamy and marriage; women must compete for connection while men have the opportunity to dally and philander.[19] The American Religious Identification Study found that Utah has approximately one hundred and fifty single Mormon women to every one hundred single Mormon men.[20] Mr. Birger states that because of a higher apostasy rate among men than women, there is some rationale to this gender gap; however, he points out the gender gap has widened significantly since 1990, when the ratio was 52:48 women to men.[21] Mr. Birger comments that the existence of this gender gap puts enormous pressure on the social norms, customs, and value systems within the church, causing a lack of confidence in our faith and belief.[22]

The imbalance between single active women and single active men is a driving factor in the church's single-adult programs today. It is the elephant in the room and the bull in the china shop, quietly and discreetly discussed but wreaking havoc everywhere it goes. If we assume the statistics cited above apply universally across the church, it is tantamount to almost three active single women to every two active single men in the church today.* What does that mean? It means that if today every active man in the church were to marry an active girl, there would still be one out of every three women with no opportunity to even become married. There are simply not enough active single men in the church to allow for a healthy and robust framework to create opportunity for all single adults to meet, interact, and develop relationships.

Put yourself in the shoes of a single sister who attends church knowing she is going to be thrust into a social and spiritual setting where she must compete for attention from the opposite gender. It becomes spurious social judgment at its worst: each step or action she takes is scrutinized, every item of clothing she wears looked at, her every physical feature constantly analyzed. It is a veritable fishbowl where physical attraction, looks, and beauty are over-emphasized and become the new standard for finding and attracting someone.

Additionally, the personal needs for connection and physical touch become strained to the breaking point and, when combined with the law of chastity, create a high sensitivity and a hypersexuality within single adults that is difficult for those who are married or outside the church to under-

---

* Little empirical data exists on the gender gap outside Utah. Still, it is reasonable to assume the gender gap is likely more skewed outside Utah because of geography and a lower presence of the church in other regions. This exacerbates the problem for those who are not close to high-population centers of the church.

stand. The extreme weight of the desire to be married and to have families does not lessen, but rather enhances and intensifies the pressure felt.

Is it any wonder Salt Lake City has 2.5 times the national average of plastic surgeons and that demand for cosmetics, hair coloring, and other beauty products are well above the demand in other comparable cities in the United States?[23] As men increasingly apostatize or fall away from the church, or either can't or won't follow the standards within the church, the women feel more pressure to follow suit as they risk exclusion or fear being ostracized from relational prospects. When we consider the negative societal trends for marriage in the United States (discussed previously), the opportunity for marriage or other connections within the church is diminished even further.

When thinking about the dearth of active single men in the church today and the opportunity to develop meaningful relationships, I often ponder the following two scriptures:

1. And *all things shall be in commotion*; and surely, *men's hearts shall fail them*; for fear shall come upon all people.[24]

2. And in that day *seven women shall take hold of one man*, saying, *we will eat our own bread*, and *wear our own apparel: only let us be called by thy name, to take away our reproach.*[25]

Both these prophetic descriptions apply and are fitting for this discussion. No doubt should exist that the church's single-adult programs struggle today to effectively maintain activity of single adults; that people, particularly men, are turning away from the church's teachings and searching for answers outside the gospel; and that imbalanced gender ratios are having a tremendous influence on these issues. As a result, there is commotion and movement in and among single adults as we reach for relevance in the church, as we grapple to have fulfilling individual relationships, and as we try to establish ourselves in families of our own.

Moreover, the emotional liabilities and inconveniences that single adults are willing to accept—and the typical relational norms and expectations we forgo, especially women, just to have a relationship irrespective of its health—are both difficult and sad. These conditions contribute to a sense of despair and futility among single adults as we strive to achieve functional and healthy relationships within the auspices of the church.

To lay the blame for the problems within the church's single-adult programs entirely on the inactivity or paucity of available single men would be both opprobrious and inaccurate. Reactivating and holding onto the single men should be prioritized and will go a long way in solving many of the issues and concerns relating to relational opportunity within the church's programs. But even we single men who remain active are sometimes viewed as opportunistic, selfish, or even lazy because we are not married when there is an overabundance of women.

Said differently, some within the church support the deleterious belief that an institutionalized lethargy has developed among the single men who take propitious and full advantage of our circumstances. We allow single women to mother and nurture us, to feed us, the assumption goes, but maintain no obligation or responsibility to ask the women out on dates, to make commitments, or to progress relationships. As a result, single men often hear direct and sometimes harsh criticism from church leaders about the evils of delaying marriage and how we should grow up by taking on the important responsibility of husbands and fathers. Local leaders also involve themselves in personal relational issues, encouraging or pressuring single men to date specific individuals without thought to the individual or the fit of the relationship. Many believe the sole purpose of the single-adult programs is for those who participate to get married, and if the men are not working toward that goal, we are failing or falling short.

Anecdotally, I once had a bishop from my singles ward approach me and suggest I should just marry a certain single sister in the ward and I would over time learn to love her. As she and I were good friends, I relayed this message to her. Her reply made me both laugh and think. She said, "I am sure you can learn to love me, but what about me?" I learned a valuable lesson from her that day: love is not automatic, and relationships are a two-way street requiring both men and women to make important and fundamental choices about who, how, and what manner of relationship we want.

The truth is, like men, women are changing and evolving in their desires and attitudes toward relationships and their basis for entering those relationships. For example, studies show women today in the United States are less willing to date and marry men who lack a college degree. The fundamental problem with this is that more women today are getting college degrees than men.[26] My purpose in discussing this statistic is not to debate educational opportunities or the gender ratio of men to women in college, or to argue whether having a college degree should be a relational prerequisite. What I am saying is, given the scarcity of eligible single men who meet the requirements that many women now have for their prospective spouse, women are not altering these to accommodate existing social dynamics and demographics.

Part of the reason for this is women today are more comfortable with their own independence. They are more capable, educated, and skilled than previous generations. They are also less willing to give up what they have currently to undertake a relational risk for fear it might be a worse situation. As a result, single women have less need today for a marital relationship to provide for their basic needs. It's not that the dream of having a happy family and children have vanished, rather the timing and selection criteria for those who will be accepted as relational partners has changed and narrowed.

Lori Gottlieb wrote a fascinating article on this subject titled, "Marry Him! The Case for Settling for Mr. Good Enough."[27] She opines that to get married and have families, women should worry less about passion or intense connection and be willing to overlook small but annoying habits that prospective or eligible men may have. Ms. Gottlieb writes that there is some difficulty today to convince women settling for a less-than-ideal man is a good thing. She comments that when she discusses the concept of settling, she is met with disapproval, shock, and disappointment. This reaction is in part because we are raised to or have a mindset to hold out for "true love."[28]

Ms. Gottlieb's article raises a fundamental and curious inquiry for single adults: given the scarcity of eligible single men in the church, why are women so picky? If men are like Peter Pan, never growing up and never taking responsibility, women are like Sleeping Beauty, holding out or waking only for their pre-chosen handsome prince. Both perspectives are detrimental to creating opportunity within the church's single-adult programs.

In chapter 6, I discussed the need for chemistry and its impacts on our dating pool, and I don't mean to debate that again here; however, I believe both men and women should honestly ask ourselves how many viable and healthy relationships we have passed by because of our own definitions of passion, chemistry, and love. Do we seek solely after a passion-filled relationship that may be temporary or less stable? Alternatively, do we seek after relationships based upon other criteria that may lead to more relational stability later? Are we better off if we disregard what we think we want for what will work?

Consider what Isaiah wrote about the last days:

> Moreover the Lord saith, *Because the daughters of Zion are haughty*, and walk with *stretched forth necks* and *wanton eyes*,

walking and mincing as they go, and making a tinkling with their feet:

Therefore the Lord will smite with a scab the crown of the head of the daughters of Zion, and the Lord will discover their secret parts.

In that day the Lord will *take away the bravery of their tinkling* ornaments about their feet, and their cauls, and their round tires like the moon . . .

And it shall come to pass, that instead of sweet smell there shall be stink; and instead of a girdle a rent; and instead of well-set hair baldness; and instead of a stomacher a girding of sackcloth; and burning instead of beauty.

Thy men shall fall by the sword, and thy mighty in the war.

And her gates shall *lament and mourn*; and she being desolate shall sit upon the ground.[29]

    My purpose in discussing this scripture is not to decry or point the finger at the wonderful and beautiful women in the church; however, it has some bearing and is worth considering as it pertains to the single-adult programs. Isaiah described a condition or a perspective that is detrimental to the establishment of productive and healthy relationships for both men and women. In this situation, it is the pride or vanity of the women that is the concern. Isaiah noted that women looked with wanton eyes, or, they demanded and sought for things that were unrealistic (i.e. they were never satisfied). They sought to lift themselves above others and to dress themselves better than those around them for gain and accomplishment. They emboldened themselves or justified their actions for what they wanted as opposed to what they needed. The consequence was not just that they lost what they sought after, but also that they lost that which was supposed to be most precious to them, their men (or in other words, their families and relationships). As a result, they were left alone to weep and wail without hope or salvation.

    Like the incorrectness of blaming the men solely for the gender imbalance, it is also incorrect to place the onus for its existence entirely on the women. Still, is not Isaiah's description analogous to the single-adult programs today? Have we not lost most, if not all, the single men in the church and are not the women left wondering where they are at and discouraged at the prospects of having relationships and families in the future? Is not part of the solution to the issues in the single-adult programs addressing how both men and women connect and attach with each other in appropriate and healthy ways? No individual is perfect, no church program capable of satisfying every need, and no relationship easy. Yet by focusing on the areas where we can make friends and develop relationships with everyone around us, we will find more opportunity and more fulfillment in our lives.

THE ORPAH DECISION

Ravaged by the scourge and depravity of famine, Naomi, Emilech, and their two sons moved from Bethlehem to Moab in the hope of establishing a new life with better opportunity. Sadly, after arriving in Moab, Emilech died. Naomi's two sons each took a wife, women named Ruth and Orpah. They continued to live in Moab where, after ten years, Naomi's two sons also tragically died. Having no husband and no sons, Naomi made a difficult and life-changing choice to leave Moab and return to Bethlehem—a choice that set in motion a series of events culminating in Ruth meeting and marrying Boaz.

Ruth and Boaz's relationship has inspired generations and impacted the course of history as their posterity produced not only David, the king of Israel, but also the Savior who was the King of Kings. As discussed in chapter 5, the story of Ruth and Boaz is beautiful not only for its message but also for its result. It is a story of devotion, sacrifice, and the discovery of love in times of tribulation. The hope of finding and developing new relationships after the loss of another relationship, the ability to cultivate great love after great sacrifice, and the overcoming of loneliness, despair, and grief to the betterment of ourselves and those around us are important messages for all of us, particularly for single adults. Despite this, we rarely talk about the circumstances and justifications that led to Ruth and Naomi's choices, and we are prone to forget another choice was made: the one made by Orpah.

After the passing of her sons, Naomi was longing to return to her homeland. Perhaps she wanted to be around family and friends, perhaps she realized there were better opportunities or support for her in Bethlehem than in Moab, or perhaps she recognized she was getting older and there was no reason for her to remain in Moab any more. Whatever the reason, when the day came for Naomi to leave Moab, both Orpah and Ruth desired to go with her. Naomi, however, tearfully entreated both to return to their parents and remain in Moab. Naomi's reasoning for this was that she was not able to have more sons for either Ruth or Orpah to marry and even if she were to bear more, it would be too burdensome for the women to forego other marriage opportunities until they were grown. Faced with this reasoning, Orpah chose to return to her family and her homeland while Ruth chose to stay and journey with Naomi. The scriptures record as follows:

> And [Ruth and Orpah] lifted up their voice, and wept again: and Orpah kissed her mother in law; but Ruth clave unto her. And [Naomi] said, *Behold, thy sister in law is gone back unto her people, and unto her gods: return thou after thy sister in law.*
>
> And Ruth said, Entreat me not to leave thee, or to return from following after thee: for whither thou goest, I will go; and where thou lodgest, I will lodge: thy people shall be my people, and thy God my God: *Where thou diest, will I die, and there will I be buried: the Lord do so to me, and more also, if ought but death part thee and me.*[30]

Oftentimes I hear taught in the church that the decision for Ruth to go to Bethlehem was a matter of her conversion and her faith in God, the opposite being true for Orpah, who was not faithful by her choice to remain in Moab. It is the proverbial spiritual fork in the road where one decision leads to the exercise of faith and salvation while the other leads to inactivity and damnation. We look at the result or blessing that came to both Ruth and Naomi as justification for the righteousness of their choice.

The view on Orpah is somewhat harsher. Ignoring or turning a blind eye, we do not think about or inquire further about her other than assuming that by not choosing to go to Bethlehem, Orpah made a misinformed choice that was not centered on God. Sadly, the scriptures are silent as to what happened to Orpah, which leads to the speculation that, like an inactive member, she fell away from the church without thought or fanfare. Perhaps this perspective is true, yet I have often reflected that the choice both Orpah and Ruth had before them was less about their faith in God and more about their chance to have attachments, connections, and family in their lives.

This is the same choice many single adults face in the church today. Many single adults live with the challenges of being single in a faith-centered environment and confront the very real choice of whether to engender meaningful relationships or to be active within the church and to prioritize God in their lives. To the church, this choice is not mutually exclusive, as the hope is everyone will become married. Yet the reality many single adults face is the availability and the opportunity to become married is either low or highly constrained. Thus, a disconnect occurs between the expectations of the church and the gospel and the real-world realities many single adults experience.

It is likely both Ruth and Orpah converted when they married Naomi's sons. This is at least a reasonable conclusion evident by the statement made by Naomi to Ruth that Orpah was returning to her people and to her gods. It gives the impression that both Orpah and Ruth changed their thoughts, perspectives, and beliefs upon joining Naomi's family; however, it is unclear whether Naomi's statement means Orpah was forsaking her new faith rather than simply returning to her home.

The fact that Naomi was encouraging Ruth to do the same indicates Naomi was not telling either of them to forsake their faith but to forsake their love of Naomi for their own personal benefit. Naomi's heartfelt grief was not for herself but for the lack of opportunity for her widowed daughters-in-law to have future meaningful relationships and families of their own. She knew that as widows their ability to find suitable spouses and to have families would be greatly diminished, if not foreclosed, if they journeyed to Bethlehem. The sacrifice both these women were willing to make for Naomi was too much for Naomi herself to bear.

A key point to remember is that Naomi herself, a devout and faithful member of the church as it existed in that time, was encouraging both Ruth and Orpah to stay in Moab. Naomi did not say that going to Bethlehem was a matter of faith in God. She did not tell them God would provide for them if they went to Bethlehem or sacrifice would bring them blessings. She also did not say to either Ruth or Orpah that remaining in Moab would mean a loss of spirituality. Additionally, I am not aware of any scriptural or theological requirement that faithful people in that time had to relocate to live in specified areas.

To the contrary, it was Naomi and her family who originally moved from Bethlehem to Moab. Naomi knew their faith was not as prevalent in Moab as it was in Bethlehem. What spiritual support or opportunity Ruth and Orpah would have had after Naomi left to practice their faith in Moab was presumably low. They would have been left to their own individual resolve to worship and to keep the commandments in an area that neither understood nor supported them. It is also likely their families, who were not of their faith, would have given them little support, if any. Additionally, if the women did remarry, it would likely be to someone outside the faith.

These aspects and influences would be heavy burdens to carry and might well factor into or result in inactivity from their faith over the long-term. Yet the fact remains, Naomi was encouraging both Ruth and Orpah to stay not for the sake of their faith, not for their relationship with Naomi, but for the chance and opportunity for Ruth and Orpah to have families and relationships in their lives. That Orpah heeded Naomi's counsel was less about a demonstration of her faith in God and more about her understanding and recognition of the environment, conditions, and circumstances she was facing. Ruth's choice to follow Naomi was more about her love and relationship with Naomi than it was about her personal faith, even though she understood the value to her faith of being in Bethlehem.

Like Orpah, however, the choice presented to single adults is whether to journey to Bethlehem (to participate in the church) or to seek after and have relationships in their lives (outside the church). The decisions single adults make to leave the church or become less active are often motivated not by our lack of faithfulness or our testimonies, but rather by the potential for relational opportunity found outside the church. It is the most agonizing and difficult choice we confront.

Regarding the sisters who, due to the gender gap, bear the increased weight of this burden, I sometimes hear taught in the church that the answer is for them is to find and convert their spouses. Missionary work is thus the solution to the problem at hand. In saying this, though, it gives great insensitivity to the reality of their circumstances; they should now have to look outside the church for marriage, something they were taught their entire lives not to do. Additionally, they must take the chance that, even if they find someone, such a person would join the church and remain faithful.

As we begin to recognize the choices single adults face and their need for connection and attachment in their lives, and the church's untapped but realizable potential to give meaningful understanding and opportunities to them, my hope is that they will no longer be presented with the heart-wrenching and difficult decision of whether to stay in the church or to seek connection outside it. Furthermore, in the event single adults do choose inactivity, it is my hope those in the church, like Naomi, will have empathy, love, and kindness for the reasons for our choice and for the complexities, and gradations, of our situation.

All things considered and all theories and analysis aside, if you use Ruth and Orpah as a litmus test for participation in the church's single-adult programs, it was fifty-fifty, with one choosing to pursue relationships outside the church and the other choosing to pursue limited relational opportunity within the church. The current reality the church faces is, this statistic is much worse for today's single adults as more and more of us, like Orpah, are choosing to pursue relationships outside the church. This reality represents a very real crisis of conscience as the church, or, better said, its single-adult programs, are no longer sufficiently meeting the needs of a large group of its membership.

The difficulty church leaders face is whether to view the single adults in these programs through the perspective of Ruth or through the perspective of Orpah. Do they approach the lack of activity for single adults as a matter of faith on our part or as a recognition of the lack of attachment or connection for us within the church and its single-adult programs? These are the hard problems and questions that must be asked and openly discussed within the councils of the church to facilitate meaningful solutions for everyone involved.

LONELINESS

Being single is tough and many married members have either forgotten or do not completely understand its impact on us, especially over the long-term. I remember chuckling at a good friend of mine who was dispirited by his wife's week-long absence. He commented that the first few days were great: he had all the freedom and time to do what he wanted. Yet as the days went by, he become bored and lonely, missing the connection and association he had with his wife. In short, he became miserable simply because he was temporarily alone and was anxious to have her back.

I have learned in my life, marriage for all its subtleties, under normal conditions, is far better than the alternative of being single because it provides both a personal and a familial connection that helps individuals face the intrinsic loneliness in our lives. Perhaps this reason is why the first question God asked upon creating Adam was whether it was good for him to be alone.[31] The answer being no, a helpmeet and companion was created, not for Adam's comfort and consolation, but for both Adam and Eve's enlightenment and elevation.

Think about people who are not able (whether by choice or situation) to have this type of relationship and who do not have this type of connection or association. Even Moroni, a Nephite general and a prophet, commented on his own struggle and difficulty of being alone. After the destruction of the Nephites, the loss of his father and family, and the weight of his responsibility to protect and finish the gold plates, he wrote the following:

> Behold, my father hath made this record, and he hath written the intent thereof. And behold, I would write it also if I had room upon the plates, but I have not; and ore I have none, *for I am alone.* My father hath been slain in battle, and all my kinsfolk, and I have not friends nor whither to go; and *how long the Lord will suffer that I may live I know not.*[32]

I often ponder this scripture and think of the terrible loneliness Moroni faced and the length and duration of that loneliness. Like waterworn rocks, the effect of loneliness on single adults may not be immediate, yet when it steadily, constantly drips onto us, it has a wearing and wearying effect that may impact our outlook and ability to perceive positive things in life. There is a tyranny and a passive brutality to loneliness that is difficult to explain.

Like the relentless tick of interest for an unpaid debt, it is unfailingly and constantly with you. When you wake in the morning, it greets you with the warm embrace of a long-lost friend; when you lie down at night it haunts you and keeps you from the sweet relief of sleep you so desperately seek. Like the signaling of a faraway whistle of a moving train, the sight of a distant lighthouse, or the sounding of an ocean fog horn, it creates a longing or yearning within your soul not for a place but to be accepted, loved, and seen.

Chronic loneliness is not just a social condition; it has detrimental physical and mental health effects, altering how we think, feel, and live in society. Without the balm of personal connection, loneliness has many varied and unseen effects on single adults. It is a form of neglect and trauma that changes our brain chemistry, impacts our emotional or psychological health, influences how we view the world, and diminishes our ability to perceive events in an optimistic light. Notably, the needed social interactions lonely people do have may be less rewarding or fulfilling than those of non-lonely people. This exacerbates the loneliness we perceive and increases the possibility of depression, suicide, anxiety, addiction, and various other forms of emotional or mental illness.

From a practical support or community perspective, isolation and loneliness impact our ability to manage the basic needs of everyday life such as getting appropriate or complete medical care, ensuring proper and sustainable nutrition, and responding to emergency situations, as well as the willingness and desire to maintain proper hygiene and healthy living conditions. Poverty and financial distress may also be issues with which we struggle. From a physiological perspective, loneliness increases stress and anxiety, impacting body functions, releasing larger doses of natural hormones and chemicals that negatively impact the body's regulatory and circulatory systems. It diminishes the ability to manage stress in life and interrupts needed sleep cycles that then disrupt the physical rest and recovery of the body from everyday activities. In short, lonely people have a lower life expectancy than non-lonely people.[33]

Loneliness isn't determined by whether someone has a relationship. Loneliness is a matter of the quality and quantity of the connections and attachments, or, better said, the lack thereof, that we have in our lives. I learned this truth the hard way as I struggled with and pursued a marriage relationship, believing having a marriage would make me feel accepted and take away the loneliness I experienced. I have since learned the loneliness I felt was not caused by a lack of a marriage or cured with it; rather, the loneliness I experienced was based in emotion and spirit. It was as if I existed within a cave, surrounded and encompassed by darkness so thick, its weight compressed and suffocated me. I was desperate to come out into the light, but I did not know how to accomplish it.

The funny thing about loneliness is that it was familiar to me, something I became acquainted with and accepted into my life. It was a chronic pain that was not alleviated, but managed. You would think loneliness would motivate me into action, but I found it to be the opposite as it disheartened, discouraged, and demotivated me. I didn't become inactive in life, but the struggle to get out of bed, to participate, to move, and to engage not only in the church but in life was just that much more difficult. Loneliness was a millstone around my neck I neither wanted nor desired. As I became older and as circumstances and opportunity to connect and attach with others became less frequent, I experienced a heavier pull and counterweight keeping and pushing me further into that cave.

When I finally did get married, I was instantly relieved. For the first time I felt like I was somebody and I belonged. Connection and opportunity within the church and life in general increased almost immediately as social interactions seemed more vibrant, communications easier, and service more meaningful. I was also called to more meaningful responsibilities in the church. It was as if I was now accepted into the club to which I so longed to belong. However, as my relationship with my wife began to decay and break down, I found myself slipping back into the cover and security of my loneliness. I finally realized the validation I sought and the connections I longed for in that relationship were not going to come to fruition. The irony I faced was, I was lonelier married than I ever was single. How could that be? This is the fundamental question with which I wrestled.

Part of the issue was that I was trying to cope with my loneliness solely and specifically through the orthodoxy or lens of the gospel. I was constantly taught that faithfulness in the church or living a gospel-centered life would be sufficient to mitigate any loneliness I felt. Loneliness was a badge of honor to be worn with dignity despite the trial and adversity it brought. By serving in my callings, reaching out to others in love and charity, I would lose myself but find peace in life. Stated differently, it was an opportunity to come closer to God, to connect with Him, and everything else would be taken care of. What I found, though, was the harder I tried to be active in the church, the more worn out I became. It was as if the gospel itself did not enhance my social connections but rather amplified my spiritual connections.

After my marriage, I tried the same model of gospel living with similar results to when I was single. While I felt the Spirit, God's help, and His love in my life, the social and relational aspects of my life were generally left to me to resolve; that I couldn't fix them left me bereft of identity and self-validation, and starving for something that I did not know how to get.

Over time this began to wear on me. Like hot butter on toast, I began to melt under intense heat and pressure; I looked great on the outside but felt hollow inside. The counsel I received from the church did little to alter this. I was told to attend the temple often and regularly, which I did; to work on family history, which I attempted; to home teach, to go to church, to serve in my calling, to read my scriptures, to say my prayers, all of which I tried as best as I could. The list seemed large and there was always one more thing to do. I was desperately chasing fulfillment but feeling I was not doing enough to accomplish it.

I would go to church on Sunday, come home, and sit in the house for hours because I was worried about keeping the Sabbath day holy but there were no church activities I could attend. The activities available to me were either long distances away, or they were not engaging or worthwhile. I would attend the temple and serve, but I never had an opportunity to sit next to or talk to a fellow patron, aside from occasional small talk. Church activity became something where I would show up, worship, and then leave without a meaningful thought or glance from others. The sad part for me was I began to expect this type of interaction as I attended church. It offered little hope and little solace for me in the future, and I struggled just to maintain my own activity.

The church is wonderful, but it operates best through healthy and functioning families. For married individuals, it's okay to focus on spiritual connections when you are at church, because when you return home, those social and familial connections are there. For single adults, the opposite is true: we may receive spiritual validation but be devoid of the social and familial interactions needed for healthy living. Often, we must balance the demands of the church while seeking social opportunities either within or outside the church. I remember once attending a single-adult dinner and dance on a Friday night. Not many people were in attendance, but I was glad to be there. Prior to the activity starting, the mid-singles coordinator stated they were going into the sacrament room to have a testimony meeting.

I was stunned and somewhat embittered. While I understood the intention, I was disappointed, asking myself how I was going to connect with others when we were sitting in a room alone listening to others bearing testimony but mostly speaking about their own loneliness. I asked myself how many church activities for married individuals and families would start out with a testimony meeting and why the single adults felt it necessary to do something more spiritual than what was provided within the regular church meeting schedules.

The issue for single adults with these types of activities is not one of faithfulness or a desire to connect with God; rather, it is one of saturation. Having a testimony meeting prior to an activity is not a bad thing, truly it isn't, but when single adults come together within the program of the church and prioritize vertical connections over horizontal connections, it can become problematic because we already have so few opportunities to socialize. Vertical connections are upward, they are those connections we generate between us and God and are spiritual in nature; horizontal connections are lateral, they are those connections we develop in and among each other and are relational in nature.

Without criticism or finding fault, my experience is many, if not most, of the activities designed for single adults in the church focus on or are intended to involve us primarily in vertical connections rather than in horizontal connections. Think about it, we even title these activities through gospel-centric themes and ideas: family home evening, break the fast, and ward prayer, just to name a few. Those responsible for the single-adult programs and activities should principally and from the start evaluate how single adults interact with each other, how we connect and attach with each other, and how we develop meaningful friendships so that when we do go to church, our opportunity and openness to the Spirit is not restricted, but enhanced.

An overemphasis on spirituality has the potential to reduce or extinguish the social aspect altogether. Let me share a personal example. My father is a wonderful man, yet his orthodoxy in the church has often prohibited meaningful connections with those around him. He views this strictness or inflexibility as part of his duty and testimony to the gospel, and in truth it helps him and many people.

Recently, he and my mother came to visit me in Minnesota for the weekend. On Sunday we went to church and spent the day together. In the evening my mother and I decided to watch a Hallmark movie downstairs. Believing watching TV was less than appropriate for the Sabbath, my father chose to remain upstairs and read his scriptures. While I was not going to judge his decision, it made me sad his choice prohibited an opportunity to participate and connect with his family. In other words, in that individual moment and at that time, he prioritized a vertical connection over the horizontal connections that were available to him.

My purpose for sharing this example is neither to debate the righteousness of mine or my mother's choice or to impugn my father's choice; rather, it is to show that how we apply the gospel may lead to spiritual edification but no connection with others. This happens too many times for single adults. In my opinion, it is one of the primary reasons the church is struggling to maintain our activity.

I have often heard people state that single adults are rejecting the culture of the church; I don't believe that. What I believe is, single adults are taught to prioritize the gospel in such a manner that it affects our ability to have meaningful connection in our lives; personal loneliness is the eventual result. What we are rejecting is this idea we must sacrifice our personal connections to have a spiritual connection. This is not meant to de-emphasize the need for spiritual activity or the importance of connecting to God in our lives. What I am trying to say is there is a need for a meaningful balance of activities within the single adult-programs of the church that meet both the spiritual and personal needs of all involved.

From where should single adults get the horizontal or social connection and validation they need to overcome their loneliness? We all need some form of love and connection with others to exist. For married members in the church who are in a healthy marriage, there is a constant presence of validation for them; it counteracts and balances their feelings of loneliness. For single adults, though, how do we build nurturing friendships, connections, and relationships within the church to have sufficient resilience for the impacts that loneliness has on us? If the church and its members are unable to provide nurturing relationships, then they should be more understanding, more compassionate, and less judgmental of others who do not have the same type of constant validation they have.

When Jezebel sought the life of Elijah the prophet, Elijah sought protection and refuge by hiding in a cave. After many days, God appeared to him and asked, "What doest thou here Elijah?"[34] I have often thought about this question as it pertains to my own personal cave and the loneliness I felt. After my divorce, I was truly lost. I neither found solace in the church nor reprieve through participation in its activities. I was alone, nursing my own introversion, bored, and struggling.

At this time, my brother Mark, who is a professional dance instructor, decided it would be good for me to take ballroom dance lessons. It was if he was saying, "Kevin, what are you doing here?" As a Christmas gift, he arranged for me to have several private and group lessons at a dance studio in Minnesota. He even gave me a pair of fancy dancing shoes. Inwardly I struggled with the idea of these lessons (I did not consider myself a dancer), but I nonetheless gave it a try.

My first lesson confirmed what I already knew: I have two left feet. Still, my instructor taught me several key points in that lesson: take one step at a time, pause, keep your head up, be confident, and smile. Over the years, dance is something I have learned to embrace and enjoy, yet these lessons have had tremendous application and meaning beyond dance itself. They have helped me to be more confident, lift myself up, and live the life I wanted, despite the loneliness I felt.

I began to step out of my comfort zone and put myself in situations that required growth, dedication, and courage. When I finally emerged from my personal cave, I didn't find a welcoming and restful oasis but a desert with the sun incessantly bearing down. Yet I was moving, trying, progressing, and that made all the difference. I have failed many times since and had to pick myself up each time. For that I am grateful. Today I climb mountains I never thought possible, reach out to those who need it, and dance where I once was still. I realize loneliness is not something that is remedied or endured; rather it is something we accept, embrace, and move beyond. I have also learned to find balance in my life as it pertains to the church, work, and life.

I am not a perfect member of the church, and I try to live the gospel as best as I can in accordance with the circumstances and situations I face. Sometimes that means saying no in order that I may reach others or participate in activities outside the church. It is a conscious effort to find meaningful attachments and connections in my life no matter where they are located. I am okay with that because I realize my life is different from what most others have in the church. Sometimes they don't understand my choices, and I am okay with that too. The battles I fight today are to embrace who I am, try new things, and be satisfied with the results no matter what they are. For I know where the cave is, and the struggle is to not go back to it.

POVERTY

Cindy is an eighteen-year-old woman and a faithful member of the church. Full of hope and optimism, she attends BYU. After her freshman year, she meets and marries a twenty-one-year-old recently returned missionary. Happy with her life, she drops out of school to work, support her new husband, and have children. After several years of marriage and multiple children, her marriage suddenly dissolves into divorce.

Cindy, now newly single, is left with the sole responsibility of raising her children with no education or job skills. She is dependent upon small or inconsistent child support as well as state and church welfare programs. She is alone, wondering desperately why she is in this predicament, and scared of what the future will bring for her and her family. If she does find a job or try to attend college, she struggles to find adequate and affordable childcare and worries about how her absence will affect her children as they grow. She is compelled by circumstance to move back home with her parents as she tries to find her way forward. Finding and committing to possible new relationships is difficult, as she must weigh the loss of welfare programs or other financial support against the risk of success for that relationship as well as the long-term financial well-being of herself and her children.

Rick is a young man who works hard his entire life, earns a college degree, and obtains gainful employment. He marries the girl of his dreams and has a family, but the marriage ends in divorce. The administrative costs of the divorce and the property settlement are significant and consume all his available savings. He is told by the court that he will be separated from his children, who are now living in a different state. He is required to pay a large monthly child support and alimony that impacts a significant portion of his real income. His wages are garnished and he has no possibility of reprieve.

Despite his employment, he can neither afford a house, savings, or money for personal care. What little money he does manage to save is spent in travel to visit his children. He is burdened with both long-term and short-term debt and has little prospect of paying it off in the near term. Living paycheck to paycheck, he transfers balances from one credit card to another to forestall payments he cannot make. He is not able to save or invest in retirement savings, which affects not only his quality of life today but also the one he hopes to have in the future. When he can be with his kids, he has difficulty finding time with them and procuring appropriate childcare for him to maintain responsible full-time employment.

What a sad and sorry state for all the individuals in the above two hypotheticals. Yet this situation and a multitude of variations happen all the time. Poverty, in its many malicious forms, robs people of their will and ability to function in life. While the individuals in the above scenarios may not be viewed as "living" in poverty, they are unquestionably able to see it from where they stand as they grapple and tussle with its onset and its impacts.

Many of us aren't prepared to live as a single adult, whether we lack the finances or the life skills to be on our own. Marriage does have many benefits that counteract poverty; it allows synergies to occur in income sharing, division of labor, and responsibility; encourages long-term savings; and allows greater efficiency for the use and acquisition of resources. Even if we are not living below the poverty line, when we are single, these efficiencies are either lessened or nonexistent, increasing the cost, time, and effort required in maintaining a beneficial and healthy standard of living. Said differently, there is significantly more red ink than black when you are a single adult.

Additionally, for those single adults who experience divorce, the process of divorce itself is one of the greatest long-term destroyers of wealth as it drains assets, creates financial uncertainty, and impacts spending and earning potential for all involved. Oddly, the outcome of this financial reality will sometimes cause us to remain in broken or unhealthy relationships out of necessity because we cannot afford the economic trauma associated with the dissolution of the relationship.

During the Savior's ministry, a poor widow came to the temple and placed two mites into the temple treasury. The Savior then called together his disciples and commented that this widow had contributed more to the treasury than everyone else, for everyone else gave of their excess and abundance but this poor woman gave all that she possessed.[35] It was a moving example of sacrifice and charity.

I have often pondered the example of this single woman who gave her entirety to God in a time of great need based solely upon her faith, and asked myself what I would do given her circumstances. This act touched the Savoir and has resonated throughout the ages with those who believe, as one of the highest demonstrations of selflessness and temporal sacrifice. The scriptures are silent though as to what happened to this woman, leaving us to believe God blessed her in His own way and in His own time.

Poverty is difficult to describe except in general terms; still, like with the widow, poverty is a fundamental and very real issue for single adults in the church. It impacts our ability to participate in church programs, to attend singles functions, and to reach out beyond ourselves and develop healthy connections and attachments. Additionally, it causes added stress and concern, especially for the raising and rearing of children when only one parent is financially responsible. Poverty often boils down to a cost-benefit analysis between the opportunity to exist, to eat, to be with family, or to seek after spiritual and personal relationships in our life.

Poverty is defined as a state of being that is extremely poor; it is the inability to provide for the basic needs of oneself and those around us.[36] It raises mental images of destitution, pauperism, indigence, neediness, and hardship. While we may debate about the parameters of the poverty line and what demographics are included within its definition, there is no doubt that poverty is a barrier to many of us in our ability to cope and exist within our communities. If our primary thought during each day is on the provision of basic life needs for ourselves or our families, it is difficult for us to prioritize or participate in other essential aspects of our life.

Many demographics and characteristics play a role in poverty, including race, income and earnings, education, family status, and gender. In the case of the widow, the scriptures point out three defining characteristics: 1) that she is female, 2) that she is single, and 3) that she is poor. Oftentimes, race is also a major factor in poverty; however, poverty can also disproportionately affect women and those who are single.

For these reasons, it is vital to talk about and understand the effects of poverty on single adults and the practical ability of those single adults suffering from it to exist and fully participate within the programs of the church. We should not assume the poverty line is the point of differentiation for what is sustainable and what is not. Said differently, we should not assume everyone living above the poverty line is doing fine; they may have minimal life-sustaining capability but be inhibited by their ability to participate in other important life activities. This is especially true for single adults. It is important to understand how single adults who are susceptible to poverty react and make choices for their personal and spiritual well-being, even if they do not meet the specific criteria for poverty itself.

In September 2016, the U.S. Department of Commerce issued a statistical report on poverty within the United States.[37] This report defines the poverty threshold as a family of four that annually earns $24,250 or less. For single adults, the poverty level is $12,486 for those under the age of sixty-five and for those over the age of sixty-five it is $11,581. According to this report, a total of 13.5 percent of the U.S. population (43.1 million people) live in poverty. Breaking this down across gender lines, approximately 12.2 percent of men and 14.8 percent of women live in poverty.

The following are statistics for poverty as it pertains to families in the United States.[38]

Families in Poverty by Type of Family

	Total in U.S.	Total in Poverty	Percentage
Total Families	82.2 million	8.6 million	10.4
Married Couple	60.2 million	3.2 million	5.4
Single Fathers	6.3 million	0.9 million	14.9
Single Mothers	15.6 million	4.5 million	28.2

The statistical analysis of families living in poverty is stunning. Of the 82.2 million families in the United States, 10.4 percent live in poverty. For single families, the poverty rate is much higher and more impactful: 14.9 percent of U.S. families headed by single fathers live in poverty and an astounding 28.2 percent of families headed by single mothers live in poverty. That is a significant increase over married couples, who have a poverty rate of 5.4 percent.

Think about that: of the 8.6 million families living in poverty, over sixty percent (60%) are families of single parents and of those, the clear majority (one out of every three) is headed by single mothers. Although families headed by single fathers are less susceptible to poverty, with one out of every six living in poverty, they are nonetheless not immune to it. We need to take a hard look at the likelihood single adults in the church are currently living in conditions that are at, below, or dangerously close to the poverty line.

Of the nearly twenty-two million single-parent families the United States, almost twenty-five percent (25%) are in poverty. Think about the ramifications of that statistic. For every four single parents you know, one of them is likely not able to meet even the basic needs of life without assistance. How many more single families exist who are not considered to be living in poverty but are strapped for resources and toiling just to make ends meet? It is my opinion that these statistics have far-reaching implications to the activity and wherewithal of single adults in the church.

Finances should not be a deciding factor in single adults' ability to access or participate with other single adults within the church. Yet all too often, it is one of the preeminent and key decision drivers we must consider. Do we want to invest the time, and money, to commute to a church activity where we know few people will attend or where we may not be edified or uplifted? Can we afford to hire a babysitter for several hours to go on a date or socialize? What about tithing and other financial contributions?

On the flip side, some single adults would love to get together at activities such as movies and eating out, but are prevented not because we can't afford it, but because other single adults cannot. Types and regularity of activities are thus generally limited to those who may afford their cost. While on the surface this may not be harmful, it places logistical limitations on the opportunity for different types of activities to occur. This creates redundancy and repetitiveness in the activities themselves that may also lead to decreased participation.

Addressing poverty generally among single adults may not be practical, as it is dependent upon so many different factors beyond the church's or society's control. Even the Savior reminded us the poor will always be among us.[39] James wrote, "Pure religion and undefiled before God and the Father is this, to visit the fatherless and the widows in their affliction, and to keep himself unspotted from the world."[40] Is the burden or suffering of the widow greater than that of a single or divorced mother or that of the single father? Is it not reasonable to then believe the practice of pure religion is to assist those in distress, to lift the hands that hang down, and to strengthen those in need?

James didn't say to solve this issue; rather, he asked us to *visit* those who are afflicted by it. We visit the single adults who are afflicted by poverty or its effects by not just helping us provide for our temporal needs but also by understanding poverty's social and emotional impacts on us: by providing opportunity, encouragement, love, and understanding for us. We can visit these single adults by providing regular childcare, transportation, and activity fees or other necessities to allow us the opportunity to participate in needed social events. By sitting by us or assisting us, as appropriate, at church or other instances when one of our children misbehaves, rather than wishing the problem would just go away. By loving us no matter what circumstances we find ourselves in, and by offering encouragement, reassurance, and support rather than judgment or marginalization.

By regularly considering the impacts of poverty in and on single adults at a local level when planning and implementing single-adult activities, it is my belief that church leaders and members will improve the capacity, ability, and willingness of all single adults to participate in the church and its programs.

ADDITIONAL THOUGHTS ON UNDERSTANDING THE NEEDS OF SINGLE ADULTS

From time to time I will hear local church leaders or even single adults state that being single is an act or form of *selfishness* because we are solely focused on ourselves. Conversely, being married is an act of *selflessness* because we are focused on our spouse and our family. The one is Christlike while the other is not. As a result, many may unintentionally view single adults in a negative light. While I am certain such perspectives are intended to motivate and encourage us to become married, these types of remarks are myopic and insensitive to the actual needs and problems of single adults. They are also counter to the purpose for which the church's single-adult programs should exist. This chapter is intended to remind us all that there are a host of bona fide and valid reasons for why we are single in the church and there are a multitude of issues and problems associated with it.

The purpose of this chapter is not to solve these problems for single adults, nor is it to define or delineate an exhaustive list of the issues and concerns single adults have; there are too many to properly touch on. Even on the topics I discuss in this chapter (opportunity and availability, loneliness, and poverty), I have some feelings of inadequacy as to my ability to state their relevance and importance to single adults. These topics are those of the highest concern to me as they pertain to my living as a single adult. Whether you agree or disagree with the importance of these topics or my thoughts on them, my hope is these ideas add to the collective discussion about single adults in the church and provide a more comprehensive understanding of the issues we face in a family-centric religion.

The danger is we will take these topics and give cursory or perfunctory thought in their application. Sometimes, in the church we look at problems from a result-oriented or end-product point of view. It's a lot like asking for a cake and being given a cake mix and told to make it. All the ingredients are there, but if it's not used correctly or applied in the proper sequence, what is hoped for may not in reality occur. We understand what the solution looks like, but we do not have the skills, capability, or wherewithal to accomplish it.

Then we sit back bemoaning the failure while pointing a finger at outward causes. Anyone who has tried crafting on Pinterest may have had a similar experience. It's not in the recognition of these issues where the solutions exist, but rather in their application both on a systemic and individual basis. By effectively applying general principals in meaningful ways to individual situations, we will provide less process-oriented opportunities and more organic opportunity for attachment and connection to grow among single adults.

Ask yourself, have we considered the needs of single adults? Have we looked at the issues and concerns single adults face? Have we thought about creative and meaningful solutions that will allow the opportunity for attachment and connection to occur and that have real impact in lives of single adults? Remember, we don't have to solve or tackle every issue relating to single adults at every activity. It may be enough to discuss, plan, and tackle one issue on an individual basis for one activity. By then learning and creatively applying these new solutions and ideas over time, a basis of trust and appreciation will grow within single adults and the church's programs. I believe, through constant and consistent review and discussion of the single adult's concerns and by innovative and meaningful application, the church will find creative and applicable solutions that provide room at God's table for all of us, married or single, so that all may partake and be edified in our lives.

8

Developing an Eternal Perspective Despite the Challenges of Being Single

Let us run with patience the race that is set before us.
—Hebrews 12:1

Several years ago, while traveling to Australia for some important and pressing work meetings, my itinerary was inconveniently altered when the flight on which I was scheduled to travel was grounded at the Los Angeles, California airport. After many hours of standing in line with hundreds of upset and angry travelers, some of whom had been there for nearly four days waiting for a flight, I began to realize my ability to reach my destination in time was in serious jeopardy.

When I finally spoke to an airline representative, I was told there were no available flights and I would have to come back the next day to see if something could be done. In a moment of panic and frustration, I anxiously called a close friend, explained my predicament, and debated whether to return home or try to continue. After listening to my frustrations, my friend optimistically encouraged me to keep trying to get to Australia. My friend told me, "It's your choice how you deal with this situation. You can look at this either in a constructive or a nonconstructive manner."

This counsel changed my perspective on the situation. I found a hotel, got a restful night of sleep, attended church the next morning, and obtained alternative travel arrangements that got me to my destination in time for my meetings. I learned an important and valuable lesson that day: we often face unforeseen frustration, obstacles, and delay in our lives causing both unanticipated and untimely difficulties. How we choose to view and react to these difficulties has a tremendous influence on our ability to manage these issues, on our success, and on our capacity to be happy.

How do we see events and circumstances in our lives, especially when hard times occur? Do we view our lives as having purpose beyond what we daily experience, or do we see them as something that is temporary? The difference between these viewpoints determines how or whether we can develop an eternal perspective in our lives.

Developing an eternal perspective is about our capacity to define ourselves in relation with deity and to find meaning in the entirety of our lives. It is the context in which we perceive facts and data and the point of reference on which we base our emotions. It is also the framework from which we choose to act. Each of us can choose what type of perspective we have. Yet the perspective or manner through which we choose to perceive ourselves and our surroundings makes a tremendous difference in how we live our lives, the choices we make, and the opportunities we create.

Take the temporary difficulty of my flight delay: I was responsible for how I viewed and reacted to the situation. Whether I viewed those difficulties in a constructive manner made all the difference in managing and resolving its impacts. So, too, it is for our ability to develop eternal perspective in our lives.

When Naaman, the Syrian captain, approached the prophet Elisha seeking healing from the scourge of leprosy, his perspective almost prevented him from receiving what he desired most. Used to the decorum and formality of kingdoms and principalities, Naaman expected Elisha to perform in grand fashion the miracle for which he hoped. With neither pomp nor circumstance, Elisha chose not to meet Naaman in person; rather, he sent a message through his servant telling Naaman he must bathe seven times in the Jordan River.

Incensed and offended, Naaman refused. He scoffed, remarking that all the rivers in Damascus were better than all the waters in Israel. Could he simply not wash himself there and be clean? Fortunately, Naaman's servant spoke to him and stated that if Elisha had asked for a great thing, then Naaman would have gladly done it. He then asked Naaman how different that is from saying, "Wash and be clean." Naaman subsequently washed himself in the Jordan River and was healed.

Despite Naaman's extreme need and desire for healing, he almost passed it by, not because of a lack of desire but because of a lack of an eternal perspective. His failure was that he did not see past his own bias to accept the blessing he sought.[1] Like Naaman, we must examine whether preconceptions and predispositions impede our ability to realize eternal blessings in our lives. Are we open to seeing beneficial opportunities, or do such opportunities become lost to us because we cannot see?

For single adults, some of the factors in developing or impeding an eternal perspective is our personal viewpoint, outlook, and disposition on being single and being married. For instance, we may view being single as living in a lesser or lower state of being, one that does not or cannot bring happiness or salvation itself. Similarly, we may view being married as living a higher, more exalted path where salvation and happiness are the result. Yet if these two perspectives are the starting point or lens through which we view our lives, it obstructs our ability today to have an eternal perspective because it means single adults cannot be happy, cannot find solace, and cannot find peace unless and until they become married. This obfuscates our ability today to make healthy choices and to appropriately react to favorable opportunities.

How many times have we expressed the thoughts *If only I were married, I would be happy* or *I will be a better member of the church when I have a family of my own*? Personally, I thought this way for many years in my life. I felt like I was stumbling around, waiting, trying to figure things out, but couldn't because I wasn't married. I passed up on useful life and relational opportunities because I saw only the burden and not the benefit of being single. These types of comparative feelings drive and influence how single adults view ourselves and the church; they form the basis for many of the important life decisions we make. Yet this view, at its core, is negative. It is viewing the gospel and our lives not through the optic of opportunity but through the mindset of failure.

Having an eternal perspective means seeing occurrences and happenings in the correct manner and in the correct context so gainful opportunities, whether relational or otherwise, may have room in our lives. It is true, despite the immense hope and desire we have for future relationships, that we may sometimes become accustomed or acclimated to being single. The fear and risk of taking relational chances, the expectation God will timely provide a proper partner (without our own effort, initiative, and self-action), or the possibility of the future failure of such a relationship often impairs the vulnerability required for us to find and enter that which is hoped for the most. As a result, we, like Naaman, may overlook, pass by without acknowledgement, or fail to understand or see healthy and beneficial relational possibilities.

Having an eternal perspective allows me to understand being single is good and wonderful. My focus is no longer on the lack of a relationship in my life, but the breadth of opportunity I have to make an effective and valuable impact with myself and in the lives of those around me. Seeing myself as single is not damaging, detrimental, or disadvantageous, but rather encouraging, enhancing, and edifying. It is central to my ability to be happy and to remain active in the church. That does not mean I don't desire or seek companionship in my life, but I am happy with who I am and what I can be, because I view myself and who I am in a healthy manner and with an eternal perspective.

I believe developing and having an eternal perspective is about four things: 1) seeing things as they are and as they can be; 2) turning curses into blessings and seeing the silver lining in every storm cloud; 3) having an absence of judgment; and 4) having and developing patience. Each of these plays an important and fundamental role in how and in what manner we view ourselves, our prospects and outlooks, our experiences, and our lives.

SEEING THINGS AS THEY ARE AND AS THEY CAN BE

Two interesting and successive events occurred for the prophet Elisha.[2] After traveling to Jordan, the prophet assisted several individuals who were cutting lumber to build housing. While working, one of the individuals inadvertently lost his axe-head in the river. Perplexed and distressed, as the axe was borrowed, this individual bewailed and bemoaned his loss to the prophet. After enquiring where the axe was lost, the prophet took a stick and tossed it into the river, at which point the heavy metal axe head floated to the surface, allowing the servant to easily and joyfully recover it.

A short time later, a much more serious problem occurred when the king of Syria came down to war against the House of Israel. Hoping to ensnare and capture the Israelites, the king of Syria laid a trap with his army. Elisha counseled the Israelite king on military strategy and tactics, which saved the Israelite army on multiple occasions and frustrated the Syrian king. When the Syrian king discovered it was Elisha who was providing up-to-date insight and intelligence into his war strategies, he sent an army to surround and capture Elisha.

When Elisha's servant saw the Syrian army he was terrified and, without hope, asked Elisha what they should do in the face of such overwhelming odds. Elisha calmly answered, "Fear not, for they that be with us are more than they that be with them."[3] Then Elisha prayed and God opened the servant's eyes so he could behold the hosts of Heaven surrounding and encompassing them. Through God's power, Elisha caused the soldiers in this army to lose their sight. He then led them away, restoring their sight once they safely left Israel.

The lessons presented in these events shed light on how we see ourselves in the context of our circumstances and surroundings. They illuminate and explain how we develop an eternal perspective as it pertains to both spiritual and temporal events and circumstances in our lives. In the instance of the lost axe-head, it was the servant's failure to see things as *they could be* that led to his despair. Granted, metal axe-heads don't normally float; yet for individuals who believe and have faith in God, it is not outside the realm of possibility that heavenly intervention can and will provide alternative solutions that will meet or exceed the need of our existing problem.

When the brother of Jared was presented with a similar issue (i.e. to provide light to the ships in their journey across the sea), he did not rely on what he knew but on what he believed God could accomplish. In other words, he reached beyond what was probable and relied on faith, believing God could accomplish what he could neither understand nor comprehend. As result, the brother of Jared saw the hand of God and received blessings that enlightened all in their most trying and difficult times.[4]

In order to see things as they can be, we must perceive and accept potential not only in ourselves, but also in those around us. It's about acknowledging what we have today while having confidence in something larger and being open to unseen or unrecognized possibility. Seeing things as they can be takes courage, faith, hope, and a willingness to reach beyond the reality we know and with which we are comfortable—to accept the possibility of effective and workable alternatives existing no matter our circumstance or predicament.

In the instance of the Syrian army, it was the servant's failure to see events and circumstances *as they are* that lead to his indecision and concern. Like the lost axe-head floating to the surface, the perception of the hosts of Heaven in real time is not something that is probable or that occurs regularly. Elisha's servant was not the prophet, and we should not expect him to have the same spiritual outlook or insight as the prophet. Still, it's not his incapability to initially see what Elisha saw that is important; it was that he did not see it at all. In other words, he did not have all the facts or a complete understanding to appropriately view or perceive his surroundings. As a result, he was not able to make healthy decisions or to undertake correct actions for the situation in which he found himself. Fear, indecision, and inaction were the result.

Having an eternal perspective means we correctly understand or perceive all, or at least most, of the relevant facts. It means we can clearly see events and are able to prioritize our responses to make useful, advantageous, and beneficial decisions. Interestingly, of all the methods Elisha could have used to defeat the Syrian army (weather, illness, etc.), he chose blindness to afflict them. In other words, he took away their vision or perspective. Despite that, Elisha did not forsake them in this condition, instead leading them away from their intended purpose, realigning them toward a more positive and beneficial outcome for them and for the House of Israel.

Likewise, God does the same for us. When we lack perspective or cannot see, God does. He can lead us to positive and beneficial outcomes, realigning us to better ways and purposes if we allow Him.

Having an eternal perspective employs more than what we think, see, or feel. It is the capacity to look within ourselves to find joy in our current circumstances, to simultaneously reach heavenward and find meaning and purpose for our lives, and to discern truth from both a spiritual and temporal viewpoint. It is the aptitude to see ourselves, others, and our experiences first as they actually are and second as they can be, unbiased and unvarnished from our own bias and perspectives.

For single adults, having an eternal perspective means not glossing over or camouflaging difficult feelings. It's about looking at ourselves in a realistic way to understand how we can grow and what changes we need to make in ourselves to be open to new opportunities and new possibilities. It's about trying new things, stretching beyond our own comforts, and developing the willingness, the proficiency, and the skills to see those things we need rather than those things we desire. It's also about seeing people and relationships for who they are and not for what they are not. When we cultivate an eternal perspective, we accept our reality while finding peace in our understanding that solutions may exist that are outside our known paradigms.

TURNING CURSES INTO BLESSINGS: SEEING THE SILVER LINING IN EVERY STORM CLOUD

When Balak, the King of Moab, sought to gain military advantage over the House of Israel, he hired Balaam, a priest, to curse the Israelites through the power of God. In a deluded and mistaken twist on the "if you can't beat them, join them" theory, Balak's thinking was, if his gods could not prevail against the might of the House of Israel, he would invoke the powers of their god, the God of Israel, against them.

Intrigued by the money Balak offered, Balaam traveled to Moab to overlook the Israelites. Along the way, God sent an angel to admonish and instruct Balaam. When the time came for Balaam to curse the Israelites, Balaam instead gave a blessing to Israel rather than a curse. Moses referenced this experience toward the end of his life, stating, "Nevertheless the Lord thy God would not hearken unto Balaam; but the Lord thy God turned the curse into a blessing unto thee, because the Lord thy God loved thee."[5]

Sometimes, as single adults, we view being single not as blessing but as a burden or detriment. The lack of attachment and connection can itself be a storm of such magnitude and ferocity that we struggle to have an eternal perspective—to see what is positive or how we can find blessing in it. For me this struggle is one of the most difficult aspects of being single. The questions for us become: *How do we turn difficulty into advantage? How do we overcome that which drags us down? How we develop the capability to be happy and to find peace despite the tempests we face?*

Having an eternal perspective about being single is not seeing it as a badge of discouragement to be worn with shame and ridicule, nor is it seeing it as a badge of honor, believing sacrifice will always bring reward. We are neither victims nor martyrs. Being single should be viewed as an opportunity to grow, to learn, and to develop, so when we stand before God to be judged we can rightly say, "I lived, I learned, I grew, and for that I am grateful." If we choose not to embrace or see the benefits of being single, or if we are a victim of our own circumstances, we run the risk of leading a less fulfilled life, one that is not truly lived or experienced. The challenge for each of us is to turn disappointment into hope, failure into success, and adversity into opportunity.

Having an eternal perspective is to see and perceive things as God sees them; it is to see the benefit even when surrounded by negative results. We are not God, and developing an eternal perspective, especially in our most trying and difficult moments, is not easy, yet doing so is possible. Eve demonstrated an eternal perspective after she and Adam were exiled from the Garden of Eden. Said she, "Were it not for our transgression we never should have had seed, and never should have known good and evil, and the joy of our redemption, and the eternal life which God gives unto all the obedient."[6] Eve chose to view her situation in the light and purpose of gaining exaltation rather than to dwell on the temporary hardships that both she and Adam had to bear.

Moses acquired an eternal perspective after the Savior visited him. When the Savior showed Moses the world and His hand in all its creation, both in the past and in the future, Moses was struck with awe and wonder. After this vision, Moses was overcome for several hours. When he regained his strength, he stated, "Now, for this cause I know that man is nothing, which thing I never had supposed."[7] Moses was a man of great stature; he was a prince of Egypt and he stood in the presence and counsel of Pharaoh. Through his experience with the Savior, he gained an eternal perspective of the goodness and greatness of God as compared to his own station in life, which was something he had not previously understood or considered.

For single adults, developing and keeping an eternal perspective in our individual lives is not always intuitive, as we do not always have the same insight and exposure given to both Eve and to Moses. Sometimes the trials and adversities we experience become so troublesome, so personal, and so taxing as to distort our view of what our lives are about. This can be especially true for those of us who struggle with the ability to enter or participate in a committed relationship or with the timing and duration of those relationships. Without an eternal perspective, we may view these hardships and difficulties as the only thing that matters in our lives.

When this happens, we focus exclusively on our sorrow without proper context or hope. We are like the one who smashes his finger with a hammer and who can only see the momentary hurt and long for nothing but it to end. We may also be like Moses, allowing our life's experiences and background to taint or subjectively bias our viewpoint away from what is real and what is true. We may allow these temporary feelings and emotions to dictate the way we receive information and experience life, thus keeping us from perceiving practical alternatives and outcomes or undertaking valuable courses of action.

The danger arrives when we replace an eternal perspective with what we think is true. Like Lamoni, who believed in the Great Spirit but nevertheless believed whatever he chose and did to be right, we can convince ourselves the choices we make, the desires we have, and the opportunities we allow to happen are right and good.[8] The Savior stated:

> Who am I that made man, saith the Lord, that will hold him guiltless that *obeys not my commandments*? Who am I, saith the Lord, that have promised and have not fulfilled? *I command and men obey not*; I revoke and they receive not the blessing.
>
> Then *they say* in their hearts: This *is not the work of the Lord, for his promises are not fulfilled*. But wo unto such, for their reward lurketh beneath, and not from above.[9]

Sometimes the greatest detriments to our developing and keeping an eternal perspective are the emotional and spiritual motes and beams each of us have that prevent us from recognizing and acknowledging our individual weaknesses and faults. When promised blessings are not immediately received, do we become bitter, lose our faith, and turn from God, or do we accept God (and his timing) in our lives and move forward? The challenge for us is to gain an eternal viewpoint while we are going through our most difficult and trying moments so we may recognize God's hand in all things, turn to Him, and be saved. To have an eternal perspective is to find happiness despite sadness, to find meaning and purpose in our journey, and to be content with who we are and what we have.

Elder Neal A. Maxwell taught, "Rather than simply passing through trials, we must allow trials to pass through us in ways that sanctify us."[10] I love this idea as it relates to the eternal perspective we gain from the trials and adversities in our lives. What matters is less about what we endure and more about whether we accept and embrace these moments as part of our lives and as opportunities for us to gain greater blessings in the future. Do we allow our trials, difficulties, and hardships to define who we are or do we use them as support in our lives to refine and forge our character for our own betterment and good? If we see our struggles, toils, and problems through an eternal perspective, we begin to realize each step we take, each fall we have, and each toe we stub gives us experience to prepare us individually to come to the Savior. With this perspective in mind we learn to accept our difficulties, our trials, and our hardships in a way that makes us Christlike.[11]

In a very real sense, learning to be happy and to have peace as a single adult is about developing the ability to see silver linings in our individual storm clouds and the capability to turn our curses into blessings and our difficulties into benefits.

HAVING AN ABSENCE OF JUDGMENT

Once during law school, I attended a lecture regarding the constitutional requirement in the United States for the separation between church and state. As part of that lecture, the professor argued that morality in society was a form or outgrowth of religion and thus had no place in institutional education, government, or law. He reasoned that morality was solely and exclusively the proper domain of churches. This reasoning struck me as uncompassionate, unyielding, and uncompromising, for it did not allow for conscience, thought, or intent as we apply the law to actions or individuals in society. Without morality, judgment cannot determine whether actions are right or wrong, only whether they are legally authorized.

Over the years, I have thought about this lecture and on what ethos or rationale we base our individual perspectives. The question for me is not just about what basis we use to make judgments for ourselves and for those around us but also about how we keep from judging others in ways that are harmful to the relationships we have with them. It's about seeing people in a positive manner despite differences we do not understand or fully appreciate.

As a natural resource attorney, I have represented controversial extraction projects for which people publicly advocated both for and against the implementation of a respective project. Often the debates centered not around the science of the project or its potential impacts, if any, but on whether such resources should be extracted altogether. Some viewed natural resource extraction from the perspective of environmental protection, while others viewed it from the perspective of the creation of needed jobs and economic vitality.

The debates both for and against these projects raged rancorously and continuously, with each side feeling they had the higher moral ground. Every aspect of these projects was viewed through the lens of which side of the debate one held. If facts were presented or decisions made that did not support one side's beliefs, they would minimize or ignore such facts altogether. If a project went through a legal and regulatory process and was approved, it was acclaimed as heroic by those who supported it and hailed as a travesty by those who opposed it. If a project was not approved, the same speeches were made but by opposite sides.

What made me sad in all of this was there was very little if no middle ground; no matter the outcome, there would be rejoicing on one side and finger-pointing, weeping, wailing, and gnashing of teeth on the other. While I was grateful people had differing opinions, as it afforded me a chance to be gainfully employed, I felt many if not all the problems and concerns could be addressed without all the emotion that surrounded the respective judgments that were made.

I realize today that we each have a choice in how we perceive facts and events and how we judge outcomes. It is a subjective viewpoint of what is right and wrong that is influenced by and based upon our emotions, upbringing, education, beliefs, and needs. Thus, an outcome is judged as correct or incorrect based primarily on the idiosyncrasies and viewpoints we hold.

As I progressed as a professional, I began to recognize that accepting and understanding opposing viewpoints was critical to finding solutions to move forward. I needed to develop the ability to move past my own emotions and viewpoints to analyze and evaluate actions and to make decisions that were in the best interest for all involved. Developing this skill was a lot more difficult than just saying or writing it; it was about sincere recognition and validation of all concerns that were expressed even if such sincerity was not reciprocated.

I have often thought that for single adults, the most difficult aspect of our participation in the church is facing the judgments, mindsets, and perspectives not only of ourselves individually but also of those collectively within the church. Being single or divorced is one of the loneliest experiences an individual may face. Whether single adults and married members recognize it, they each have idiosyncrasies and perspectives relating to the church and the gospel that influence or bias their judgments and behavior.

It can be incredibly hard for single adults to relate to family-centric perspectives and for married members to have sufficient understanding and empathy for the uniqueness of the challenges single adults face in that environment. For both, learning how not to judge each other and how to expand each other's view (or at least for all to be open to a larger perspective about the intent of the church and its reality for single adults) is key to more compassion and better understanding. With increased empathy from both sides, we will find common ground for all. It is also an important element for the ability of all to have an eternal perspective regarding the lives of single adults and for our continued activity within the church.

After Joshua and the House of Israel conquered the Canaanites and had retaken possession of the Promised Land, Joshua divided the respective lands among the twelve tribes as an inheritance. Despite the charge to remove any residual Canaanites, many of the tribes chose not to continue a complicated military campaign; rather, they made peace, requiring instead tribute from the remaining Canaanites.[12] Perhaps the reasons were an unwillingness to continue a prolonged military conflict, the monetary benefit of allowing these people to remain, or a desire to coexist peacefully. Whatever the reasons, Israel demonstrated a willingness to accept or tolerate the beliefs and practices of others who were not of their faith based on convenience and social pressure.

Shortly thereafter, a serious event occurred that almost plunged the House of Israel into civil war. Two tribes, Reuben and Gad, as well as half of the tribe of Manasseh received inheritances in the Promised Land on the far side of Jordan—lands that contained geographic characteristics that physically isolated them from Jerusalem, the tabernacle, and the congregation of Israel. When these tribes took possession of their lands, they built a great altar on the border for all to see. When the other tribes of Israel saw this altar, they took great offense, believing it to be rebellion against the House of Israel and apostasy from God. As a result, the congregation of Israel gathered themselves together and prepared collectively to go to war against these tribes.

A delegation consisting of Phinehas, the son of the high priest, and ten important and influential men were sent to discuss the matter with these tribes. Upon arriving, Phinehas enquired why these tribes had trespassed against God in building the altar. He admonished them, stating that the greatest threat to the House of Israel was not from external forces but apostasy against God. He stated that if these tribes were to rebel against God today, tomorrow God would be angry with the entire House of Israel. He then reminded them of Achan's trespass and the resulting consequences to the entire House of Israel. Phinehas's offer to these tribes was that if their lands were unacceptable, they should relinquish them and take possession among the other tribes.

Surprised by Phinehas's words, these tribes stated that they had not built the altar to perform ordinances outside the tabernacle or to rebel against God. Rather, they built the altar as a pattern or symbol to future generations to remind them of the importance of the rightful tabernacle and the link they had with the other tribes. It was a witness of their faith and of the bonds that united and tied them together with the House of Israel to stand guard against future generations wondering or asking what role they had with the God of Israel. Upon hearing this declaration, Phinehas and the House of Israel were greatly pleased, and the House of Israel disbanded its intention to destroy their brethren.[13]

This story is tragic, and it involves and describes the sort of misunderstandings single adults may experience within the church, particularly relating to how they are perceived. Like the tribes of Reuben and Gad and the half tribe of Manasseh, there are geographical, spiritual, emotional, relational, and other barriers that can prevent single adults from full participation in the gospel. For single adults, there is a desire to be a part of the church, yet a separateness that is difficult for married members to perceive or understand.

As a result, the church and its members may view us not in context of our individual circumstances but in context of the program of the church as it applies to those who have functioning families. However unintentional, it is a collective groupthink on what is right and wrong as viewed by the majority in the church. This creates problems that leave single adults feeling like we are on the outside looking in, wondering what role or place we have in the church.

Often family, friends, and church leaders will approach or interact with single adults through the topic of our ability to become married and to have families. Many times, the conversations they have with us start and relate to whether we are dating; if we are, who we are dating; or, really, whether the relationship we have will lead to marriage. If we are not dating, inquiries for the reasons may be requested or demanded. If we are not forthcoming or do not provide a satisfactory answer, those asking the questions may make or infer negative assumptions or non-meritorious speculations about the causes.

If we bring a friend of the opposite gender to church, ward members may make assumptions that we are in a relationship. Gossip, rumors, and otherwise may spread irrespective of their accuracy or truthfulness, creating at best awkwardness and at worst barriers for connection. Sometimes well-meaning but unsympathetic advice is given to us like, "You stress too much about being in a relationship," or "There is plenty of time to find someone in the future." This type of advice lends comfort to the advice-giver but little, if any, comfort to those of us receiving it.

I have often thought the basis for these questions and situations, like Phinehas in his approach of the outlying tribes, lies not in a caring for the individual, but a concern for the benefit of those asking and for the program of church. Even if the conversations are well-intended, single adults may become burdened or feel even more excluded or misjudged because our issues and concerns are not understood in the correct context.

How should married church members interact with single adults? I believe most people in the church are good people who try their best to be helpful, yet struggle to understand what single adults experience. My intention is not to create a list of what to say and what not to say, but rather to point out that social judgment, especially relating to our relational status, whether implied, perceived, or unintentional, impacts how we relate and communicate with those in the church.

Sometimes single adults feel inadequate or inferior in a family environment. We compare our worst to your best. We know what we want internally and measure ourselves against what we perceive others have externally. Healthy interactions with married and single adults is about normalizing our relationships with each other. Removing social judgment is not about looking at ourselves or others as better or worse, married or single. It is also not comparing our inside feelings to everyone's outside appearances (for we never really know what level of difficulties the other has).

It's about daily knowing, accepting, and understanding each other and recognizing the external realities we portray are often different from the realities we live. It is about seeing things through the eyes of the other, walking in our shoes, lifting and carrying when required, and engaging in healthy interactions and connections where genuine friendship is fostered and engendered. By understanding how judgment effects the interactions with single adults, we can have more meaningful and productive connections.

Additionally, sometimes single adults face a dilemma when dealing with individual mistakes or sins, as church leaders will counsel or judge us without a full understanding or comprehension of our circumstances. Like the House of Israel's willingness to accept the beliefs of those outside their faith but to harshly impose death and destruction on those within their faith, single adults may face the brunt or burden of different perceptions within the church. Being hurt and alone, single adults come to priesthood leaders hoping for love and acceptance but may be met with overreach and misunderstanding. As a result, we may develop a sense of unfairness and an unwillingness to reach out for future help. This can lead to inactivity or complete withdrawal from the church.

I do not say consequences should not be warranted for inappropriate behavior, nor do I mean the church should alter its stance on how it regulates moral activity; however, I have learned not every situation or circumstance is the same. Without a fulsome understanding and comprehension of the pressures and issues single adults face, severe or lengthy consequences may have the appearance of protecting the needs of the church rather than those of the single adult. The outcome is a protected church and a loss of single adults.

Remember that when the House of Israel determined to destroy those within its own faith for their perceived dereliction, it was less concerned about the effects of any perceived apostasy on the two and a half tribes and more concerned about the perceived consequences to the entire congregation of Israel. Thus, their judgment was not based in love of the individual tribes, but in concern for themselves. Phinehas had to change his perspective on the intent and actions of the two and a half tribes so that a correct understanding and an appropriate action could occur. Had he not, the results would have been catastrophic for all.

One final thought as it pertains to the application of judgment. After the fall of Adam and Eve, God placed an angel to guard the way to the Tree of Life.[14] He did this so Adam and Eve would not immediately partake of eternal judgment and thus He gave space, time, and opportunity for them and for us to progress and grow. I often think about that and believe by giving space, time, and opportunity to single adults through understanding and through the appropriate absence of judgment, we will all be enabled to gain an eternal perspective of the church and for ourselves.

HAVING AND DEVELOPING PATIENCE

Have you ever stood in line at a grocery store and watched the checkout lines around you move at a faster pace? Have you ever been stuck in the wrong lane of traffic or been prevented from changing lanes so that you miss your desired exit? Have you ever wondered how life will continue if there is no immediate Wi-Fi access to connect you to needed or desired electronic media? These and many other like situations have occurred and often do occur in my life. When problems or issues do not satisfactorily or expeditiously resolve themselves (and they frequently do not), feelings of frustration, annoyance, or irritation are usually the result. Really, what I feel or experience in those circumstances is impatience.

Sadly, I see this mindset more and in greater degrees today than when I was younger. We live in a time of convenience that demands just-in-time results or instantaneous blessings before they are earned or deserved. We expect on-demand information, prompt answers, and continuous comfort and satisfaction, yet are befuddled or discontent when self-determined outcomes or solutions do not timely present themselves. As a result, we become impatient and susceptible to trading tomorrow's happiness for today's triviality.

Think of families who rapaciously acquire debt at the expense of tomorrow's financial security, individuals who having just graduated from school and without experience demand extraordinary remuneration at their first job, or individuals who enter unhealthy relationships because they cannot bear the loneliness or the stigma of being single. Many of the problems we face today in and out of the church are a direct result of diminishing patience in our lives.

After two years of missionary service in Switzerland, during my mission exit interview, my mission president counseled me to get married upon returning home. He also counseled me to marry the person I date "after four seasons of dating." I took that advice to mean I should get married within a realistic time frame but make sure I had at least one year of dating to safeguard the viability of the relationship. This advice seemed reasonable and from my perspective not a major issue as I, at the time, had many years of life ahead of me.

As the years progressed and as the duration of my being single increased, I began to worry this time frame was unrealistic and would impact my ability to find someone, to develop a relationship with them, and to have a family. The older I became, the greater effort it seemed to wait a full year to become married. As a result, I began to subjectively interpret what that advice meant. I told myself "four seasons" could mean a season of joy, a season of sadness, and a season of peace. I even joked that all I had to do was get someone mad at me once and we would be good to go. Even though I had no dating opportunities, I was justifying the timing I felt was required to alleviate my own longing and loneliness.

For single adults, patience—especially as it pertains to having and developing relationships—is one of the more onerous and laborious aspects of being single. We tread a delicate balance between the immediate expectation and hope for a relationship while striving to be happy in our current state. When all others around us seem to have found a faster way, or have greater success developing and maintaining relationships, we may become impatient with ourselves, the church, and with others.

As I grew up, I was taught patience is a virtue. Patience is something that we consistently strived to achieve. It was the ability to wait when all around you is in commotion. Despite the trial, despite the difficulty, patience was constant, unyielding diligence dutifully performed. Even if we were not immediately successful, if we continually strived for what is good and right, we would eventually achieve the desired goal. Perseverance or endurance was thus synonymous with patience.

King Benjamin stated, "Nevertheless the Lord seeth fit to chasten his people; yea he trieth *their patience* and *their faith*."[15] I have often thought about this scripture as I have lived as a single adult. Sometimes I told myself being single is a trial God wants me to have; it is not my timing but God's timing that mattered most. I must wait until His timing is right for me. This thought gave me hope as it meant God was constantly in in my life and what occurred was for my benefit. I believe this; yet this thinking always struck me as odd as it lessened my own responsibility and accountability in striving for a healthy relationship.

As I wrestled with finding a relationship in my life, I would tell myself, *I will wait six months and endure it no matter what but when that six months comes, I am done trying, done waiting, done hoping for a relationship in my life*. I suppose having those milestones in front of me gave me a sense of hope as I moved forward, something to strive and work for amid all my futility; yet, when these milestones came and went, and they always did, I was left wondering what to do and where to go. Patience became a relentless battle for me and one that I seemed to always lose.

I learned that having an eternal perspective wasn't just about marking time or measuring the progress in my own journey, it's about how I lived it. Patience was no longer just about waiting on God, but rather finding patience with myself. It was finding joy in the moments and experiences I have, not in those I hoped for but didn't have. It was learning to be patient with others in their trials and struggles, to love them for who they are and not for what they are not. It wasn't about whether my burden was fair but about developing sufficient character to stand in my own moments of trial. It was also about finding a steadiness, a balance, and a healthy perspective in my life. It was the ability to enjoy who I am and those around me despite what I felt inside.

ISRAEL'S GREAT PROVOCATION

Consider the events surrounding the House of Israel as they struggled for religious and societal independence. After the miraculous and monumental salvation of the Israelite people from the ruthless and tyrannical grip of

Pharaoh and the intensity and bitterness of Egypt's enslavement, the Israelites were for the first time in centuries cast into a new and unfamiliar role of self-determination and of exercising and implementing their own sovereignty. Their exodus, and the extraordinary events surrounding it, represent the birthplace of liberty and freedom that still inspire and captivate us today. Moses was faced with the herculean task of developing a new society while kindling and strengthening the fire of faith within his people; yet, the condition and length of the Israelites' bondage caused the Israelites themselves to be ill-prepared to accept both the opportunity and the weight of the responsibility that came with these entitlements.

Upon arriving at Mount Sinai, the Israelites turned to unrighteousness, revelry, and idol worship as Moses communed with God on their behalf. Like misbehaving college freshman initially free from the repercussions and structure of their childhood and exercising their newfound autonomy, the Israelites chose self-indulgence, anarchy, and chaos rather than the peace and comfort offered by and through the gospel. Because of the Israelites' unwillingness and inability to recognize and accept the saving principles of the gospel, God instituted the Law of Moses, a lesser law of prescriptive ordinances and practices intended to remind and teach the Israelites the importance of the Savior, to prepare them to receive the fullness of the gospel, and to enter the salvation and rest of God.[16]

With the terms and conditions of their spiritual progression firmly implanted into their minds and hearts, and having covenanted with God to undertake it, the redirected Israelites, filled with a new sense of determination to press forward, continued their journey in the wilderness. They eventually arrived on the borders of the land of Canaan, the land promised to their forefathers. Yet this land was not empty space, hosting people and communities that had lived and progressed there for centuries. Still, based upon the covenants of God to their forefathers, and the unrighteousness of the people currently in possession of the land, God commanded the Israelites to go forth and take possession of it.

In preparation to undertake this endeavor, Moses sent twelve spies, one from each of the tribes, to search and report back on the condition of the land itself and on the strength and weaknesses of its people. These individuals searched the land for forty days and reported back to Moses. Ten of these spies reported of the great bounty and plenty the land provided; however, they were skeptical based on the strength of the inhabitants. They saw the high walls and stout defenses of the Canaanite cities; the condition, size, and military strength of the inhabiting people; and returned to Moses with only doubt and fear. They concluded that the Canaanites were stronger than the host of Israel and the Israelites should not go into the Promised Land. Two spies, Caleb and Joshua, also gave a glowing report of the land and its abundance; however, they took a different view despite the military and physical adversity presented to them, arguing in favor of moving forward, because they were "well able to overcome it."[17]

Whether induced by a deficit of faith or excessive timidity, the Israelites, after hearing all the reports, seized solely upon the negative conclusions of the ten spies and refused to enter the Promised Land. This revolt was so contentious, the Israelites even sought to stone Caleb and Joshua and to supplant Moses as their leader. Their purpose and intent was to return to Egypt, believing it better to live in captivity than to perish in the wilderness. Having just demonstrated their spiritual immaturity at Mount Sinai by rejecting the fullness of the gospel, the Israelites were now rejecting the blessings of the gospel itself, that of entering the Promised Land despite the covenants they had made in respect of the Law of Moses.

Not only were they rejecting God's blessings, but they were actively seeking to return to the bondage from which they had toiled and endured for centuries, thinking it better than what God offered to them. Despite the wonders and miracles they had seen in the convincing of Pharaoh to allow them to leave, despite the many symbols and signs given them in the wilderness, despite the crossing of the Red Sea and the destruction of Pharaoh's army, despite the daily nourishment bestowed upon them without price or cost, the Israelites now were turning away from God based solely on their emotions rather than exercising faith. These events are referred to as "the provocation in the days of temptation while the children of Israel were in the wilderness."[18]

It was for this reason God revoked and changed His initial commandment for the Israelites and gave them a new commandment to wander in the wilderness for forty years, one year for every day the spies had searched the Promised Land. God decreed that the Israelite children would enter and inherit the Promised Land, but all the adults in the congregation, except Joshua and Caleb, would not enter the Promised Land and would perish in the wilderness. Upon hearing this, the Israelites realized their sin and, confronted with the stark reality of the consequences therefrom, chose not to accept and follow the new commandment. Instead, they desired to follow the original but now revoked and inapplicable commandment, and proceeded to do what they should have done in the first place.

The problem was, God was not with them and they failed in their attempt. The Canaanites forced them into the wilderness, where the judgments of God came to fruition. The Israelites' sin of rejecting God and His commandments was now compounded by rejecting the consequences once they were pronounced. They failed to distinguish between what was required of them in the present and what was required of them in the past. They rebelled against God not once but twice, and He did not attend to them like He would have had they initially obeyed. As a result, they were driven and smitten by their enemies.

The Israelites' troubles were not immediately over, as shortly after this event sedition occurred when several Levites—Korah, Dathan, and Abiram—and 250 of the popular leaders of the congregation rose up and demanded from Moses the rights not only for civil leadership but also for the Melchizedek Priesthood. They accused Moses of being out of touch as a leader, placing himself above the needs of the congregation. They argued that the congregation itself was holy and God himself was with Israel. They subsequently accused Moses of bringing the House of Israel out of Egypt, a land full of milk and honey, for the sole purpose of putting himself into power. Additionally, they incongruously accused him of failing to bring them into a land comparable to Egypt or bestowing them with an inheritance. Because of this uprising, God, in an unmistakable demonstration of His authority, swallowed the three Levites in the ground and consumed the 250 leaders with heavenly fire.

We should feel empathy for Moses as he dealt with the multitudinous issues surrounding his leadership of the Israelite nation. Of the vexing and disturbing issues that the Israelites imposed upon themselves, the most basic seems to be an inability to have an eternal perspective, leaving them incapable of making correct and healthy decisions. Their failure to have an eternal perspective in real time caused them not only to reject the benefit of the gospel but also to pass by desired blessings and opportunities that would have blessed them and their posterity. Additionally, they were unable to recognize the authority and power of God and believed they themselves should define and dictate righteousness and, at their whim and discretion, control the powers of Heaven. Jacob in the Book of Mormon perspicaciously stated:

> Wherefore we labored diligently among our people, that we might *persuade them to come unto Christ*, and partake of the goodness of God, *that they might enter into his rest*, lest by any

means he should swear in his wrath *they should not enter in*, as in *the provocation in the days of temptation* while the children of Israel were in the wilderness.[19]

For single adults, like the House of Israel, it can be tough to develop and maintain an eternal perspective. Sometimes we can be like the Israelites, seeking to return to the captivity we know rather than the freedom we do not, or we can be like entitled Dathan who demanded reward and inheritance. Do we sulk in the pain of the past, the heartache of the present, and wish things were different, or do we look forward to future opportunity? Do we say, "I am active in the church. I have a temple recommend. I live the commandments. I am entitled to be married in the temple"? Such perspectives may take away our ability to see things for what they are and may prevent us from seizing upon and developing blessings God hopes to give us.

What does it mean for single adults to develop and maintain an eternal perspective as they strive to live the gospel in a family-centric environment? At least in part, it means that we learn to accept and be happy with the reality of our situations, to not become embittered at the church when we feel we don't belong, to believe and hope in times of our trials while trusting God can and will provide for our needs. It is also learning to live in the present, day by day, being content with what we have while believing opportunities exist of which we are not yet aware. It is also developing patience—not judging ourselves or those around us for those things we still need or have opportunity to obtain.

ADDITIONAL THOUGHTS ON DEVELOPING AN ETERNAL PERSPECTIVE

When developing an eternal perspective, it is important to keep a favorable outlook no matter the circumstance. Immediately after the fall of King Noah, the conquering Lamanites placed King Limhi and the remaining Nephites into bondage and imposed significant burdens upon them that were grievous to bear.[20] All military attempts to defeat the Lamanites had failed with tremendous casualty and suffering. Despite the calamities that had befallen his people, King Limhi never became discouraged or failed to try to free his people.

When an expedition from Zarahemla found King Limhi's people, they did again attempt to free themselves from the Lamanites. After the many failed attempts to escape the Lamanites' barbarism and slavery, the loss of life to his people, and the despair they endured, King Limhi gathered his people together and stated:

> O ye, my people, *lift up your heads and be comforted*; for behold, *the time is at hand, or is not far distant*, when we shall no longer be in subjection to our enemies, notwithstanding our many strugglings, which have been in vain; *yet I trust there remaineth an effectual struggle* to be made.[21]

King Limhi knew, as do we, all things are possible with God. With the help and assistance of God, there are always beneficial and effectual struggles to be made that will have eternal significance and advantageous outcomes on our lives and on those around us. Keeping an eternal perspective is not necessarily knowing what the future holds; rather it is a willingness to keep our heads up despite overwhelming failure, possessing the readiness to listen to the Spirit, and having the desire and faith to take an initial step and find out what God has in store for us. After all, we never know what opportunities or blessings God has for us just around the corner. Remember, the Jordan River did not part for Joshua or the Israelites until they stepped into the water.[22] Is this not a lesson for each of us that we must first take a step on our own, sufficient in scope to allow God to help us overcome our barriers and obstacles that prevent us from entering our own Promised Lands?

Finally, for us as single adults, developing and maintaining an eternal perspective is essential to our ability to see and reach each of our eternal destinies. Emerson once wrote that life is a succession of lessons that must be lived to be understood.[23] Personally, I like to think of life as an inward sojourn into the defining of one's soul—an existential look, if you will, into one's search for meaning in a large and often imperceptible universe. Each experience we encounter here in mortality is an occurrence that gives us insight and perspective into who we are and why we are truly here. How we view those lessons and the perspective we gain are what define us and what provide the emotional and spiritual footing for what we can become.

Having an eternal perspective means seeing the forest through the trees, perceiving individual facts and circumstances while considering a greater whole and purpose. Having an eternal perspective is about learning to see ourselves as God sees us. God's name is Eternal, and having an eternal perspective means understanding how He perceives and reacts to us.[24] I think all single adults need to believe in the goodness and realness that we are okay today just as we are. That if we could see God today, He would entirely accept and love each part of our being—no conditions, no expectations, no requirements, and no limitations. Period!

God loves us not only for who we are but also for who we can become. When we develop an eternal perspective, not only do we have a more complete understanding of who we are, but also an ability to unlock our potential, to know where we can go, and what heights we can reach.

9

Being and Becoming Saints of God

And now abideth faith, hope, charity, these three; but the greatest of these is charity.
—1 Corinthians 13:13

A tender moment occurred during the Savior's ministry when a distraught father brought his child who was vexed by debilitating physical and spiritual problems to the Savoir for help and healing. So uncontrolled was this child's condition, that he was in constant danger of hurting himself, requiring nonstop care and supervision. The father's plea to the Savior was for help for both the child and their family, "but if thou canst do anything have compassion on us and help us." Full of love and understanding, the Savior responded by teaching the man all things are possible to those who have faith.[1] Tearfully the man replied, "Lord I believe, help thou my unbelief." After which the Savior healed the child.[2]

Each of us can feel the vehement and violent pain suffered by both the child and the father. The child whose body and mind were tortured and tormented by crippling conditions, and the father whose soul was bewildered and beleaguered by the powerlessness to help one he so dearly loved. As single adults, sometimes we face overwhelming situations and conditions we can neither control nor overcome, and sometimes we are like the father, compelled to helplessly watch as those we love suffer through adversity, trial, and hardship. This event helps remind us that, no matter the scorching nature of our individual circumstances, it is by and through our hope and faith we must approach the Savior and it is by and through our hope and faith He is capable of healing us as well as those around us. I often ponder the humble response of that father who recognized the faith he had and the help he needed to gain more.

But what are hope and faith, what importance or purpose do they have, and what do they lead to in our lives? Hope and faith are interconnected and interrelated. Just as you cannot slice a piece of cheese so thinly that it does not have two sides, you cannot have faith without hope, and vice versa. Yet despite these similarities, hope and faith are not the same, nor are they matching or correlative in function or scope. By better understanding the differences between hope and faith as well as their respective roles in our spiritual development, we are more able to realize our own worth and to assist both ourselves and others to find inner peace and come closer to the Savior.

Hope is the foundation of an eternal perspective and a building block for faith. It's a state of mind that sees positive things occurring rather than negative. It's the belief that good outweighs difficulty, that light is stronger than darkness, and that all things have purpose and meaning. As Mormon stated, "How is it ye can attain unto faith, save ye shall have hope?"[3] Faith is more than just a positive perspective; it is movement. It is the activity and action we undertake because of the hope we have.

When used together, faith and hope combine to create synergies that enhance our ability to grow, enabling us to reach outside ourselves and to increase our capacity to obtain or cultivate additional faith and hope. They are reinforcing agents that, when appropriately utilized and synchronized, create spiritual expansion and development. Whether hope comes before faith or faith comes before hope is academic and less important. What is important is our recognition that they are interdependent and intertwined; like a muscle, the more we exercise them, the stronger they become and the less we use them, the more they atrophy. Thus, fence-sitting or postponing the development of either faith or hope in our lives is not a neutral activity, rather a negative one.

When thinking about the relationship between hope and faith, I sometimes consider two books in the Old Testament: Nehemiah and Ezra. These books of scripture are like the Book of Omni in the Book of Mormon, passed over without thought and recognition or rarely discussed or quoted in the mainstream practice of our religion. As a result, we may forget their relevance or think they have little importance or doctrinal standing, yet together they chronicle the House of Israel's significant and historic return to Jerusalem after their Babylonian captivity. They are a record of the House of

Israel's effort to reconstruct their society and to reclaim their religion after a lengthy trauma and harrowing tragedy.

The most important aspect of these two books is not the specific words that are written but what they document: the struggle to rebuild the temple and to restore the wall surrounding Jerusalem. The Book of Ezra recounts the rebuilding of the temple while the Book of Nehemiah recounts the restoration of Jerusalem's wall. The reconstruction of the temple is an unambiguous representation of the rebuilding and restitution of faith and belief in ourselves and in God; the repair and mending of the wall is a profound representation of hope and its role in surrounding, supporting, and protecting that faith. Just like the rebuilding of Jerusalem's wall and its temple, hope and faith are critical even though they have different roles and serve distinct purposes in our lives.

Interestingly, while contemporaneous, Nehemiah and Ezra each record one of these two events: the effort to rebuild the wall or the effort to rebuild the temple, but not both. This demonstrates that faith and hope are complementary of each other but separate in and of themselves. In both efforts, the Israelites faced stiff opposition not only from the local Samaritans who militarily and diplomatically opposed the re-establishment of the Israelites in the region, but also from their previous captors, who politically debated whether it was good to allow a nation to grow that might rebel against them in the future, especially one that had fortifications like Jerusalem and a faith that was different from theirs.

For single adults who struggle under the weight and trauma of being single, faith and hope are the resources and the infrastructure we must construct and utilize in our lives no matter the difficulty or opposition. Yet what good does it do us to focus exclusively on our faith if we leave it unprotected? What power can our hope have if we focus completely on the defense of our faith but ignore its use or its benefit? If faith is the lighthouse, piercing the darkness, beckoning and lighting the way for all to see, hope is the jetty that protrudes into the deepest and darkest depths of the sea, breaking the waves and calming the storm, providing invitation, protection, and safe harbor for all who wander and journey.

I love the comparison Lehi made to his two oldest sons, Laman and Lemuel. Said he to Laman, "O that thou mightest be like this river continually running into the fountain of righteousness." Said he to Lemuel, "O that thou mightest be like this valley, firm and steadfast and immovable in keeping the commandments of God."[4] If hope is the valley firm, immovable and steadfast, faith is the river, mobile, constantly flowing, and moving our souls toward the Savior. Throughout our lives, they provide both a firm foundation and a fluid means to ebb and flow, to proactively address or appropriately react in positive and healthy ways to the individual subtleties and ever-changing vicissitudes of life.

The product or outcome of both hope and faith is charity. Charity is love itself and it is what we develop through the application of hope and faith in our lives. Thus, hope and faith lead us on a personal journey to grow, to improve, to be better today, or at least motivate us to make the effort to do so. Said differently, hope is what we perceive, faith is what we do, and charity is what we become.

Paul states that we receive grace from Christ and those who have faith in Him are called by Him to become saints.[5] It's a charge to move, to grow, and to become something more than what we are today. That is the purpose of the gospel: to inspire us to strive and to stretch, to expand and enlarge our propensity to love so we may stand before God wiser, more capable, and more charitable toward others than what we were previously.

For single adults, the destination of this journey is no different than for those who are married, for it is not what we have but who we are and who we become that matters to God. Still, for those who are single, we can be like the father of the vexed child, at wit's end, with only a margin of hope or faith to move forward. We are apt to feel isolated, alone, and adrift in a deep and unknown sea, like refugees marooned or displaced without home or place to rest. The opportunity and challenge for us is not to give in to the idea that all is lost but to develop hope, exercise faith, and accept and grow where we are.

A SUFFICIENT HOPE

Have you ever heard someone stand up in a testimony meeting and say, "I know the atonement applies to you, but I am uncertain whether it applies to me." Have you ever personally wondered where you belong in the church or in society? Have you ever thought you were taking one step forward but in doing so had to take two steps backward? Have you ever failed and asked yourself whether you can go on? Have you ever believed that you were of no worth to those around you or to God? Whenever I hear statements or sentiments like this, I feel sad, particularly if it's from a single adult, because I know that individual is viewing events and circumstances from a negative perspective rather than from a positive perspective. They are wrestling not with their faith but with their hope.

As I considered the interrelatedness of faith, hope, and charity, and how they apply to single adults, I reviewed the definitions for each that the church provides in the *Bible Dictionary*. To my surprise, I found faith is well and robustly defined, charity has a good but short description, but hope is not defined and has no entry whatsoever. My initial thought was amusement, thinking perhaps this oversight is poetic or symbolic, as hope is more individual, subjective, and not as easily characterized as is faith or charity; however, that hope was not delineated or defined at all in the *Bible Dictionary* surprised and caused me to think about the importance and role of hope in our lives.

Do we place a high emphasis on faith at the expense of our hope? If someone is struggling, do we get caught in the trap of trying to help their hope solely by focusing on or increasing their faith? Do we, without thought or context, tell them to read their scriptures, say their prayers, attend the temple, etc., believing by doing so they will feel inspired? These activities and actions are no doubt important and helpful, and should not be discounted in our lives; however, we should at least ask whether we are applying the appropriate therapy to the correct issue.

Are we giving an aspirin to someone with a broken leg? Are we providing provisional or temporary relief while overlooking or not addressing the underlying issue or fundamental problem? Are we providing the proverbial window-dressing that papers over deeper and more significant matters? Just as a doctor must understand the primary cause of a malady to provide an appropriate treatment, so too must we understand what an individual requires before we can move forward. It is for this reason that whenever I talk to someone who is struggling, my first inquiry is about what they see and how they perceive their lives and their circumstances. My main objective is to help them develop a positive perspective rather than a negative perspective, both temporally and spiritually.

Having a positive perspective, means seeing things that are constructive and beneficial for us. Alternatively, viewing things from a negative perspective means to see only difficulty, hardship, and harm. It is the difference between seeing opportunity rather than burden in the experiences we have in life. Each of us can choose whether we have a positive perspective or a negative perspective. Still, maintaining a positive perspective takes more work and effort than that of having one that is negative.

In his book *Hardwiring Happiness*, Dr. Rick Hanson comments that there is a natural bias toward negativity that is a normal part of our psychology.[6] It's a defense mechanism wired into our brains that is meant to provide both emotional and physical safety. When dealing with our negative bias in perceiving events and circumstances, Dr. Hanson writes, we generally make two types of mistakes. The first mistake occurs when we are overly protective, perceiving constant danger and feeling fear. For example, it is refusing to ever cross the street (or doing so in an excessively defensive manner) for fear a car might hit us. The second mistake Dr. Hanson points out occurs when we are overly optimistic, devaluing or deprioritizing legitimate risk. It is the opposite of the previous example where we rush across the street without looking, or thinking nothing will occur. When we choose this perspective, we do not have the burden of fear, but we are caught unawares and unprotected when real danger presents itself.

Dr. Hanson argues that we as individuals and society collectively have evolved psychologically toward the perspective in the first mistake. We are overly cautious or guarded, always seeing danger where none exists, because it provides greater security and protection to us in the near term. We default to this viewpoint emotionally because it means we are at least safe and protected; however, by so doing, we may, over the long term, overvalue or misconstrue threats that may be less risky or more manageable than we perceive. Alternatively, we may overlook or marginalize favorable circumstances or opportunities that are more beneficial than we anticipate.

What does this mean for our perspectives regarding the attachment and connections we hope to develop? It means our default position psychologically is to cocoon ourselves away either emotionally or physically, particularly as it pertains to relationships or connections. Walling or hedging ourselves emotionally, we are less willing to be open and vulnerable to others or in relationships because we are afraid of being hurt or unaccepted. To put it another way, we may forgo deeper or meaningful relational connections because we ourselves are too scared, too afraid, or too anxious to take the emotional risk, or we do not even see the opportunity at all, passing a potential partner by like two ships in the night. We keep our personal relationships at arm's length, giving brief acknowledgement or a few well-meaning courtesies, but eventually withdrawing to continue the journey, never again converging or connecting.

By never having to risk vulnerability, we have gated ourselves through self-imposed emotional isolation. Yet we are okay with being risk-averse because we never have to take a relational chance and we are fine being apathetic because we are ignorant of the opportunity lost by our emotional safeguards. We then are free to pursue relationships we know will have a high potential for failure or become negative because we know the relationship won't go anywhere and because it meets an immediate or short-term need.

Just ask yourself the next time you are looking at online-dating profiles whether you accept more people than you reject (do I swipe more to the left than to the right?). If we are rejecting more people than accepting on a frequent basis, we might at least ask ourselves whether we are viewing people and relationships more from a negative viewpoint rather than a positive viewpoint. We are each capable of having or developing a positive perspective, but the starting point for us from an emotional, biological, or psychological view is one of safety rather than vulnerability. In other words, it is easier for us to perceive negativity than positivity and easier for us to see suffering than hope. It is also much safer to assume failure rather than success because if we do, we are never disappointed.

The real challenge for single adults is to apply ourselves in such a way and in such a manner that we can overcome our natural tendencies and biases to develop hope. We must create an emotional viewpoint or positive perspective where crossing the street is possible and becomes a routine experience if we are self-aware and if we take appropriate precautions to recognize, to adequately mitigate, or to altogether alleviate the risks. It takes hard work and effort that is not accomplished through inaction or passivity. The key is to find enough positivity in people, in sufficient scope, that we are willing to be vulnerable with them and take the risk of having a relationship. We must find and prioritize the positive reasons to be in a relationship more than the negative reasons to not be in a relationship.

Hope means we believe our life has meaning and purpose despite hardship. Thus, the ability to have hope is conditioned on how we see and perceive events and outcomes. Do we see these in an optimistic light or, alternatively, in a harmful light? The loss of hope, or, better said, the loss of a positive perspective has deleterious consequences, for it drives us to short-sighted or short-term actions that are more likely to be defensive or negative. If our short-term views are routinely more negative than positive, having or maintaining a long-term positive perspective will be especially challenging. Said differently, if we see nothing but darkness today, how do we expect to see light tomorrow? For single adults, whether we have a positive or negative view impacts how we perceive and interact with the church, its members, and its activities because we see it as either safe or unsafe. How we see things, how we perceive them, and the level of hope we develop will largely dictate how we respond to the connections and relationships we experience.

After the terrible and calamitous destruction of the Nephites, Mormon wrote as follows:

> Wherefore, I would speak unto you that are of the church, that are the peaceable followers of Christ, and that *have obtained a sufficient hope by which ye can enter the rest of the Lord*, from this time henceforth until ye shall rest with him in heaven.[7]

I have often thought about Mormon's choice of words. I find it curious Mormon used hope as the basis for our ability to enter God's rest, rather than faith. He certainly did not say he wanted to speak only to those who have demonstrated sufficient faith in their lives. Mormon's statement does not diminish the need for faith or say it's not relevant to our ability to qualify for salvation; however, he specifically chose hope as the precursor by which we are enabled to enter Heaven.

Similarly, Paul taught that we are "saved by hope."[8] Thus, the evaluation isn't of whether we accomplished or did enough, but rather, have we developed sufficient capability to perceive good in our lives and in those around us? Have we the emotional fortitude, spiritual capability, and internal character to look beyond our natural biases, to patiently wait for desired outcomes and results, to endure trials and difficulty, and yet be happy? Developing a positive mindset is the best and most effective way we can take into ourselves the fullness of the gospel, the blessings of the atonement, and the love God has for each of us. Both single adults and married members of the church should ask whether each has enough hope to facilitate our ability to receive God in our lives.

Hope is a lot like the windows in my house. During the day, I open the window shades to let the light in, but if I forget to close the shades at night, the light is let out; the existing house light is diminutive or less effective. Like accessing the available light in my house, I need the individual capacity to allow positivity in during the day and to have sufficient reserve to retain it during the night. Paul states,

> but we glory in tribulations also: knowing that tribulation worketh patience; *and patience, experience; and experience, hope: And hope maketh not ashamed.*[9]

Hope is thus a learned and practiced behavior of consistently seeing positive elements and outcomes in my life experiences despite difficulty and negativity. It is a sifting and narrowing process both for recognizing the positive aspects in my life and for learning to accept them sufficiently to have meaningful effect in it. Developing hope is also about minimizing or altogether eliminating negative perspectives or thoughts. This does not mean the elimination of negative emotions, but rather the elimination of negative perspectives deriving therefrom. It is maintaining a positive perspective despite negativity in any of its forms.

When the Israelites built a tabernacle in the wilderness, God commanded them to maintain a constant and continuous light inside.[10] I love this imagery because it pertains to me and other single adults as we continually work to enlighten our minds and our souls. The more light we can access in our lives, the more hope we have and the greater capacity we have in retaining it. Hope is the one counteraction and redress that may nullify or ameliorate the toxic effects of shame in all its varying shades and degrees in our lives. As single adults, the challenge for us is to make developing hope and positivity a daily habit or core focus—to motivate ourselves to continually close the shades at night and to reopen the shades the next day so we may let light in our life and hold on to it when the dark comes.

Previously, I discussed the importance to single adults of receiving individuals and relationships into our lives. Receiving hope is no different except instead of being sufficiently open and vulnerable to receive others, we must be sufficiently open to receiving a positive viewpoint and perspective in our lives. Receiving hope in our life isn't just the pursuit of acquiring it, it is learning to recognize it and accept it. Like leaven in bread, hope penetrates the heart, permeates our thinking, and pervades our souls, infusing itself into each experience and thought process. Hope becomes an inward extension of who we are and what we want to be.

Finding joy and happiness in the church as a single adult is likewise a constant and continuous exercise in discerning and receiving the goodness of life and the blessings of God in them. It is about allowing and instilling beneficial, productive, and helpful events and circumstances into our daily lives so we may recognize and see the light, accept it, and become like it. The Savior said, "Behold, mine arm of mercy is extended towards you, and whosoever will come, *him will I receive*; and blessed are those who come unto me."[11] Having hope as single adults allows us to receive not only ourselves and those around us, but also the church and the Savior as well.

After my divorce, I was met with a stark and difficult reality, one I did not want to accept. The anxiety, fear, and loneliness combined in such a manner to overshadow everything else in my life. What I really lost was hope. I was going to church, attending the temple, and reading my scriptures, but I couldn't see past the hurt and I couldn't see anything positive in the experience. It was a slow and agonizing process to again find myself and to allow hope back into my life. I had to relearn how to stand in my pain, accept it, and move forward.

Developing hope wasn't a magical overnight realization but rather a conscious choice of picking myself up when I failed and putting myself on an upward rather than a downward trajectory. I would intentionally go back to locations where events, difficulties, or traumas in my marriage occurred just to create new positive memories on which I could lean. I returned to restaurants, theme parks, and movie theaters just to be there and to have a positive experience. It wasn't about replacing the old the memories but about enabling myself, for the first time, to choose which memory to think about and upon which to base my emotions. It was about learning to recognize physical and cognitive responses to difficulties and to control them in a manner that did not control me.

I realize today, hope is a fickle thing—easy to lose and difficult to obtain. It is like the stock market, where returns grow slowly over time but can be lost quickly and in large amounts. I failed many times trying to develop a positive mindset in my life. Each time I would stop and look at a situation and ask if I saw that situation in a positive or a negative light. If it was negative, I did not get down on myself, I simply reminded myself how I could view things in a more positive light the next time a similar situation occurred. Gradually, hope came back to me, my sense of identity returned, and I found a strength and capacity to see potential where I once thought only hopelessness existed.

WHAT IS IT WE SHALL HOPE FOR?

Chapter 8 defined and discussed the importance of developing an eternal perspective. Having an eternal perspective is about the manner and framework as well as the purpose and meaning with which we see ourselves. It is the road map or guidelines that we follow as we experience life. Having hope, at least for purposes of this discussion, is more general in nature and relates to what context, either positive or negative, we perceive facts and circumstances. It is quite possible to develop hope in your life but not have an eternal perspective—we can hope for a better job, peace in the world, opportunity for our children, or better relationships in our lives without seeing things in light of our standing with God or without seeing a higher purpose and meaning in life.

For members of the church, hope is more refined and focused on spiritual matters. Within the context of the gospel, hope is not just about how we see things but upon what, or, better said, on whom we base it. As both single and married members of the church increase our hope, we are also increasing our reliance on and association with the Savior. Hope is an embodiment of the principles He taught and a realization of their benefit for us. It is also in understanding where we come from, the purpose of our lives, and the potential for it afterwards. I have often thought that the reason part of the temple ordinance is called an "endowment" is because its purpose is to give knowledge and understanding of spiritual things in our lives, things not generally received or accepted by those outside our faith. The true endowment, though, is hope: hope in the Savior, hope in His plan, hope in His purposes, and hope in ourselves. Perhaps this reason is why the temple is so important to us, not only because it is a holy place where holy things are accomplished, but also because it instills a greater hope in those who attend.

I have always been intrigued by the Book of Abraham in the Pearl of Great Price. Part of that fascination is based on the fact it is the only book of scripture that uses three drawings or facsimiles to convey thought, doctrine, and meaning. It is a unique scriptural method to illustrate and intimately teach us about God and His plan for us. While each of these facsimiles has its own meaning and purpose, generally they depict: 1) Abraham was saved by God; 2) he had the power of God; and 3) he understood God's plan for us.

Abraham recognized that God knows each of us personally and He has the love, capacity, and desire to save each of us both temporally and spiritually. Abraham understood the priesthood and held the keys to its administration. He knew its purpose was to empower and bless us in this life and to facilitate and enable us to return to God in the next. He also understood the Great Plan of Happiness, which provides opportunity for us to grow and progress and to connect and attach with each other in the eternities, as well as providing a place for each of us to reside and belong.

Facsimile three vividly illustrates the Savior's role in God's plan for us: He is central to God's thoughts and vision for our lives. The Savior's atonement brings to pass the ability for us to once again stand before God to be judged, not just for what we have done but also for who we have become in our lives. It is the mechanism by which we are snatched from the jaws of eternal justice and given opportunity to progress. It is the bedrock of our hopes in the church as well as the method and the opportunity by which we may lay claim to the same never-ending happiness that God enjoys and that we all strive to obtain.

As a young teacher at the Missionary Training Center, I was once presented with a challenge from a demotivated missionary whose hope was wavering, whose desire to serve was waning, and whose perspective negatively impacted not only him but also the spirituality of those in his missionary district. While pondering on how to help this missionary, it became clear to me this missionary needed to be individually loved and to personally recognize and feel that love for him to open his heart and to be receptive to the Spirit. As a result, I met separately with each member of his district and set a goal for them to find ways to express love to this missionary and to teach him the gospel. I reminded them they had a perfect opportunity to be missionaries even if they were not yet in their assigned mission areas.

Afterwards, this missionary district went to work. They turned frustration into opportunity, they expressed unconditional charity and love, they shared faith and testimony, and they constantly reached out to this struggling missionary in unseen but impactful ways. While change did not occur overnight, it did occur. After his eleven weeks at the Missionary Training Center were complete, this missionary had changed his perspective, laid the groundwork for a personal testimony, and developed the desire to remain on his mission.

I do not know what became of this missionary—I do not know if he stayed on his mission or if he allowed spiritual growth to continue in his life—but what I do know is, at that time and in that moment, the love and efforts of a small group of individuals to reach out, embrace, and connect personally with this missionary opened a window into his eternal soul that provided an opportunity for him to see things anew and to gain hope. It also gave an entire district the opportunity to learn the true meaning of missionary work and the gospel.

Helaman taught:

> Yea, we see that whosoever *will may lay hold upon the word of God*, which is quick and powerful, *which shall divide asunder* all the cunning and the snares and the wiles of the devil, and lead the man of Christ *in a straight and narrow course across that everlasting gulf of misery* which is prepared to engulf the wicked.[12]

Consider the precious insight, important life principles, and gospel understanding Helaman articulates. What is the basis for ourselves, our families, friends, acquaintances, and others to "divide asunder all the cunning snares and wiles of the devil"? How do we develop the capacity to withstand and weather the tricks, traps, and temptations of the adversary? What motivates, provokes, and causes us to progress and to proceed forward on that straight and narrow path? What empowers and enables us to have hope, to bridge that terrible and everlasting gulf of misery, and to finally put behind us the shame, guilt, and trauma of our lives? As Helaman points out and explains, it is our willingness, capacity, and ability to "lay hold upon the word of God."

What is "the word of God" and what does it mean for us to lay hold upon it? Nephi related and compared the word of God to an iron rod, observing those who persistently held fast to it would prevail and overcome whatever spiritual snags, difficulties, and complications they faced.[13] At a minimum, Nephi meant that laying hold of the word of God incorporates understanding the precepts, standards, and doctrines of the gospel as written in the scriptures, as taught at church, in our families, and as taught through God's prophets. These give insight and perspective into our lives and our spiritual development, and they provide principles to guide our steps and decisions. They are a Liahona or compass that points, directs, and corrects us in our chosen course as needed and as required.

May I also suggest and advocate to you that both Helaman and Nephi's statements encapsulate a much larger principle than individual appreciation of, knowledge regarding, and constant study of the gospel. I believe they also meant that laying hold upon the "*word* of God" relates to establishing, cultivating, and investing in a personal connection with, attachment to, and relationship with the Savior, who is himself the "Word of God." Consider the following two scriptures:

1. In the beginning was *the Word*, and *the Word* was with God, and *the Word* was God.[14]

2. ... and *his name is* called *The Word of God*.[15]

Laying hold upon the Word of God is about aspiring to, grasping upon, and abiding in a personal and individual relationship with the Savior. It is about knowing and receiving Him in our lives. Just like that wonderful young missionary who so long ago struggled with his own hope, the basis by which we gain hope in our own lives, the way we motivate ourselves and grow spiritually is through our connections and relationships not only with others but also with the Savior. Hope in ourselves and in the Savior is the means through which we hold on to positivity and healthy perspectives in our lives.

Moroni stated:

> *And what is it that ye shall hope for?* Behold I say unto you that *ye shall have hope through the atonement of Christ* and the power of his resurrection, to be raised unto life eternal, and this because of your faith in him according to the promise.[16]

For single adults who struggle with hope, my sincerest desire is that we lift our heads, elevate our perspective, make good and positive choices, and develop healthy connections, attachments, and relationships in our lives. I also hope we are content with our station in life and we take charge of our own inadequacies, to reach beyond ourselves and lay hold upon our own personal and individual relationship with the Savior.

FAITH:
WHAT IS IT AND WHY IS IT IMPORTANT?

Faith is a spiritual gift of God that emanates from Him and transcends the borders of mortality. It is the underpinning and the substance of our ethics, values, ideals, and morality. It is an important influence in our lives that shapes our actions, thinking, and decisions toward ourselves and others. It is an adhesive that collects and combines individuals and groups, allowing people, communities, and societies with a common understanding and a shared belief to interact and commune with each other and with God in meaningful and synergistic ways. It provides structure for and access to a grander and vaster paradigm and an expanded reality, giving meaning and purpose to those who strive to reach outside themselves to touch and connect with divinity.

One of the greatest principles of the gospel is that each of us lived with God before coming here. Relatively little is known about this existence; however, Abraham taught that in the pre-existence, the Savior and the adversary presented two different and opposing plans for the development and salvation of our souls. The purpose of the Savior's plan was to provide opportunity to prove whether we would be willing to follow and do all things God commanded us. It was a test of faith. If we exercise faith in this life, we will have the opportunity to receive additional opportunity and blessings.[17]

The adversary's plan was devoid of individual choice, having the benefit of saving all but denying us the opportunity to gain experience and to learn responsibility for our own actions and choices. It was a plan of force and compulsion rather than a plan of faith and choice. Abraham points out that the primary purpose for our being here in mortality is to be tested and to exercise our right to choose. It is fascinating to realize that every thought, deed, and action undertaken in this life is an assessment of our individual agency and faith. Like the Robert Frost poem "The Road Not Taken" we each stand at an unseen crossroad with every decision we make. Each choice made here in mortality has an eternal consequence and affects our personal relationship with the Savior; thus, the goal of mortality is not only to choose, but to choose wisely.

To create a condition whereby we could freely choose, a spiritual veil was established to preclude any previous or prior knowledge of God.[18] This partition allows us to make our life's choices free from bias and based on own our own desires, after our own purposes, and after the intents of our true selves. As a result, faith is the standard and the definitive means by which we rely on God and choose to follow him. It is the opportunity to stretch our understanding, to rise by our own merit and effort, and to move forward. President Hinckley stated, "The challenge which faces every member of this church is to take the next step, to accept that responsibility to which he is called, even though he does not feel equal to it, and to do so in faith with the full expectation that God will light the way before him."[19] What a humble thing to know and understand that we are the masters of our own fate, the choosers of our own course, and the drivers of our own destinations.

For sure, we will all face adversity in life, yet how do we keep from losing faith altogether or from believing faith is illusory? Additionally, in those times that are damaging and destructive, how do we maintain faith's importance and relevance in our lives? Faith is how we chose right over wrong despite the many and varied challenges life presents to us. It is the one true blanket in which we may wrap our souls and shield ourselves from the deleterious effects of the adversary. It is the measure of our character and the quality to act when outcomes are unknown or uncertain. It is the last defense and bastion when we confront our greatest fears and obstacles. It is the motivation by which we obey God's commandments and reach past the tumult of this life. It is also how we touch and embrace the elements of divinity within each of us.

But what is faith? Faith is the first principle of the gospel. By and through faith are all things made possible. It was through faith Adam offered sacrifices. It was by faith Noah entered the ark, Enoch was translated, and Abraham received his inheritance. By faith David slew Goliath; Shadrach, Meshach and Abednego withstood the fiery furnace; and Daniel survived the lion's den. It was faith that healed Naaman from leprosy and allowed Peter to give sight to the blind. By faith the brother of Jared saw the hand of God. Faith empowered Moses to free the Israelites from bondage and led Lehi to the American continent. It was unwavering faith that protected the armies of Helaman as they battled overwhelming Lamanite forces. It was also through faith that the Savior himself atoned for our sins in the Garden of Gethsemane and on the cross at Golgotha.

Today, faith may seem less imperative or important because technology, science, and human advancement support and sustain much of the business and hustle in our lives. As a result, we may tend to view faith from the perspective of something that is extra, unneeded, or a remnant and relic of a time long past. At its best, society tolerates faith but looks at it with dubiousness and leeriness. At its worst, society views faith as implausible or the product of a misdirected or frenzied belief. Like Thomas who lacked faith and doubted, demanding to see before he believed, society may also demand tangible proof of God's existence prior to its exercise of faith. Yet this demand is not an exercise in faith at all, rather one of risk mitigation. Why risk faith when other explanations are plausible or easier to understand? The lessening of faith in our lives deadens and desensitizes us, at least in part, to the wonder, beauty, amazement, and possibility of this world, the cosmos, and ourselves. It prohibits or at least limits us from recognizing God's hand in even the smallest things or in the order of all creation.

As members of the church, we worship and exercise faith in a God who is all-encompassing, who is unchanging, unceasing, and ever-present in all that we do and all that we are. We do not see Him, but His existence is manifest in our lives, our families, our children, and in our faith for a better life both in mortality and in the eternities to come. The creation of the world, the regularity and consistency of the solar system, and the enormity and vastness of the universe itself all point to a higher order and design as well as a higher state of being, not happenstance. As Alma points out, even the regularity and motion of the planets around the sun demonstrate there is a God.[20] The pursuit of knowledge, technology, and science is truly a blessing and may unlock the secrets and wonders of how the universe was created, but it will never provide the answer to why it was created nor will it give us the opportunity, as the exercise of faith does, to appreciate and comprehend the beauty of its purpose.

Despite what those without faith claim, it is neither illogical nor irrational. It is the binding link between mortality and eternity. It is a mooring or anchor to our souls that stabilizes and steadies us while preventing us from being carried out with the tide. It is a unifying force that allows us to collectively and individually come together for a common cause and outcome. Paul defines faith as the substance of things hoped for, the evidence of things not seen.[21] Without hope for a better place, without thought of a life after this, we may be cast into a depressing and fatalistic view for this existence. Without faith we can rationalize our relinquishment to the natural man, dabbling into every carnal and temporal preference. Even the world's cry of, "Eat, drink, and be merry, for tomorrow we die," is hollow and devoid of opportunity for a lasting and permanent happiness.[22]

Faith is the soothing and healing balm that gives us the ability to look forward, to see the light at the end of the tunnel, and to become better. It gives us the courage to stand up and be counted for something rather than succumbing to the impulse, capriciousness, and vagaries of negativity. Despite failure, it is the drive within us all allowing us to say, "I will try again tomorrow."

OBTAINING FAITH: IT'S IN THE DOING

Several days after Lehi and his family left Jerusalem to embark on a difficult and lengthy journey to the American continent, God commanded Lehi's sons to return to Jerusalem and retrieve the brass plates from a rich and powerful man named Laban. Upon hearing this directive, Laman and Lemuel bitterly protested, complaining it was a "hard thing" God required of them. Nephi, on the other hand, was resolute and determined when he so famously stated he would go and do whatever God commanded because he knew God would not abandon them to their own devices, rather provide opportunity and means to accomplish what He asks.[23]

The purpose for Lehi's sons obtaining the brass plates was to preserve a written record for future generations so they might know and understand how to come to the Savior. If the brass plates represented such an important and integral part of the development of Lehi's family and future generations, why did God require Lehi's sons to obtain these plates only after they had departed Jerusalem?

It certainly isn't that God forgot them or that He was incapable of providing new scriptures in the same manner He had previously to the House of Israel. No, this was a test of their faith. Nephi's humble yet unswerving answer demonstrates the faith he had and is the reason why he was successful in retrieving the brass plates while Laman and Lemuel were not. Nephi's example of unwavering faith and willingness to perform his duty, even in moments of inconvenience, blessed himself, his family, and an entire nation of people, and prepared the way for the bringing forth of the Book of Mormon in our day.

As we grow in faith, there also grows a simultaneous and profound sense of responsibility or duty that quickens our minds, lifts our faculties, and intensifies our desire and willingness to act. When the impoverished and imperiled Saints in Missouri needed help, the Prophet Joseph Smith expressed an overwhelming sense of personal responsibility or duty to them. He called it "an imperative duty" to God, to our families, to the rising generation, and to the pure in heart. I have often thought about what having an imperative duty means and how that relates to my own faith and willingness to act and do, especially in times of need.[24]

Similarly, Brigham Young stated:

> An individual who . . . continues faithful to his calling, who delights himself continually in doing the things God requires at his hands, and continues through life in the performance of every duty will secure to himself not only the privilege of receiving, but the knowledge [of] how to receive the things of God, that he may know the mind of God continually.[25]

We learn from President Young that those who find joy in their service to God and who diligently perform that service will grow, learn, and develop spiritually until they understand God and receive Him in their lives. As a result, our constant and vigilant efforts over our entire lifetime to learn our duties and to willingly and freely perform them have a direct impact on our ability to have and develop faith and to be saved in the kingdom of God.

I am not saying faith is an obligation or implying the underlying incentive for our actions in the church, in our callings, or in other activities should be motivated solely by and through a sense of responsibility or duty. Such a formula over the long-term may demotivate rather than motivate individuals, particularly single adults. What I am saying is, the development of faith is propelled by and through our actions; it's through the applying and doing that we learn and gain more. I am reminded of my previous stake president in Wyoming who would often quip upon the calling of a new bishop that it was good we called the bishop first and trained him second because if the new bishop learned what his duties were before he was called, he would never sign up to do them.

As a missionary, I once wrote my mother and asked her what it was about the church that inspired her to join. She told me she joined the church initially because of the fellowship of members and her appreciation of the values and emphasis on the family found in the gospel; however, it was only after learning and applying the principles of the gospel that she increased in faith and gained a testimony. She had to pay tithing to realize its blessing in her life, and she had to live the Word of Wisdom to feel the Spirit witness to her of its truthfulness. She gained her faith and testimony line upon line and precept upon precept and then only after she was willing to apply those teachings in her life. This pattern of learning should be found in our lives as we strive to increase our faith.

Sometimes we may develop an expectation that because we have some faith, we are entitled to receive all blessings and benefits from God. Early in the work of translating the Book of Mormon, Oliver Cowdry had a great desire to translate the record himself. Perhaps Oliver's desire was in part based on a righteous need to be equal to the prophet in his calling and his work or he was curious to know what it is like to function in that capacity. Whatever the reasons, Oliver became impatient. As a teaching moment, God gave him the opportunity to translate the record. Oliver sat down and tried several times to read and interpret the record but could not. God lovingly taught Oliver he was assuming God would just grant him power to do what Oliver wanted in the moment that Oliver wanted to do it. As a result, God taught Oliver he needed to exercise thought and effort on his part to do the work, so he could be prepared to receive the inspiration and ability to undertake the task.[26]

Because of Oliver's faith, he was given the right and the opportunity to translate the record, yet he failed because he did not recognize the spiritual, mental, and physical preparation required from him. His difficulty came not in his faith but in applying himself to his faith. Despite his virtuous and honorable desire, Oliver's expectation was one of remissness and stolidity.

Sometimes I think we have a similar expectation whenever we are called to a new calling, or have strong desires to exercise our faith; we assume we are automatically capable and qualified to the task at hand.

While it is true doctrine that whom God calls God qualifies, He does so only in the manner and capacity He determines to be correct and then only based upon our exercise of faith and diligence. We are expected to ask God what our duties are, to search the materials and information that He has provided, to pray, to work, and to apply our own individualism and character to the issues so we may grow and so all of us may be better for it. It is in and through the exercise of our faith that we gain opportunity to bless the lives of ourselves and others. It is also by and through the exercise of our faith that we can strengthen, grow, and gain greater faith in our lives.

When I was a young Boy Scout, I learned a valuable lesson from an inspired scoutmaster and a willing and faithful senior patrol leader. After arriving late at our campsite, our troop found the conditions to be miserable. The rain was torrential and the campsite covered in mud. Several of the boys had come unprepared for such conditions and struggled to set up their tent. As a result, they inadvertently broke the main support pole for their tent. Rather than solve the problem himself, the scoutmaster turned to the senior patrol leader and asked, "What are you going to do about this?"

The senior patrol leader thought for a few minutes, and then took his tent poles, gave them to those who were in need, helped them set up their tent, and then went and found another place to sleep. I am sure this scoutmaster could have solved the problem himself. He could have made comfortable those who stood in need of comfort; however, by allowing this senior patrol leader to exercise faith, judgment, and service in a time of great difficulty, he taught an entire troop what the exercise of faith is and how to be a Boy Scout.

The Book of Mormon records a miraculous instance regarding the two thousand stripling warriors. Untested and untried in the vigor and sacrifices of human conflict, this band of faithful boys was assigned to lead away from the city of Antiparah the largest and strongest army of Lamanites. The strategy was to draw out this Lamanite army so the Nephite army, led by Antipus, could recapture the city and strike this Lamanite army from behind. However, the strategy did not go as conceived because once this Lamanite army discovered Antipus's forces, the Lamanite army desired to first catch and destroy the two thousand stripling warriors and then to face Antipus's army.

Helaman recounted that the Lamanites were intensely and tenaciously pursuing the two thousand stripling warriors, forcing them to retreat in haste because of the exigency of the situation. In fact, both armies were moving as fast as possible in a straight line as both were afraid of being caught from behind; the two thousand stripling warriors were afraid of being caught by the Lamanites, and the Lamanites were afraid of being caught by Antipus. None resting, none deviating, and none conceding, these three armies played an exhausting and deadly game of cat and mouse the entire day until darkness came.

The next day, before dawn arrived, the Lamanites were close to catching the two thousand stripling warriors, and they fled for their very lives. Seeing their danger, Antipus marched his army at an increased speed but at great cost, for when Antipus finally caught the Lamanite army, they were weary from their long and speedy march. As a result, when the battle ensued, Antipus and his army were in danger of being overcome.

Not knowing why the Lamanite army halted, and fearing a strategic trap that would entice the two thousand stripling warriors into battle, Helaman was left with a bitter and difficult choice to make: to continue to flee to safety or to engage a superior force with inexperienced boys. Faced with the enormity and weight of this decision, Helaman went to them and asked as follows: "Therefore what say ye, my sons, will ye go against them to battle?" Their faithful answer to do and to go no matter the cost is an inspiration for all of us. Recounted Helaman:

> And now I say unto you, my beloved brother Moroni, that never had I seen so great courage, nay, not amongst all the Nephites. For as I had ever called them my sons (for they were all of them very young) even so they said unto me: Father, behold our God is with us, and He will not suffer that we should fall; then let us go forth; we would not slay our brethren if they would let us alone; therefore let us go, lest they should overpower the army of Antipus.[27]

Helaman knew great danger existed by having the two thousand stripling warriors engage in battle with the Lamanites. He was their leader, their prophet, their general. He knew they would go and do whatever he commanded. Yet he went to them in their moment of greatest danger, when their very lives hung in the balance, and asked them what they should do.

He gave them the choice and allowed them to exercise the faith they had been taught by their parents. Because of that decision, the army of Antipus was saved, the Lamanite army defeated, and not one of the two thousand stripling warriors fell in battle. The opportunity Helaman gave to these boys to exercise their faith and the ensuing righteous choice they made allowed God to bless and to save.

To a large extent, we control the outcomes and destiny of our individual lives. When we sit still and do nothing, we become inactive and fail to progress. Our commitment to increase our faith sufficiently to meet our daily needs—and our choice to act like the two thousand stripling warriors—will bring meaningful success to our lives no matter the odds or the extremity of the circumstance. Oftentimes, the call to act or to exercise and apply faith comes quietly, without fanfare. When we magnify our responsibilities, we learn we are not just performing obligations that have been placed upon us; rather, we are engaging in God's work and thereby learning love, charity, and service to others.

But how long must we strive to have faith and to apply ourselves? Isaiah struggled all his life in duty and service to God. His goal was to bring the entire House of Israel to the Savior, yet his efforts were met by constant rejection and continual apostasy from those he was called to teach. In a moment of doubt and uncertainty, Isaiah exclaimed that he had labored in vain and spent his effort and strength for nothing. God reminded Isaiah that the outcome is different than the journey and the result less important than the amount of individual faith applied, when he stated:

> And now, saith the Lord . . . *though Israel be not gathered, yet shall I be glorious in the eyes of the Lord,* and my God shall be my strength. And he said: *It is a light thing that thou shouldst be my servant* to raise up the tribes of Jacob, and to restore the preserved of Israel.[28]

I love the phrase "though Israel be not gathered, yet shall I be glorious in the eyes of the Lord." Even though Isaiah did not accomplish his goal, his faithfulness and his steadfastness in performing his duty sanctified his soul and made him beautiful in the sight of God. We learn from this that whatever the outcome of our efforts in this life, the final resolution of God's work is run and directed by Him. Our privilege and blessing are to apply our talents and gifts in His service so we may grow spiritually.

Through the life-long exercise of faith our hearts are softened, our spirituality grows, and our nature changes. We become more charitable, we learn to love, and we are better members of the church, more loving and caring friends, spouses, and parents. We are better neighbors, better employers and employees, better citizens, and better people. We learn to put off the natural man, to become Christ-centered rather than self-centered. We receive the countenance of the Savior in our lives and are spiritually born again as His sons and daughters. We no longer fear what the world imposes upon us; rather, we rejoice in the future opportunity to live and be with God and our families forever.

For single adults who may wrestle with our faith—who, like Isaiah, may struggle to achieve a desired goal or to find companionship and marriage in the gospel, who may wonder how long we must endure, who may ask how far we must go, or who may worry about going the distance and failing—I truly believe the exercise of our faith, no matter how great or small, has eternal benefits and rewards. Its value cannot be measured but is felt and experienced. May we all have the courage to step into the darkness when there is no perceived light, to steadily move forward, to pick ourselves up after we fall and say, "I am okay despite everything." May we also say, "I will do my very best, but if I fail, I fail knowing I tried and that God is the true master of all outcomes."

BECOMING JUST: FAITH, WORKS, AND GOD'S JUDGMENT

I remember a unique youth activity that my ward put together when I was a teenager. Upon arriving at church, I found the cultural hall filled with many different booths and carnival games like ring tosses, Go Fish, and other arcade-type activities. In the middle sat a long table with wonderful prizes—a new bike, a Walkman, popular clothes, and other treasures kids only dreamed about. The buzz and excitement permeated the air as we prepared for what was going to be the greatest of all church activities.

We were told all the carnival games were for us to play; we could choose which games to play and how often. Depending on our success in the carnival games, we would be given coupons as a reward. At the end of the activity, we could use the earned coupons in an auction for the prizes in the middle. There were also doughnuts and other great refreshments available for purchase with the coupons we earned. We were also told that in each corner of the gym were stations that did not give coupons but blessings. These blessings could be redeemed or exchanged for extra coupons later. These stations were not carnival games but mini Sunday school classes. If we participated in the classes and answered gospel-related questions correctly, we earned these blessings.

Like gleeful kids starting an Easter egg hunt, everyone tore into the cultural hall with noise and jubilation. People generally focused on the carnival games and were earning coupons quickly; they were also spending them just as fast. I realized early on that the exchange rate of the blessings to coupons was higher than trying to earn them individually at the various carnival games. As a result, I strategically focused my efforts on the four corners of the cultural hall believing if I earned more blessings, I would have more coupons than everyone else, thus giving me advantage in the auction for the most desirable prizes. Over time, the gym seemed less noisy and active, but I didn't mind as I was singularly focused on my task.

Peripherally, I noticed people dressed in white clothes walking in and out of the gym, but I paid them no attention. Eventually, one of them came up to me, tapped me on the shoulder, and asked me to come with them. I was led into the bishop's office and asked to give an accounting of the blessings I had earned. I handed them all to the bishop, who was surprised at the high number I had accumulated. He then told me I had passed away and this interview was a judgment about where I would be and who I would be in the next life. He told me that based on the number of blessings I had earned, I was assigned to the celestial kingdom. I was then led into the sacrament room, where everyone else was sitting. I noticed most of the kids were assigned either to the terrestrial kingdom or telestial kingdom rows, and only two others and I were assigned to the celestial kingdom row. Bragging, I raised my hands in victory and walked triumphantly to my seat, where the bishop proceeded to teach us about God's judgment and the effects of our choices in this life.

Over the years, I have reflected on this activity. What I learned most from this activity was we cannot earn our way into Heaven. The judgment of God is not a total or sum of the deeds we accomplish or do not accomplish in this life; rather, it is an evaluation of who and what we are. Even though I had earned more blessings than anyone else and achieved the highest reward for the activity, I had done it for the wrong reason. By every outward measure I was successful, yet my actions did not align with my motive.

Today, I realize the motives for my actions do matter: what I do and how I do it are just as important as why I do it.

We cannot paint over a rotten barn and call it good. The purpose of our faith is not to look righteous; it's not about playing as much as we can or earning a great reward. It's not about whether we come in first or whether others do. It's about exercising our faith in such a way and in such a manner that we qualify for the highest blessing God may bestow to us. If we do good through an evil motive, we are judged by that. If we do good for a charitable motive but do not have the desired effect, we are judged by the effort rather than the outcome.

Faith is the enzyme that facilitates the implementation and the benefit of the atonement in our lives; it is the first step in allowing its effects to change our nature and to prepare us to receive God's judgment. Paul teaches that the Gospel is the power of God unto salvation, both for those in and out of the church if they will have faith.[29] Think about that. The gospel has universal application irrespective of one's church membership or marital status and is the model or standard by which we are all measured. Paul states that God is righteous because he allows the gospel to save all those who are just and that the just "live" or are saved by faith.[30]

What does this mean? It means God is righteous because he judges all—men, women, members of the church, Jews, Catholics, Protestants, singles, marrieds, etc.—based upon the same set of criteria to determine who shall receive salvation. The measure of our faith is really a measure of our intent in our actions. The goal for each of us is to develop sufficient faith and then to exercise it in such a manner that we become justified.

What does it mean to be just or to become justified? When Jacob was fleeing his brother Esau in the wilderness, he saw a vision of a ladder that extended from the Earth to the Heavens upon which angels ascended and descended.[31] This vision is a representation of the touch points and binding links that connect us with Heaven and the progression and process by which we all develop and improve. It represents the way and the method by which we return and stand before God. It is a vision of the atonement and the propitiation it gave to each of us. It is also a vision of the justification process where the exercise of our faith allows us to elevate ourselves step by step, rung by rung, stage by stage, level by level, and covenant by covenant to rise above and overcome the effects of mortality.

Justification is thus the procedure, means, and timing by which God's judgment is applied to each of us. It includes the many ordinances and covenants we enter in this life, such as baptism, the sacrament, priesthood, and temple marriage, as well the daily efforts to seek after salvation not only for ourselves but also for our families and for those around us.

As a lawyer, I often point out that the application of civil judgment is not always about the issue or controversy before the court but about the authority, process, and manner by which that tribunal renders judgment. For example, to qualify for adjudication, legal controversies and complaints must be ready for a final determination, the proper location and venue must be decided, and the court must have jurisdiction both over the subject matter and the individual involved.

The application of God's judgment is similar: it fairly and rightly applies eternal judgment through a preordained process at the correct time, in the correct sequence, and in the correct place. Remember, those who do not exercise faith during mortality will be judged at a different period and through a different procedure than those who do not exercise faith.[32] Thus, whether and how we exercise faith has a bearing on the scope, manner, and timing of the judgment we receive. This does not mean the standard is different but the application, process, and timing of the implementation of God's judgment is different for those who are righteous than for those who are not.

God's judgment is always against ungodliness and unrighteousness. It is against those who have the appearance of good but have evil intentions. It is against those who know what is right but who intentionally change eternal standards to fit what is convenient or what is desired. As a result, it is our individual desires and personal choices in this life that lead to actions that either build faith or destroy it. God allows us the space to make these choices in our lives, but it is not His fault if we choose counter to what He intended. How wonderful it is to realize we are judged not by what other people do, but rather based upon what we do and who we are. It is an individual responsibility and accountability that allows us to have confidence in the course we fashion and chose. Would you have it any other way?

Sometimes it is easy for us to judge others for their actions or circumstances; yet in doing so, we lose self-perspective and think we are in a position of power or determination and therefore we are ourselves exempt from God's judgment. It is a misguided and incorrect validation of our own wrongs and deficiencies. Sometimes it is the hardness of our own hearts, our unwillingness to accept God's judgment, that prevents us from obtaining mercy or the full effects of the atonement. God's judgment is not according to partiality or bias, but rather based in truth. After all, He doesn't sin and

His judgment in all cases should be sought after, not feared or rejected. He is the one true arbiter of our souls and our faith. He gives and blesses according to our faith, especially to those who are patiently and constantly trying to do good.

How should single adults view God's judgment in our lives? Are we to look forward to it or be concerned by it? If being married is an indispensable part of our salvation, what happens if we live the entirety of our lives without becoming married? What happens if we exercise faith all our lives but are single or divorced when we die? Will God constrain us to a judgment that did not take this condition into consideration? Will we be prohibited from achieving a fullness of joy because we failed at marriage, we did not have the opportunity to be married, or someone else did not choose us for a marriage partner? Surely not—yet these are the questions that burden our faith and our hopes. By more fully understanding the conditions and grounds upon which God judges us and the purpose for which we exercise our faith, we can have a more stable basis for hope and faith in our life and in the opportunity for love, relationships, and connections that extend far beyond what we perceive.

Regarding God's judgment, Paul taught that those individuals who only "hear" the word of God are not just; however, those who are "doers" of the word are justified.[33] What does this mean? It means that faith is a principle of action, movement, and effort. It means that even if we have the gospel in our lives, we cannot sit still and expect salvation to occur. Faith is not waiting for the sun to set before we begin the day's work. It is not to carry the lazy man's load because we are hurried or unwilling to put forth greater effort. Sometimes we will contemplate whether faith is separate and distinct from our individual works and whether one may be saved with faith but without action. For me this is doctrinal hair-splitting. Faith is both word and deed. It is in our hearts as well as in our hands. It is felt through our conviction but seen and expressed through our actions.

Paul further taught:

> For when the Gentiles, *which have not the law, do by nature the things contained in the law*, these, having not the law, *are a law unto themselves*:
>
> Which shew the *work of the law written in their hearts*, their conscience also bearing witness, and their thoughts the mean while accusing or else excusing one another.[34]

What does this mean? It means those who do not have the benefit of hearing the gospel in their lives, who do and act by their own nature in concert with the principles of the gospel will be a "law unto themselves." Stated differently, God will judge them in accordance with their circumstances by the same criteria by which He will judge those who are faithful. This means they will have the benefit of the gospel even if they did not have the opportunity to accept it in their lives. Thus, the challenge is the same for all: to act and to do. It is to develop our hearts and minds in such a way and in such a manner that we can receive the blessings and benefits God has for each.

Through Paul's teaching, we learn that if we as single adults strive for, live for, and continue to hope for an eternal marriage in this life but are denied the opportunity, we will have the benefit of it tomorrow if we will but exercise faith today. If God can save those who are not baptized in this lifetime, He can do likewise for those who are not married. If those who do not have the covenant of eternal marriage in their lives still do that which is in the spirit or nature of that covenant, it is counted for good toward them, not for evil. While this does not replace the actual law, they become, as Paul described, a law unto themselves—they reap the benefit as if they had made the covenant themselves.

Is this not beautiful? Is this not fair? Is this not what the gospel is about and intended to be for married and single adults? Paul reminds us that making and keeping covenants in our lives is an outward and needed manifestation of our faith but the true test of our faith is not just what we do but whether these things are incorporated into and made a part of who we are. It is not the act of circumcision that counts; rather, it is a circumcision of the heart that God requires.[35]

God's judgment leads to one immutable thing: repentance. Our faith in Him is how we put aside our earthly nature, to be better, and to become saints, expressing and demonstrating the same love and charity to ourselves and to others that the Savior has for us. Alma stated as follows:

> He that exercises *no faith unto repentance* is exposed *to the whole law* of the demands of justice; therefore only unto him that has faith unto repentance is brought about to the great and eternal plan of redemption.[36]

Incomplete faith may be a result of incomplete repentance on our part. Repentance is not a hindrance to us; rather, it is how we overcome spiritual obstacles and make progression toward eternal life. Repentance is why we cling to the iron rod and continue down the straight and narrow path to the Savior. Repentance is not an ordeal that is begrudgingly endured, but a sincere offering of oneself to God with the hope He is mighty to save. Justification, the exercise of faith, and the prospect of repentance are less about good versus evil, right versus wrong, or a fear of failure on our part; rather, they are each an exercise of conviction and confidence in the capacity we have to change for the betterment of ourselves and our opportunity to reach for and receive Heaven's help in troubled and difficult times.

As it pertains to the outcome of the justification process and the application of God's judgment, consider this personal experience. Both my parents are converts to the church. As a result, my extended family are not members of the church. When I went on mission, I truly believed that if I was faithful and worked as diligently as possible, God would soften the heart of my grandparents and develop in them a desire to join the church.

Serving in Switzerland was a tremendous experience, yet it was a place where little conversion occurred as compared to other places in the world. The difficulties I faced there were offset by the optimism that my efforts would influence my family at home. This belief came crashing down when halfway through my mission, I received a call that my grandmother had passed away. I was devastated and didn't know how to react or respond. I inwardly felt a failure and pained myself at the belief all was lost for her in the next life. I thought it was my fault she didn't have a better opportunity to find the gospel in this life. I am grateful I learned differently.

Later, I read the parable of the Master and the Vineyard, which gave me a new perspective on faith and God's judgment. Here, the Savior compares Heaven to a man who went out early to the market place and hired workers to assist in his vineyard. This man promised these workers a fair day's wage, to which they happily and eagerly agreed. Subsequently, that same day, the man went again to the marketplace and found individuals who were not as fortunate and who had not found employment. These he also hired and promised he would pay them a fair reward. The man repeated this process two more times during the day.

When the day was done, the man offered each worker the same reward. Those who had worked longer in the vineyard complained, as they had toiled when others had not. The man replied that he had not treated them unfairly and they had received just compensation for just work; it was his right to be charitable to others who had contributed less.

I learned from this parable that whoever qualifies for the celestial kingdom should rejoice in the kindness and charity the Savior has for each, no matter the amount or timing of faith exercised in mortality. If we have the benefit of a full day's work, we have a surety of a reward; for those of us who struggle and strain, we have hope for the same type of salvation because He loves us for the faith we do have and for the faith we will have in the future. For single adults, I believe this parable is important as we all have the same reward and the same opportunity even if we must wait the day or are left behind hoping for a chance to work and be in an eternal relationship.

I also believe that we should never be surprised at who will qualify for the celestial kingdom, as that increased charity may be more for us than for the others who are there. The Savior did not say those who had been given a more charitable reward were less qualified for the work, nor did He say the work they provided, no matter how short, was of lesser value or lesser quality than the work the others provided. Irrespective of whether we have two mites or many, irrespective of whether we marry or are not able, what we can give, if we through our faith give it, is sufficient for and of worth to God.

SANCTIFICATION: THE CHALLENGE TO BECOME SAINTS

The exercise of our faith is not just the opportunity to prepare ourselves to receive God's judgment; it is also the opportunity to benefit from the results of that judgment through the atonement, our choices, and our efforts in living a righteous life. It is actual immortality and the opportunity to receive eternal life. The word "sanctification" means to make holy, to purify, or to overcome worldliness. It is an eternal course for us to be and to become saints of God. Paul states:

> But God commendeth his *love toward us*, in that, while we were yet sinners, Christ died for us. Much more then, *being now justified by his blood*, we shall be *saved from wrath* through him.[37]

What does this mean? It means God is not stationary regarding us; He moves and reaches toward us in thought, plan, and principle for the betterment of our souls. It means He gave us the Savior, who condescended below all things, who left His own heavenly state of being, to take upon himself the cloak of mortality for the sole purpose of showing love and charity to each of us. Through His triumph over physical death, we now have the potential to receive not justice, but mercy as a judgment. We are saved not just from the effects of the fall but also from the effects of our choices and the exercise of our agency in our life.

Does this mean all who are justified are also sanctified? Surely not. Justification is about the application of judgment; sanctification is about the consequences (or, said differently, the removal of such) from the judgment we receive. Even those who do not qualify for the first resurrection will still be justified as the resurrection also blesses and benefits them and brings them back into God's presence.

I suppose one could argue sanctification is also applied, at least in part, to those who do not inherit the full blessings of eternal life as they will receive a degree and a measure of glory in God's kingdom. Having said that, one should not think receiving only a portion of the benefit of the atonement is what Paul had in mind. Paul is teaching about receiving the fullness of the atonement, the opportunity to live as God lives, not because we earned it but because we have become like Him in thought, word, and deed. Paul further taught:

> For *when ye were the servants of sin*, ye were *free from righteousness. What fruit had ye then in those things* whereof ye are now ashamed? *For the end of those things is death.*

> But now *being made free from sin*, and become servants to God, *ye have your fruit unto holiness*, and the *end everlasting life*. For the wages of sin is death; but the *gift of God is eternal life* through Jesus Christ our Lord.[38]

I love these words by Paul. He teaches that while we are in mortality, we are subject to its effects—we are governed by the state or condition in which we live. In mortality, we are servants to a temporal or natural condition that includes unrighteousness and sin. Within the context of this condition, we are in some sense free from the effects of righteousness or eternal life but such freedom is deceptive and illusory as it has no lasting benefit or fruit. Paul is quick to point out that all we reap as the result of this condition is a separation from God. The atonement, however, frees us from the effects of this worldly condition and allows us to become servants, or, better said, saints of God. The fruit unto holiness Paul speaks of is the opportunity to be sanctified, to be holy, and to qualify for the benefit of eternal life itself.

Moses taught:

That *by reason of transgression cometh the fall, which fall bringeth death*, and inasmuch as ye were born into the world by water, and blood, and the spirit, which I have made, and so became of dust a living soul, even so *ye must be born again into the kingdom of heaven*, of water, and of the spirit, and be cleansed by blood, even the blood of mine Only Begotten;

that ye might be *sanctified from all sin*, and enjoy the words of eternal life in this world, and eternal life in the world to come, even immortal glory;

For by the *water ye keep the commandment*; *by the spirit ye are justified*, and *by the blood ye are sanctified*.[39]

Moses reinforces the doctrine that through the fall we are subject to the state or condition of mortality. He also teaches that we must be born again, not physically but spiritually, to sanctify us from the effects of sin. There is a lot of discussion in the church today about the symbolic nature or meaning of being born again through water, blood, and the Spirit. I think these are all great discussions and helpful with understanding the individual elements of the atonement and how it applies to us.

For me, being born again can be explained simply. It is a process that begins with our hope and faith and is made effective through the making and keeping of spiritual covenants, all of which allow us to be both justified and sanctified in this life and in the next. In short, we have changed our very nature to become something different from what our circumstances dictate.

Joseph Smith taught the doctrines of justification and of sanctification are true doctrines and are important and essential for all members of the church.[40] Why are these doctrines important for single adults to understand in our daily lives? They are important because we need to understand what the atonement is, what it overcomes, and how we as individuals relate to the Savior. It is also germane in understanding that the atonement applies to us each day. The benefits of justification and sanctification are not unforeseen future events but are ongoing and continual processes in our lives.

The atonement encompasses and drives the doctrines of both justification and sanctification. It is through justification that we are brought back into the purview of God's law and through sanctification by which we are advantaged from it. It is a spiritual progression we make to claim an eternal heritage and a divine destiny. I think Jacob saw this progression and process in his vision of the ladder to Heaven. This process was an important and essential part of Jacob's purpose and meaning in life, not only for him, but also for all the generations of the world who would benefit through his posterity and through the eternal covenants God made with the House of Israel. As Moroni so perspicaciously stated:

> And again, if ye by the grace of God are *perfect* in Christ, and deny not his power, then are *ye sanctified in Christ by the grace of God*, through the shedding of the blood of Christ, which is in the covenant of the Father unto the remission of your sins, *that ye become holy, without spot.*[41]

If we substitute the word "perfect" with "justified," we have a more complete and a higher understanding of what Moroni meant and what the atonement is and does. It grants to us the opportunity to be justified and the potential to be sanctified, today, tomorrow, and forever.

My wish for all the single adults in the church is that we think about and understand the justifying and sanctifying effects of the gospel and the atonement in our lives; that we are always willing to take upon ourselves the name of Christ; that we constantly remember the breadth, depth, and magnitude of His life and the impact of His atonement in our lives; and that we expand our willingness to enter into spiritual covenants and increase our desire in understanding and in keeping the commandments He gives to us—for they truly lead to eternal life. The sanctification process is less about the death of the Savior; rather, it is about His continued life and the way He currently lives it. It is the power to heal our souls, mend our broken hearts, and forgive all our sins if we will but turn to Him.

FINAL THOUGHTS REGARDING FAITH

After the Savior had taught the multitudes, He sent His disciples ahead of Him in a small boat. A terrible storm arose while they were at sea, and the disciples were frightened for their lives. Seeing their distress, the Savior walked toward them on the water. The disciples, believing the Savior to be a spirit or aberration, cried out in terror. The Savior straightway called to them and stated, "Be of good cheer, it is I, be not afraid." Then Peter answered the Lord in his usual brash manner, "Lord, if it be thee, bid me come unto thee." The Lord answered as He has always done for all mankind, "Come!"

Peter sprang from the boat with his eyes riveted to the Savior, but as the monstrous winds whipped his hair and the boisterous waves splashed his clothes, Peter took his eyes from the Savior and began to sink. Peter cried out to the Savior and the Savior stretched forth his hand and lifted the drowning disciple with this gentle charge: "Oh thou of little faith, wherefore didst thou doubt?"

So often, as mariners of mortality, our lives are tossed about in the tempestuous sea of uncertainty and doubt. We see the terrible waves of hardship and loneliness crashing about us and can feel the winds of adversity pushing us away. In such moments we are apt to sink into the deepest depths of despair. During these times, when our difficulties are the darkest, our loneliness the most pronounced, when our journeys seem endless and our outcomes uncertain, I hope that each of us, whether single or married, may develop the faith necessary to stretch out, to reach for the Savior and hear His supernal plea, "Be of good cheer, it is I, be not afraid."[42] In so doing we are enabled to lift our souls, to stand in the rage of the storm, and to rise above the fathomless abyss that is always there to engulf and drag us down.

DEVELOPING CHARITY: BEING AND BECOMING LOVE

If faith is the genesis of applied grace, charity or love is its result. If hope is a state of mind and faith is a state of action, charity is a state of the heart. Charity is the noblest basis for what and how we feel, the origin of empathy, and the doorway to acceptance, tolerance, and broad-mindedness. Charity is about how we live and experience life and it's the quality that most defines us as human beings.

It is the characteristic that members of the church embrace and seek after and is the beginning, middle, and end of our discipleship and devotion to God. Of all the attributes embraced by God, charity is the most distinguished, the most elevated, and the most virtuous, for God is Himself love. As a result, the only accurate measure of our souls is the degree and magnitude of our love for ourselves and for one another. As Moroni stated:

> And charity suffereth long, and is kind, and envieth not, and is not puffed up, seeketh not her own, is not easily provoked, thinketh no evil, and rejoiceth not in iniquity but rejoiceth in the

> truth, beareth all things, believeth all things, hopeth all things, endureth all things.
>
> Wherefore, my beloved brethren, *if ye have not charity, ye are nothing*, for charity never faileth. Wherefore, cleave unto charity, which is the greatest of all, for all things must fail—
>
> But charity is the pure love of Christ, and it endureth forever; *and whoso is found possessed of it at the last day*, it shall be well with him.[43]

Charity is not something one purchases or acquires in life; neither can it be found in a list of donations, contributions, or accomplishments, no matter their importance or greatness. Charity, at its very essence and core, is something we become. For me, that is simple to say and difficult to explain or realize. It requires a lifetime of learning to love, learning to accept, learning to see events, circumstances, and issues as others see them, to express sympathy, empathy, and love no matter another's perspective. It is learning to extend connection, friendship, companionship, and comfort rather than hate, isolation, and detestation. As we develop true charity in our lives and in our relationships, we become one with the Savior and with each other.

Charity is manifest in the "pure love of Christ." It is an outcome, outgrowth, or occurrence that happens because of both faith and hope. As Moroni stated:

> There must be faith, and if there must be faith, there must be hope and if there must be hope there must also be charity. *And except ye have charity ye can no wise be saved in the kingdom of God; neither can ye be saved in the kingdom of God if ye have not faith; neither if ye have no hope.*[44]

For members of the church, true faith and true hope always moves and leads its possessor to charity; therefore, one cannot have either faith or hope without also having charity.

I wrestled with describing or defining charity, at least beyond the scriptural definition, as it is challenging to fully scope and adequately circumscribe the magnitude, range, and scale it comprises. When thinking about how to define charity, I felt like Jarom, who when tasked with writing something of worth in the small plates, stated, "For what could I write more than my fathers have written?"[45] Describing charity is a lot like describing Heaven. Charity is something small that has the power to grow into something larger and more meaningful; it imbues and imbibes itself into the essence and character of our souls and lifts and raises our perspective; it is a treasure of great worth to those who seek after and recognize it; it is a net that gathers and collects the hearts of those around us; it is all-encompassing, never tarnishing; and it embraces both the old and the new and is part of everything that was, that is, and that will be.

When I looked for specific examples of charity in the scriptures, I wondered what actions or examples best defined it. Was it the sacrifice of the widow's mite, the philanthropy of the Good Samaritan, the teaching of the Sermon on the Mount, the blessing of the woman at the well, the Savior's visitation to the Nephites, or any of the many described events and miracles? When thinking on these, I asked myself whether the actions of the individuals involved were faith-based, humility-based, duty-based, or something else? I began to realize I was looking at this topic in too narrow of a viewpoint and that each of these instances exemplified charity in some form. In my mind, charity distills down to three fundamental elements: 1) what we give; 2) what and who we accept; and 3) what we forgive.

What We Give

Whenever I think of charity, what I give is usually the easiest part to understand. An array of formal charities exist today, and many of us across the world generously donate services, money, or goods for a variety of reasons. Some are motivated by philanthropy; for others support for a cause they care about; for some it's business or commerce related; some want to set an example and inspire communities, families, and friends; and still others give to charity for tax reasons or even to improve their ability to better manage finances.

For members of the church, charitable giving is generally fixed in and motivated by both faith and compassion, where the only benefit sought is spiritual and the only reward is the joy of helping those in need. The offerings we make are symbols of our faith and demonstrations of our willingness to become like the Savior. The trick for us is to come to that state in our lives where we give without thought of temporal reward, without compulsion or coercion, but by pure and simple love of God and for others.

When it comes to giving, there are two doctrinal concepts to consider: the law of sacrifice and the law of consecration. While both doctrines are related, there are differences: the law of sacrifice is about *what* we give, and the law of consecration is about *whom* we give (ourselves) and *for what* purpose. Together these doctrines define how we dedicate and offer ourselves to God.

Immediately after the fall and the expulsion of Adam and Eve from the Garden of Eden, God gave Adam and Eve the law of sacrifice and commanded them to make an offering of the firstlings of their flocks. Adam was faithful and obedient in every respect to these commandments, but he did not wholly understand the purpose of this sacrifice. After some time, an angel appeared to him and asked why he was making sacrifices to God. Adam honestly responded that he did not know why, except God had commanded him to do so.[46] Sacrifice of at least some of our material possessions is a requirement of the gospel during mortality, even though, like Adam, we may neither understand the significance and importance of it nor perceive any immediate benefit therefrom. The most important aspect of sacrifice is not what we give but our willingness to do so.

The scriptures are replete with examples of righteous individuals who sacrificed. Noah sacrificed his friends, family, and his society when he entered the ark. Abraham was willing to sacrifice his son Isaac upon God's command. Nephi sacrificed all his family's wealth to obtain the brass plates. Ruth sacrificed her comfort and family to stay with Naomi. Esther sacrificed her safety to save the Israelites. Abinadi sacrificed his life in testimony to King Noah. Truly the list of the sacrifices made by individuals in the defense and the establishment of God's kingdom is endless. Likewise, church members sacrifice through the payment of tithing and fast offerings, the time we give in callings, church and institute attendance, and the service we provide to friends, family, and others. It is also in the time, effort, and labor spent in ministering to others, the covenants we make, and our efforts to improve ourselves.

Sacrifice is a choice. It is also a choice that is not always easy to make. We are often presented with opportunities to be charitable, yet it is up to us whether to follow through. When a rich man approached the Savior and inquired what he must do to gain eternal life, the Savior instructed him to keep the commandments. This man indicated he had been faithful but further queried as to what he additionally lacked. The Savior responded by asking this man to sell his possessions, give them to the poor, and to follow Him. This man was troubled by the Savior's teaching and walked away.[47]

How sad that this man, when asked to contribute to God's work, in that moment chose not to. I often ask myself whether there is something I hold back when dealing with God. Am I truly prepared to sacrifice and to consecrate myself to the purposes God has in store? Personally, I think we get so caught up in ownership issues in mortality, we forget the only item we can offer God is ourselves. God created this world and everything on it. He has literal title to all things and everything we have is borrowed from Him. The only thing God has given us ownership over is our personal agency. By choosing to follow God, we are offering ourselves to Him. The scriptures refer to this as a broken heart and a contrite spirit. It is a consecration of ourselves, our abilities, and our choices to the betterment of the church and the building of hope and faith among all His children.

We often refer to the Savior's atonement as the great sacrifice; in that same vein, I also like to think of it as the great consecration. The Savior both consecrated His life and sacrificed it for the well-being of our souls. Is this not love? Is this not charity? As we likewise do for the betterment of others (in the manner, capacity, and method in which we are able) we come to know Him. Any service, sacrifice, or consecration that we may make in mortality, whether great or small, is minor in comparison to those the Savior made. Yet by following His example and by implementing these principles in our lives, it will bring greater happiness, increased spirituality and satisfaction, and greater appreciation of the atonement in our lives. When single adults exercise charity, we are filled with the love of the Savior and we experience firsthand that charity truly never fails.

What and Whom We Accept

The parable of the Good Samaritan is the narrative of a Jewish man who was beaten, robbed, and left for dead. It tells the story of the depravity of those who were supposed to deliver and provide aid, but who for their own pride and bias declined to help, passing by without consideration or compassion. It also is the account of a Samaritan man, who despite social custom and prejudice, offered needed care, without thought of himself, to one who was rejected and desperately in need.[48]

But why is this parable so important and so moving to us? What is it that touches our heart and makes us want to be better? Is it the immediacy of the need of the wounded man or the way that need arose? Is it because of the absence of relief and refusal of assistance shown by others who were charged to give it? Is it the timing and amount of the aid given? Each of these play a role in this parable's importance, yet the defining characteristic isn't what was given but what was accepted that allowed and facilitated the Samaritan to give charity.

The Samaritan's basis for extending charity was his ability to set aside what differentiated him from the wounded man and to accept that which made them alike. A man who was supposed to hate put aside his own predilections, partialities, and predispositions, and, instead, he loved. The Samaritan saw the wounded man not as a Jew, not as a risk, not as a burden, but as a human being and his neighbor.

Why is acceptance so important for our ability to extend charity? The answer centers on what charity is, or, better said, what it is not. Charity is the absence of pride. Pride is the love of ourselves over others. It is the prioritization of our desires, our ambitions, our actions, over the collective betterment of those around us. Pride is siloistic and divisive by nature, for it is individual and singular in its objective. Satan fell from Heaven because he chose to elevate himself over all others. If pride is the love of ourselves, charity is its opposite, for charity is the love of others over ourselves. If pride divides, charity collects; if pride excludes, charity includes; if pride rejects, charity accepts. As a result, receiving, accepting, and including others, who they are, what they stand for, how they feel, and what is important to them is fundamental in developing and applying charity in our lives.

Paul recounts a disconnect that occurred with Peter, the prophet, when he visited the saints in Antioch. Paul and Barnabas had worked hard and had much success in preaching the gospel and growing the church among the gentiles. When Peter came to visit these saints, he dined with them; however, when other influential members of the church arrived, who were Jews, Peter withdrew from eating with the convert gentiles, fearing the new arrivals would be offended. As a result, all others in attendance who were also Jews followed Peter's example and withdrew from the meal.

Angered by Peter's dissimulation, Paul dramatically and publicly confronted Peter, accusing Peter of duplicitousness, for Peter himself was Jewish, but as a member of the church, he was no longer living after the manner of the Jews. If that were so, why would Peter compel the gentiles to live as the Jews do? In other words, why did Peter force Jewish beliefs, bias, and prejudices onto new members of the church when he did not follow them himself?[49]

Here, there was no malfeasance or malintent with Peter's actions. Certainly, as a Jew, Peter was raised on the belief that to dine with non-Jewish people was improper. Peter showed positive personal growth by initially putting this belief aside to eat with the gentiles. Still, when confronted with the perceived judgment of others, Peter reverted to his original belief and withdrew. Even though Peter had received direct revelation regarding the gospel and the gentiles, his acceptance of them as equals in faith was still a work in progress.

What a difficult situation this action created and how sad for all involved. How would you feel if you had recently joined the church, exercised faith in the Savior, accepted Peter as a prophet, and then had him leave your dining table because he valued the opinions of other people who considered you as less than worthy? Peter's inability in that moment and at that time to accept and to receive those who were with him prevented him from extending love and charity in real time to those who needed it. He saw these people not as members of the church, not as people with a common faith, a common covenant, and a shared hope, but rather he saw them through the biased lens of his upbringing as a people who were of a different class and heritage than he.

What do we learn from this situation? At a minimum, we learn there is a difference between tolerating something and accepting it. Tolerating something is not bad, but it falls short of truly understanding or accepting something. Dr. Jefferson Fish states, "You can tolerate something without accepting it, but you cannot accept something without tolerating it."[50] What this means is, toleration is more surficial. It is acknowledgement without connection, tacit allowance without position or opinion. It allows one to say, "I am okay with another's actions, beliefs, or status so long as it does not impact me."

Acceptance, on the other hand, is more personal. It is an understanding and reception of individuals irrespective of what they do or believe. It is a belief in the goodness of people, their humanity, and who they are. Acceptance does not mean affirming actions but affirming actors.

In gospel parlance, you can hate the sin but still accept the sinner. This is seen through the Savior's acceptance and treatment of the woman caught in adultery as He loved her despite everything she did. Peter was certainly willing to tolerate his discomfort with eating with the gentiles so long as it was not public; yet when the moment for decorum or public opinion arose, he placed himself, his needs, and his partiality above the needs of others and failed to accept and to receive them for who they were.

Previously, I discussed the need to remove judgment and the importance of receiving people in relationships. Both principles are also crucial in our ability to have charity with those around us. I am reminded of a conversation I once had with a young single woman who, when asked whether she would consider a relationship with someone to whom she was not attracted, stated, "I can date ugly for one night, but marriage is forever."

While I often laugh at the candor of this truthful response, it made me think about whether I am tolerating individuals or accepting them in the relationships I have, or in the relationships I hope to have. Am I like Peter, dismissing opportunity based upon personal need or want, or am I open to new possibility and opportunity irrespective of where it arises? Do I look for the good in people rather than passing them by? Do I look for reasons to have a connection or to be in a relationship, or do I look for reasons not to be in one? The answers to these questions affect my ability to have and develop charity in my life. President Monson taught:

> Charity is having patience with someone who has let us down. It is resisting the impulse to become offended easily. It is accepting weaknesses and shortcomings. It is accepting people as they truly are. It is looking beyond physical appearances to attributes that will not dim through time. It is resisting the impulse to categorize others.[51]

As we learn to accept others, as we learn to be more open to them, as we find the good and accept it, we will find a heightened and enhanced capacity to love and to be loved.

What and Whom We Forgive

The most challenging aspect of charity is forgiveness. It is how we respond to things that have wronged us, to instances that have hurt us, and to individuals who have disappointed us. Forgiveness is not just a choice, it's a journey. Just as hope is about choosing how or in what light you see things, forgiveness is about choosing how you respond and react to those things.

The Old Testament's account of Joseph is often discussed and viewed in the church as a story of triumph over imposed adversity, the ability to stay true to our own self and to God regardless of circumstance, and the glory of God in creating good despite extremity. This account is also about the ability to forgive and to provide salvation despite the infliction of significant and substantial hurt by those who were supposed to love and care for us. It is a blueprint for the overcoming of our emotional and spiritual afflictions and the restoration and reestablishment of peace in our soul.

Joseph was the favored son of Jacob. Although he was the eleventh-born son, Joseph held the birthright after the eldest, Reuben, forfeited it. Sadly, Reuben's forfeiture led to a competitive and contentious game of thrones between Joseph's older brothers, who were both jealous of the preferred status Jacob gave Joseph and covetous as they themselves jockeyed for their own status and entitlements to their perceived inheritances.

When the opportunity presented itself, Joseph's brothers conspired to murder him for their own advancement and benefit. Fortunately, the greed of some of his brothers saved Joseph, who, rather than kill him, sold Joseph into slavery for gain and profit. After returning home to their father, Jacob, the remaining sons lied, stating a wild animal had tragically killed Joseph. They then presented Joseph's prized coat, which they had soaked in blood, to substantiate their claim and to hide their subterfuge.

Joseph, meanwhile, was indentured to Potiphar, an important and ranking individual in Egypt. Joseph did not bemoan or sulk because of this situation; rather, he put shoulder to the wheel, worked hard, and was eventually promoted to great status within Potiphar's house. This was a blessing to both him and Potiphar as Potiphar profited greatly from Joseph's work.

Later, after Joseph refused the inappropriate advances of Potiphar's wife, and after she unjustly and spitefully accused him of misconduct, Potiphar had Joseph placed into prison. Once again, Joseph found himself on the short end of the stick for having done nothing but what was right and good. He was stripped of the benefit of his labor and cast into prison for what might have been the entirety of his life. How hard must this have been for Joseph, who was wrongfully and materially burdened not once but twice by the actions of others. Despite this setback, Joseph again worked hard and was again promoted within the confines of the prison to a position of high responsibility and importance.

Despite Joseph's difficulty, these circumstances and responsibilities were the impetus to his eventual freedom as, during the performance of his duties, he had the opportunity to correctly interpret the dreams of two prisoners. Because of Joseph's demonstrated insight in prison, years later, when Pharaoh had a dream that perplexed him, Joseph was summoned to Pharaoh's court to interpret it. Inspired, Joseph saw in Pharaoh's dream that Egypt would face several years of plenty followed directly by several years of famine. Because of Joseph's inspired interpretation, Pharaoh placed Joseph at his side and charged him with the management of Egypt's affairs going forward. Joseph used the years of Egypt's plenty to prepare it for the future famine.

When the famine came, that preparation saved Egypt's people and brought great glory and wealth to it. Even Joseph's brothers came seeking relief and food for their family. As his brothers stood before him, Joseph had the choice to either seek retribution or confer forgiveness. To seek justice or grant mercy, saving their family from starvation and ruin. What internal agony Joseph must have felt to see again those who had harmed him and those who were supposed to love him.

When Joseph revealed himself to his brothers, there was no bitterness in his soul, no lingering hatred or animosity, only love and kindness. He attributed their wrongs to him as God's instrument to save them all from calamity. How beautiful this must have been, how relieving for all, both Joseph and his brothers, to reunite, to put away harm, jealousy, and family animosity, and to move forward in love and respect. The greatness in Joseph is not in his astonishing achievements and his overcoming of individual adversity, but in the love and charity he extended when he could have given the alternative. Compassion, not bitterness; mercy, not justice; and kindness, not resentment were bestowed despite Joseph's induvial suffering, trauma, and ordeal.

How many of us have been in family, marital, or other relationships that were dysfunctional? How many of us, as a result, have borne the painful and difficult consequences, whether spiritual, financial, emotional, or otherwise, from choices that others in that relationship have made? How many times have the repercussions of those consequences cascaded into the rest of our lives, placing us in situations where we wondered if we ourselves have been imprisoned, whether we will again see the light of day, and whether we deserved the outcomes? How many times did we ask how long must we endure and how long must we wait for relief? These are the questions that many single adults ask ourselves, especially after failed relationships occur.

My divorce was a very bitter pill to swallow. While I was not faultless in the breakdown of the relationship, I faced judgment I did not deserve, financial stress that was not required, and the devastating loss of friends and family. Not only did I lose a marriage I valued, I was contemporaneously laid off from employment I had held for nearly fifteen years. It seemed as if my entire identity was consumed in turmoil, chaos, and confusion. I was angry at my situation and thought I didn't merit what happened. Anger, bitterness, frustration, and fear were my new companions, and I wrestled to find positive means to put them behind me.

For years, not a day would go by when I wouldn't think of my ex-wife and ask myself why this happened and wonder what could have been. For a long time, I thought I didn't deserve to be back as a single adult facing the same situations and conditions I faced prior to my marriage. I felt punished well beyond the measure of my deficiencies. I felt like Sisyphus, continually pushing a boulder up a mountain only to have it roll to the bottom each time I reached the summit. I was Charlie Brown, always trying to kick a football that was ruthlessly taken away or was never there in the first place. Failure, disappointment, and a lack of motivation were all real challenges for me.

I suppose I could have stayed in that condition in perpetuity, but I found a better way. I began to look at life differently, to accept my role in the breakdown of the relationship, to place a proper and healthier perspective on events and circumstances. I began to wish for beneficial outcomes for my ex-wife. I hoped and prayed she would find positive and meaningful relationships in her life, even if such were not with me. I placed her name on the temple role each time I went, not for reconciliation, but to have forgiveness in my heart for her.

I wish I could say forgiveness came overnight: it did not. I was like Nephi, who immediately and outwardly forgave his brothers for their hurtful actions yet internally wrestled with anger toward them for the long-term consequences he and others needlessly bore.[52] I realized the person I had to forgive the most was not my ex-wife but myself. I had to learn to let go of my expectations and emotional burdens, to find rest in my journey, and to become who I was meant to be. I found charity was the healing balm, the salve that brought peace and joy again to my life.

The Savior's parable of the Prodigal Son is another powerful example of how forgiveness and charity work together in our lives. Perhaps it's the intimacy of the rift between the father and the son with which we each can relate. Perhaps it's the inward struggle to find oneself after difficult and deleterious choices. Perhaps it's the overcoming of grief, jealousy, and resentment to find love and compassion. Here is a son, broken, lost, bereft of understanding for the great and good things given to him. His only thought was for himself and for his immediate pleasure and satisfaction. As a result, he lost everything that he received and he suffered greatly through his own volition. Still, that suffering had some purpose as it allowed him to come to himself and to recognize the deleterious effects of his choices. Sometimes the hard things in our lives force us to be humble, to view events and conditions in a different perspective, or to long for different times and for different places. If it leads to this end, such trauma is good for our personal development.

But what of the hurts and traumas of those left behind? The Prodigal Son's choices did not end solely with himself. The loss of the relationship, the anger and hurt, left a wake of destruction and devastation with those around him. How do these individuals overcome their own issues and concerns? Most likely, the older brother—the one who was faithful, obedient in all things—felt sorrow and grief over the loss of his brother. If he had not cared for his brother, why would he then have strong feelings and concerns upon his return? Perhaps he saw the rift growing between his father and brother. Perhaps he chose sides in the family conflict—we do not know.

And what of the father? Not much is made of the father except he forgave and showed love. Perhaps this is the true meaning of the parable. Certainly, the son asking for his inheritance was inappropriate. What entitlement or right did the son have for things he had not earned? What reason did the father have in granting the unwarranted demand of his son?

Perhaps he knew what his son needed and felt that giving him his request would be constructive to him in some manner. Perhaps he wanted his son to find happiness. Maybe he felt guilt for the broken and fragmented relationship and believed honoring his inheritance would give his son an opportunity to improve outside their relationship. Whatever his reasons, the father granted the request. I have often wondered how the father felt about the choice he made. Did he have regrets or did his feelings change as time passed? Was he angry at his son's demand? How did he feel inwardly about his son's leaving for what he must have felt was a permanent separation?

When the opportunity for reconciliation came, however, the past hurt, trauma, and conflict was no longer important to either the son or the father. What had the greatest worth and impact was the unending love, forgiveness, and charity shown to each other and to themselves. How do we accept those back into our lives or forgive those who have caused hurt or wrongs in our life? Are we like the father who showed unqualified and unconditional love, or are we like the faithful son who held onto the past? Each of us at some point will have an opportunity to make this choice. How we react, the forgiveness we give, and the love we bestow has important relevance in our personal growth and our ability to have and develop charity in our lives.

Paul taught:

> To whom ye forgive anything, I forgive also: for if I forgave anything, to whom I forgave it, for your sakes forgave I it in the person of Christ; Lest Satan should get an advantage of us: for we are not ignorant of his devices.[53]

Forgiveness is the key to charity. I have learned you can't change the consequence of the choices of others but you can change how you react to them. So many times, I hear single adults blaming their ex-spouse for the breakdown of relationships. Irrespective of the causal reasons for the termination of the relationship, each of us may look with kindness and charity on those who have wronged us. Sometimes the most charitable action or outcome may be to terminate an unhealthy relationship so that both parties may stand on their own and grow. Just like the parable of the olive tree, a new grafting and replanting may lead to better and healthier situations for all.

Today, I realize my ex-wife's filing for divorce was a tremendous blessing and not a burden in my life. It gave me opportunity I never thought possible and provided growth I scarcely realized was needed. Regardless of whether I agreed with her reasons, I recognize that she did something that was needed and that I could not have done myself; for that I am truly grateful.

There is no need to justify to others why we are single, no need to perceive fault or sin from divorce or to validate to others the reasons for ending a relationship. What is needed is an outpouring of love and charity for each person involved. How we love, how we forgive, and how we see and react to others are the threads and weaving in the tapestry of our own happiness today and the basis of salvation for ourselves and others tomorrow.

10

The Opportunity of One

That they all may be one; as thou, Father, art in me,
and I in thee, that they also may be one in us.
—John 17:21

What does all this mean? Where do we go from here? If the gospel is so important to helping us develop hope, faith, and charity, why do so many single adults struggle to participate in and feel a part of the church? If salvation is dependent upon who we become and the charity we engender, how does the church as an institution matter in our lives, especially if it is family-centric? How do both single adults and the church find symbiotic, practical, and helpful paths forward so that all are edified and brought closer to the Savior? These are the questions I have considered as I have lived as a single adult in the church. These questions condense into one salient discussion: What is the value of the church as an organized religion to single adults?

At least some of this debate requires us to understand and recognize existing societal trends concerning the value of and need for organized religion. According to the Pew Research Center, organized religion is becoming less important to more individuals in the United States. Fewer people today than in previous years exercise a belief in God, pray, or regularly attend church or other religious services.[1] Despite a high percentage of people in the United States who accept or believe in a higher power, an increasing number of people no longer affiliate with a specific organized religion.[2]

Interestingly, though, these statistics show an increase in the number of people in the United States who feel they have a spiritual connection irrespective of their religious beliefs. For example, in 2014, sixty percent (60%) of responding individuals reported they often felt "spiritual peace and well-being" and forty-six percent (46%) of responding individuals weekly felt a profound appreciation for the "wonder about the universe"; this represents a seven percent (7%) increase over previous years for both statistics.[3]

What does this mean? It means that while people in the United States have a *belief in God*, their *practice or observance of that belief* is performed less through religious institutions than in previous years. Americans increasingly perceive themselves as less religious yet more spiritual. Said differently, individuals are progressively defining their spirituality or connections with God through their everyday experiences and observations rather than through institutional opportunities. People today are finding more spiritual connection through activities that engage with nature (going to the beach, walking in the woods, sitting by a river, etc.) or by meditating on some fact or issue rather than through established or organized practices. As a result, the societal definition of what it means to be religious is changing and evolving.

The following three charts are intriguing and show the decreasing trends in the United States toward organized religion.[4]

In 2007, eighty-three percent (83%) of people in the United States identified themselves with an organized religion, while sixteen percent (16%) did not. Yet by 2014, these numbers had shifted to seventy-six percent (76%) of the people identifying with an organized religion while twenty-three percent (23%) did not. That is a seven percent (7%) swing, over a seven-year period, of people in the United States who no longer affiliate or identify with religion in any manner. Additionally, attendance at religious services are trending down in frequency and duration over the same time frame. These are remarkable and staggering statistics that clearly show people decreasing their activity for participating in religious services and moving away from religion altogether.

Interestingly, population growth is in part contributing to this shift. In 2007, the number of adults in the United States was 227.2 million, with approximately 188.8 million adults who affiliated with an organized religion. In 2014, the number of adults in the United States increased to 244.8 million, yet the number of adults who affiliated with and organized religion decreased slightly to approximately 187.3 million adults.[5] Much of this decline is due in part to a rising generation of people who are less religious and more secular in their beliefs.[6]

While most people believe in God, the importance of organized religion and the practice of faith and belief is more important to older generations than to younger generations. Assuming these trends continue, we should

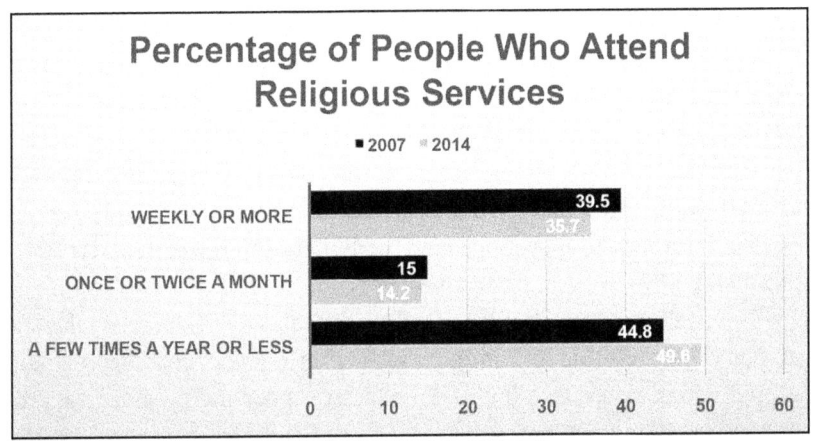

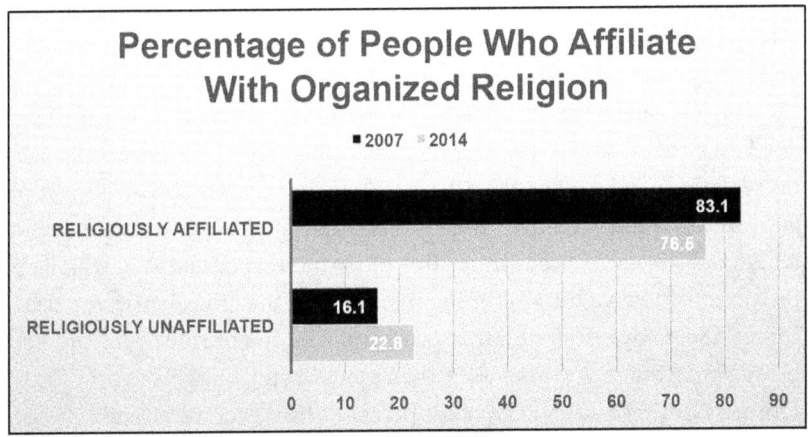

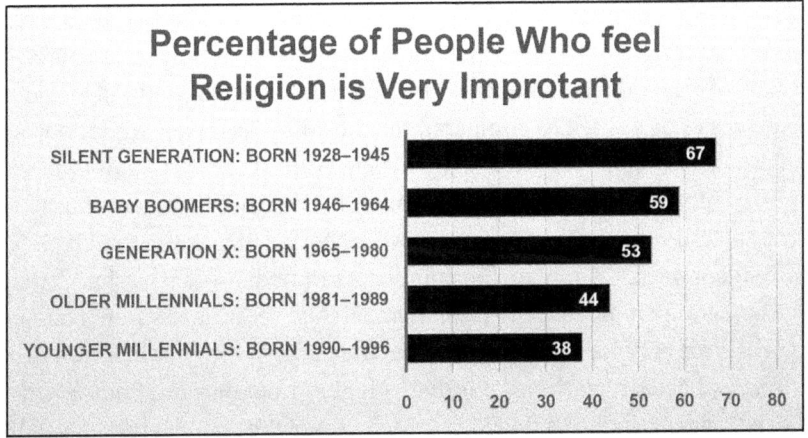

ask ourselves what impacts or effects this will have on organized religion as the younger generations age. True, we may tend to be more open to organized religion or its importance may change or become more of a priority the older we get. As a result, these statistics may reflect more about the participants' ages than their generation. Still, these statistics speak volumes about the difficulty that organized religions face today to encourage people, especially those who are younger and single, to be interested in and to practice their faith.

Despite this, many people in the United States feel organized religions play an important role in communities by 1) bringing people together and strengthening community bonds, 2) helping the poor and needy, and 3) protecting and strengthening morality in society. Conversely, many who are unaffiliated with a religious organization state that some of the reasons for their unwillingness to participate in or their disenfranchisement from organized religion are that it is too concerned with money, power, and politics, and it has a high adherence and rigidity to rules.[7]

One can argue about the accuracy or preciseness of the results from the Pew's research, yet the trends it identifies are important indicators of the willingness of individuals to participate in religious organizations and activities. The statistics from the Pew research cited herein are based upon a national survey of about thirty-five thousand respondents, of which approximately twelve hundred were members of the church. Among other things, the study also found that gender plays a major role in the practice of religion: women are more likely than men by wide margins to pray (sixty-four percent [64%] versus forty-six percent [46%]) and to attend religious services (forty percent [40%] versus thirty-one percent [31%]).[8]

When analyzing the specific scope or intensity of members' activity in the church, the study showed positive marks for the church as compared to other organized religions. According to the study, seventy-seven percent (77%) of responding members of the church indicated they attend religious services once a week as compared to Jehovah's Witnesses, who reported eighty-five percent (85%) attending weekly, evangelical Protestants who reported fifty-eight percent (58%) attending weekly, and members of historically black Protestant congregations who reported fifty-three percent (53%) attending weekly.[9] Granted, the number of respondents for the church may be small as compared to its total membership, yet even assuming a margin of error in these responses, it's clear members of the church have a high degree of activity in their faith that is higher than nearly all of the organized religions in the United States. Members of the church also reported a higher regularity of feelings of spiritual peace and well-being than most other organized religions.[10]

Sadly, this study did not distinguish the activity and willingness of people to participate in organized religion based upon marital status. I would love to see how these statistics varied based on that indicator across the different religions in the United States and specifically to see how—or whether—it varied within the church. Certainly, we know the activity rate for those who are single in the church is far less than it is for those who are married and the older an individual becomes while remaining single, the lower their activity rate becomes.

How can this be for a church that has such a high degree of activity everywhere else? The church is facing the perfect storm of issues where the rising generations in society are less willing to accept organized religion and where marital and other family values are shifting. When combined with the dissonance of being single in a family-centric organization, it creates an environment where we rely more on what we self-determine to be spirituality while becoming less inclined to practice our faith through the organization, programs, and policies of the church. This leads to more subjectivity in how faith manifests itself in the lives of single adults, leading to decreased activity and participation in the church. The hard reality we all must face is, improvement must and should be made in all facets and fronts of the uphill battle for the souls of single adults in the church.

As a natural resource attorney, I am often amazed at the comparisons mining companies will make when describing their operations to the public: *We have the largest equipment, the greatest output, the biggest mineral reserves.* Often the recitation of these facts is rhetorically powerful and tells an important public story, but it overshadows what people really want to know: What, if any, are the impacts of the operation? What safety protocols are in place? Is there sufficient regulation and supervision to prevent harm or accident to individuals, the environment, and communities?

Sometimes I think members of the church, like these mining companies, become enamored with large generalized organizational statistics, like the size and growth rate of membership of the church, the number of missions and missionaries around the world, and the number and location of temples. I love these statistics as well, yet I often wonder whether the meaning of these statistics tell the world and ourselves how big we are, without considering the lived reality of church members or portraying on-the-ground issues and concerns to individuals and groups like single adults.

Do we assume that all is well in Zion, because the larger story surpasses a significant and real problem? Do we sail under different colors hoping everything is fine and that no one will notice? Do we postpone needed or preventative maintenance and allow disrepair because we tell ourselves one thing that is true but miss the mark on the reality of something else? My biggest concern is that single adults in the church are not just losing in the realm of participation and activity in the church but, in line with current societal trends, are at statistical risk of moving from being affiliated with the church and organized religion to un-affiliation with organized religion altogether. I truly hope not.

What is it that single adults and the church must do to appropriately recognize and address these trends? This is a hard question because there are no one-size-fits-all or one-stop-shop solutions, and neither is there a secret ingredient or hidden recipe to achieve success. There are few new strategies or policies and even fewer easy explanations. It comes down to how the church relates to single adults, how much opportunity is given to us to develop connections and attachments, and how single adults are treated and viewed within the context of the gospel.

It is not about treating single adults as if they were the youth or viewing them through the perspective of those who are married and who have families. It is about the church creating, generally, conditions that allow for the nuances and perspectives of being single while empowering local leaders to apply those things in a fair and consistent manner that creates the best opportunity for success. It is about using common, practical solutions that take into consideration the needs of those locally, recognizing blanket approaches may seem good on paper but when applied to individual communities may have a watered-down efficiency that has little or no effect. On the flip side, improvement requires single adults to become more open and vulnerable in their lives, recognizing and developing healthy relationships irrespective of whether they lead to marriage, and finding positive reasons to belong to the church and a normal and good balance between the routine of our lives and our activity and service within the church.

Great challenges often provide great opportunities. I mention these statistics not to deter, to cause dismay, or to give a negative outlook on an issue that is not easily discussed or resolved. What I am here to say is the opportunity for single adults to be one not only with the church but also with themselves and with God is something worth considering and discussing. Unity is a theme for all members of the church. It resonates with us and it's a goal for which we strive; yet how do we unify ourselves, our thoughts, our perspectives when there is so much difference and diversity in these areas in the world and in the church?

The opportunity for each of to become one begins with all of us collectively and individually trying to understand each other in compassionate and loving ways. It is less about trying to give ourselves quick and standardized answers, but rather it's about listening to what others are struggling with and recognizing where the weaknesses are, both individually and institutionally. It is about adapting to the needs of single adults and learning sufficient personal and relational skills so we may receive each other as saints of God and respect each other as individuals.

BEING ONE WITH THE CHURCH

Have you ever asked yourself why you are or continue to be a member of the church? Have you ever considered what it is the church as an institution provides to you and to your well-being? Paul recognized that if we are saved by and through our faith, by who we are and what we become, some might argue there was no need for the church as an institution. In other words, some would contend, spirituality itself is the means to achieve salvation, thus replacing or at least minimizing the need or requirement for a church as an organization. Considering the statistics and trending views of spirituality and religious affiliation discussed above, we see at least a form of Paul's concern growing and manifesting itself today.

Based upon this concern, Paul asked and answered the following question:

> What advantage then hath the Jew? or *what profit is there* of circumcision? *Much every way*: chiefly, because that unto them were committed *the oracles of God*.[11]

Let me restate Paul's question in terms of single adults: What advantage or benefit do single adults have in being a member of the church? What gain or increase do they acquire through making and keeping gospel covenants (i.e. participation in the church)? Perhaps Paul's question is at the core of many of the struggles for single adults. The utility of faith, spirituality, and organized religion in our lives is a question of individualism versus collectivism. It is a question of whether the benefits both individually and collectively are sufficient to counteract the respective burdens of membership in the church.

Paul's answer is significant because it puts into perspective what the church is and what it represents. He stated that being a member of the church, making and keeping covenants, is of benefit primarily because to the church is given the oracles of God, or better said, God's prophets. These prophets hold the keys (the authority and power) to administer the priesthood today. In other words, the priesthood provides the primary benefit, which is the organization and medium by which we apply our faith. Thus, the church as an institution or as an organization is tremendously important to our individual salvation because it drives and facilitates our ability to worship in authorized and meaningful ways. It's like a Christmas tree, providing a structure and a base upon which we may hang the moments of our lives, and without which there is no decoration, no beauty, and no celebration.

Paul reminds us the church and its stakes, wards, and branches provide access to and authorized use of these essential priesthood keys. He taught the Ephesians that the church is "built upon a foundation of the apostles and prophets, with Jesus Christ himself being the chief corner stone."[12] The sole purpose of these individuals—for the priesthood keys these individuals hold—is, as Paul also taught, "to gather together in *one* all things in Christ, both which are in heaven, and which are on earth."[13]

Thus, the purpose of the priesthood is to unify us and make all of us one with the Savior. These priesthood keys bless our lives in ways unseen but are most certainly meaningful and felt. They are necessary to unlock revelation, heavenly gifts, and blessings, as well as to administer the saving ordinances that will justify our souls in the eternities. These keys also allow us opportunities to grow spiritually and to improve. They provide structure for us to exercise our faith and to strive to be better. They facilitate our ability, like the people in the city of Enoch, to receive the greatest blessing God has to offer, eternal life.[14]

These keys give us real power to strengthen and solidify the kingdom of God on Earth, without which we would be subject to the whims and wiles of the adversary here in mortality. Without the priesthood, efforts to improve our station would be received just as Uzzah's in ancient times who, with neither right nor authority, stretched forth his hand to steady the ark and was cursed by God.[15] The true purpose of the priesthood is to bless each of our lives. It magnifies each of our individual efforts, irrespective of their size and scope, making all one and incorporating us into a much greater whole.

Having said that, the church must recognize that difficulties and insensitivities, while unintentional, may arise within the culture of the church that affect how the priesthood is applied to single adults and how we receive it. When discussing the culture of the church, it is important to realize single adults may view ourselves as more independent or individualistic than those who are married. In other words, we are likely to have a more pronounced and sovereign view of ourselves, our identity, our roles and circumstances, and how we interrelate with the church. Often, we may view ourselves as part of, but separate from, the body of the church; define ourselves more through self-determined character traits; and make important decisions with more autonomy from the construct of the church's programs and organization.

On the other hand, married individuals in the church may view themselves from a more collective or group perspective. They may see themselves as connected to the body of the church, defining themselves through the organization and programs of the church as well as the family and other interpersonal relationships they have and develop with those around them.[16]

I have often thought this difference in viewpoint is in part why the church and its members wrestle to understand why single adults may not completely or immediately accept church programs and policies. Sometimes in the church, the group perspective takes precedence without thought or consideration of the individual. Married individuals tend to see church programs and policies through the perspective of the whole as opposed to the individual.

Have you ever asked yourself why married members will ask single adults why they aren't married or ask newlyweds when they will start having kids? It has little to do with the answer to the actual question and more to do with what the answer reveals about how quickly we will become part of the mainstream of the group. Many of the insensitivities or misunderstandings that occur within the culture of the church are a matter of the viewpoint (whether collective or individual) through which facts, circumstances, and events are perceived and experienced. This is also true of the ways local priesthood leaders advise, interact with, and apply the priesthood to single adults. Understanding these differences will go a long way in bridging the divide with us.

Please understand that having either an individual or collective perspective is not more important or better than the other; they are simply different. Consider Mark's account of the Savior as He was teaching in a crowded house in Capernaum. When a group of individuals wanted to bring a man afflicted with the palsy to the Savior, they were prevented by the number and size of the crowd in the house. Exercising faith and some ingenuity, they removed the roof of the house and lowered the sick man to the Savior. When the Savior saw their faith, He told the sick man his sins were forgiven. The many people in the house were shocked and offended at what the Savior said, saying only God could forgive sins and the Savior was blaspheming. The Savior responded to the entire group by asking whether it was easier to say, "Thy sins be forgiven," or to say, "Arise, take up thy bed, and walk?" After which the Savior healed the man, and all were amazed and glorified God.[17]

This account is illustrative of the Savior's ability to simultaneously love and teach people with differing needs and perspectives, whether as individuals or as a group. In this case, the Savior focused first on the individual and told him his sins were forgiven. I have often wondered why the Savior made this statement rather than directly heal him. Was it that the Savior knew the thoughts, perspectives, and lack of faith of those in attendance and wanted to teach them a gospel principle? Perhaps the afflicted man thought his disease was a result of sin itself; the Savior recognizing this concern provided him the means to heal not only spiritually but also physically.

Whatever the reason, the Savior taught, healed, and testified to all in attendance in such a fashion that all recognized and glorified God. Is this not a lesson for understanding the individual and collective perspectives when dealing with single adults? Is it not possible for the church, its leadership, its membership, and single adults to concurrently address and validate both perspectives so all are edified and blessed from the Savior's love? I truly believe it is.

Single adults must also remember the church as an organization is not a perfect institution—it's an evolving one. God is unchanging, unceasing, and ever-present in all we do and all we are. He instituted immutable doctrines of salvation regarding the creation, the fall, the atonement, and the resurrection. Yet, given the unchanging nature of these doctrines, does this mean their application in our lives and in the daily practice of the gospel through the programs of the church will always stay the same? Absolutely not.

It is within God's discretion to tailor and to apply the unchanging doctrines of the salvation in a manner suited to the changing and developing challenges and trials we face today. I have observed, sometimes, that when revelation or inspiration occurs and changes are implemented to our practice of religion, some dispute the veracity of the revelation or the character of those who are rightfully charged to receive and implement it. By doing so, they may not enjoy the benefits of recognizing or following that revelation and slowly lose faith in God.

Members of the church, married and single, should not marvel or wonder why change occurs in the church or in the application of its doctrine in our lives. There is no malfeasance in the church's intent as it adapts and changes to new environments and new circumstances, especially when new liabilities and new societal issues arise. The church itself and its programs, policies, and practices must change to adapt to a society that is itself full of change. It is not about whether the church changes but when and how much it will change. True, we all get used to doing things in a particular way, relying on routine to give us comfort and security, but whether the church and its programs, policies, and practices are the same today as they were yesterday is less important than the exercise of our faith and the hope, charity, and service we develop and give.

There are many examples of changes in the daily practice of the gospel that are recorded in the scriptures. For example, the institution of the ordinance of circumcision with Abraham, the coming forth and establishment of the Law of Moses and its fulfillment centuries later, the institution of the sacrament at the Last Supper, the preaching of the gospel to the gentiles, and the eventual discontinuance of the ordinance of circumcision after the Savior's resurrection. Think about the importance and impact these practices had on the individuals who lived during that time. How would you feel if you had been circumcised and then years later you were told it was no longer required for membership in the church? Would you become angry, embittered by your hold on past practices, or would you embrace and rejoice in the revelation of God's commandments?

Today, changes in the gospel happen every day. A few examples include the establishment of the Relief Society, implementation of the Word of Wisdom, the bestowal of the priesthood to all worthy men in the church, the method of sending missionaries out into the world, the basis for gospel teaching, how we worship in the temple, how the priesthood is organized, the retiring of the programs for home and visiting teaching, and the restructuring of church worship services. These things are all based upon the inspirations given by God to His prophets to bless the lives of His children and to strengthen their faith in the Savior as they walk in difficult and changing circumstances. These changes in no way alter the underlying doctrines of salvation.

How grateful I am for a God who is living and breathing and who communicates with us so that we may know how to grow and progress. Because our goal is to become like Him, we should always keep in mind that it is not God who must change; rather, it is us. We must change in accordance with His purposes and His plans.

Does that mean there is no room for flexibility or improvement? Does that mean we should thoughtlessly accept everything that church leaders say and what the church provides? Heavens no! It's important for each single adult to take that which is offered to them from the church and its leaders and to apply individually that which is good and beneficial to them. Space must also be given so those who struggle with change can safely and with transparency experience it in their own manner and fashion. Hopefully, single adults look forward to additional and continued institutional changes in the church pertaining to how it relates to single adults, the hope being that such changes will make easier the connections, interactions, and activity among all who are involved.

Consider what Ezekiel taught about the latter days:

> And say unto them, Thus saith the Lord God; Behold, I will take the children of Israel from among the heathen, whither they be gone, *and will gather them on every side*, and bring them into their own land:
>
> And *I will make them one nation* in the land upon the mountains of Israel; and *one king* shall be king to them all: and *they shall be no more two nations*, neither shall they *be divided into two kingdoms any more at all*.[18]

After the scattering of Israel in ancient times, God promised and covenanted to gather once again His people in the latter days. This gathering is happening today by and through the priesthood and the spreading of the gospel. As the pure in heart are sought and brought to the knowledge of the gospel, they are gathered from the clutches of the adversary and placed under the protective canopy of the gospel. We are, in a very real sense, one people, with the Savior as our head. This gathering is not just for people who are outside the church; rather, it is for all of us. As both single adults and those who are married within the church learn to better understand each other and grow together, we will no longer be two differing nations. We will be united and made one in the great circle and whole the gospel provides.

For me, being a part of and becoming one with the church as a single adult is a constant, continuous, and personal choice I make each day. I choose to be associated with others who have similar desires and beliefs. I choose to find a healthy balance between the realities of my life and applying the gospel in advantageous, positive ways, even if others in the church do not understand the intent and motivations behind my actions. I also chose to accept the weaknesses of those in the church, in the organizational programs and practices of the church, and in the individual application of the gospel. Not because I blindly exercise faith, but because I recognize their opportunity to grow as well. By so doing, I am able find greater purpose and meaning in my life, connection with God, and peace with my soul.

BEING ONE WITH GOD

On July 21, 2015, in Becker, Minnesota, a seventeen-year-old young woman failed to stop at a red light while driving, causing a vehicular accident that killed a father and his ten-year-old daughter. These events forever altered and tragically changed this young woman's life, the lives of those involved, and the lives of their families. The cause of this accident was that the young woman was using her cell phone while driving and did not see or appropriately respond to the conditions and circumstances on the road. Passengers reported repeatedly asking this young woman not to use her cell phone prior to the accident. Evidence later established that this young woman was posting to Facebook seconds prior to the accident.[19]

Distracted driving is a difficult and frequent problem today that represents a substantial public health and safety threat with serious implications on how we drive and utilize technology today. In 2015, distracted driving in the United States claimed the lives of 3,526 people and it was the causal factor in over 391,000 vehicular injuries.[20] According to the National Safety Council, vision is the single most important ability required for the safe operation of a motor vehicle. Drivers who use cellular phones while driving fail to see up to fifty percent (50%) of the information required to safely navigate their surrounding environment. It is an intriguing but sad phenomenon; those who use cellular telephones while driving may "look at" but not "see" objects and circumstances.[21] In a very real sense, we are looking past our primary objective, blinded from our most important and fundamental task by our current use or reliance on external and less important things.

This phenomenon is a perfect example of a common and everyday occurrence where people are actively engaged in a task but not connected to what they are doing. It is a situation where we are present physically but not mentally, where we look at but do not see or comprehend events and circumstances that are necessary for our safety and that of those around us. Ask ourselves the following: *What do we see and what is our vision? What distracts us from seeing events and circumstances around us? In what manner or scope do we connect our thoughts to the actions and intents we undertake?*

Many of the relationship problems and issues discussed in this book relate to the manner and depth we connect with ourselves and with each other. What I worry most about is the level and degree to which we engage in these relationships: Are these relationships built on a high degree of connectivity, or are they defined by low activity and low attention? The answer to these questions provides a general guide or roadmap for the success or failure of those relationships.

When it comes to a relationship with God, I think the same analysis should be considered. In other words, as we in society become more spiritual and less religious, we may be more inclined to carelessly drive through the intersections of our lives without the proper spiritual perspective, without the correct understanding or a complete set of facts upon which to make important and timely decisions. We are in a very real sense distracted living, becoming more casual or superficial with our connections to God impacting or impairing our ability to become one with Him and His purposes.

At the Last Supper, directly prior to the events comprising the Savior's atonement, the Savior offered what is known as the Great Intercessory Prayer. That prayer is one of the most meaningful in all scripture, as the Savior not only prayed about His relationship with God the Father but also pleaded that each of us would gain eternal life and have the same opportunity, like Him, to be one with God the Father.

> Neither pray I for these alone, but *for them also which shall believe on me* through their word;
>
> *That they all may be one*; as thou, Father, art in me, and I in thee, *that they also may be one in us*: that the world may believe that thou hast sent me.
>
> And the glory which thou gavest me I have given them; *that they may be one, even as we are one*: I in them, and thou in me, *that they may be made perfect in one.*[22]

Why is it important for us to have the opportunity to be one with God? And, if it is so important, what is it we need to understand to accomplish it? Personally, I like to believe that becoming one with God is about three things: believing and exercising hope and faith in the existence of God, understanding the nature of God, and understanding God's plan for us.

Consider the intense and powerful doctrinal debate between Amulek and Zeezrom found in the Book of Mormon.[23] Zeezrom, a skillful and adept lawyer, stood forward to publicly challenge Alma and Amulek as they attempted to teach the gospel to the people of Ammoniha, a people who had rejected not only the gospel but also their allegiance to the Nephites.

Amulek's public defense of Zeezrom's belligerent and vituperate attempts to impugn the gospel of Christ is insightful and applicable for us in our daily lives because it exposes the depths to which the adversary will go and the shrewd strategy he will utilize to mislead each of us. It also provides us with the insight and knowledge necessary to recognize and overcome the primary obstacles and challenges that affect our faith and our capacity to develop a relationship with and become one with God. Zeezrom's folly originates in his unsuccessful attempts to legitimize the city's physical succession from the Nephites and to justify its citizenry's spiritual apostasy from God.

Zeezrom first began his attack by offering Amulek a large sum of money if Amulek would deny the existence of a Supreme Being.[24] This attempt was a direct assault on the actual and literal existence of God. Perhaps the easiest way for the adversary to ensnare the souls of men is to blind their hopes and faith and discount their belief in the existence of God or a higher power. When we believe there is no God, we are left to our own genius, strength, and devices for our survival. Without God, we are justified in seeking solely after that which is most self-centric or that which is most pleasing, because there is no final judgment or concluding sentence to be passed.

As Lehi taught:

> And if ye shall say *there is no law ye shall also say there is no sin*. If ye shall say there is no sin, ye shall also say there is no righteousness. And if there be no righteousness there be no happiness. And if there be no happiness there be no punishment nor misery.
>
> *And if these things are not there is no God*. And *if there is no God we are not*, neither the earth for there could have been no

creation of things neither to act nor to be acted upon; wherefore all things must have vanished away.[25]

How grateful I am to Amulek for his righteousness in refusing Zeezrom's offer of payment to deny that which Amulek knew was true; how grateful I am for Amulek's humble and steadfast testimony that God truly did exist and that He watched over us in our daily lives. By awakening our senses and faculties to the existence of God, we realize there is a greater purpose to life and we begin to reach heavenward and thus strive to be better and to do better. Our own recognition of His existence is the first step for us to become one with Him.

After failing to discourage Amulek on the existence of God, Zeezrom utilized a two-pronged legal attack to both confuse and conflate the nature of God with the plan of God. Zeezrom next challenged Amulek on whether there was more than one God. Amulek answered that there was not. Zeezrom followed up by asking whether the son of God would come to save everyone? Amulek simply answered yes.[26]

Zeezrom's question to Amulek about whether there was more than one God was a perversion of the truth. It was a direct attempt to twist Amulek's first answer about there being only one God with his second answer that God would send his son to save us. According to Zeezrom, how could there be only one God, if God was to send his son to earth. To some members of the church, Amulek's answer that there is only one God may seem odd, as we believe the Godhead is comprised of three separate and distinct individuals, the Father, the Son, and the Holy Ghost.

Amulek's answer, however, demonstrates he had an intimate and personal knowledge about the nature God. Amulek did not say Heavenly Father, the Son, and the Holy Ghost were the same entity; rather, he said they were one in purpose, one in thought, one in power, and one in glory. The Savior said it best himself when He prayed to God the Father, "We are one."

If you step back and think about it, the universe and our existence could not operate with any meaning or regularity if the members of the Godhead had separate and differing agendas or views on what should occur and how salvation should come to pass. Today, many of us are caught in the same intricate web of confusion spun by Zeezrom's question. When we do not understand the nature or character of the Godhead, when we do not understand who they are, we cannot fully comprehend the fundamental and basic truths of the atonement. We can therefore never come to fully comprehend our own nature or the eternal worth of our immortal souls. By understanding who God is and in understanding His nature, we can accept Him and become one with Him.

Zeezrom's final attack related to the plan of God when he asked whether God would save His people in their sins. Amulek answered God could not for it was impossible for Him to deny His word. Zeezrom then boldly made his closing summation to the people by stating:

> See that ye remember these things; for he said there is but one God; yet he saith that the Son of God shall come, *but he shall not save his people—as though he had authority to command God.*[27]

Amulek rebutted by teaching:

> And I say unto you again that *he cannot save them in their sins* for I cannot deny his word and he hath said that *no unclean thing can inherit the kingdom of Heaven*; therefore, how can ye be saved except ye inherit the kingdom of heaven; therefore *ye cannot be saved in your sins.*[28]

Zeezrom's inquiry and argument is about whether there are conditions or limitations on salvation. He hubristically assumed all should be saved no matter their choices in life. The notion all will be saved irrespective of our actions is not new—it was debated in Heaven long before the world began. In fact, the war in Heaven was essentially a disagreement on how agency should be applied to God's spirit children. As discussed previously, Satan's plan was based on that ancient boast that not one should be lost and all would return to live with God. Satan's plan deprived all of us of the opportunity and right to choose. It would have forced us into a course of action that inevitably would have made the purpose of mortality irrelevant.

Amulek understood and knew that God not only created our existence but also that He had a purpose and design for it. Long before our time on this world, God gave us life and the ability to choose and direct that life. God's purpose in creating this world was to allow us opportunity and space to exercise that agency to see if we would use it in a manner that is beneficial to us and in harmony with and in the same manner that God uses His. The Savior's purpose was not to save us in the sins we commit but to save us from the spiritual effect and consequences of those sins. He bridged the gap that separates us from eternity; thus, salvation is attained separately by and through the choices we make throughout our time in mortality. Amulek's clear and unambiguous answer to Zeezrom was that entrance into Heaven is not predicated on what one acquires in life but rather on what one does and who one finally becomes.

The interaction between Amulek and Zeezrom is important. It demonstrates to us that through our recognition of God's existence and through our increased understanding of both His nature and His plan for us, we can have a greater understanding and appreciation of ourselves and our relationship with God. Through our application of the gospel in our lives, we are enabled to come closer to God. Even the word "atonement" itself describes and connotes a state of unity with God. It is literally a state of at-*one*-ment with Him. Is there any better way to demonstrate through language the impact, purpose, and effect of what the Savior did for us? How wonderful, how profound, how beautiful is His atonement for us and how benevolent is He to allow us the opportunity to become one with Him.

BEING ONE WITH ONESELF

Once, while sitting on a plane waiting for a flight, I noticed an elderly couple struggling down the aisle with multiple pieces of luggage and several unruly kids in tow. It was apparent this woman loved these kids but she was frustrated with their restlessness and with the intricacies of air travel. Their seat was directly behind mine, and as they attempted to get settled, one of the children obstinately asked why he had to put on his seatbelt. The woman curtly replied, "Because life is cruel and then you die."

I was at first shocked and then amused at the directness of this statement, yet the sentiment this woman expressed has been on my mind for some time. Granted, not everything we encounter in life is intended for our contentment and comfort; however, do the trials and adversities we face or the difficulties and obligations we experience in mortality become so wearisome and so strenuous as to taint or distort our view of what our lives are about?

It's a cliché statement but true: life is not supposed to be easy, it's meant to challenge us so that we can grow and improve. Yet as a single adult, I have often wondered whether life was supposed to be *this* hard and whether its endurance is supposed to be *this* long.

I have been single most of my adult life. I know when I get home from work there will be no one there to greet me. I know when I go to bed tonight and wake in the morning there will be no one there to rely on or with whom to connect. I recognize that at forty-seven, my opportunity to have a family, to be a father, and to have a posterity are waning and less likely. I also understand the chances of that changing anytime soon are small and less than they were previously in my life. So how do I find happiness in my life? How do I get out of bed each day with a positive outlook? And how do I move forward and participate in the church, at work, and elsewhere when incessant, unremitting loneliness surrounds all I do?

To be honest, it is not easy. I find the most important thing in my life is to accept and to be okay with who I am—to find inner peace and to be one with myself. I realize it's okay to be single and it's okay to be alone. Even though I strive to change this condition, I am satisfied I have done all that I can, no matter the result.

I once took a master dance class from a world-famous ballroom dance teacher and choreographer. The lesson focused on how people should connect with each other when dancing. It was about how to hold your frame, how to move, and how to find balance and stability with your partner, in the dance steps you take together. Said he, "Before you connect, you must get over yourself and find balance."

Of course, he was talking about dance technique on how we hold our shoulders, arms, and head in a dance position and about finding balance on the appropriate leg so the proper movement and support could occur. Still, his lesson resonated with me in that for us to connect with our environment, with those around us, with God, with our families, and with those we love, we must first *get over ourselves* and second *find a strong balance in our lives*. I suppose if there is any advice I would give to single adults who struggle, who are alone, who wish for better days and better circumstances, I would say finding balance with yourself is the means to finding happiness, joy, and contentment, no matter where you are or where you are going.

Being one with yourself, as a single adult, is about letting go of expectations and outcomes not only for yourself, but also for others, for God, and for the church. Part of my experience in trying to be one with myself developed out of a desire to escape emotional pain. Many of my personal disappointments and failures came because of unrealistic self-expectations that did not meet or conform with the reality of the circumstances I faced. I had to learn to love myself as God loves me. To find harmony and resonance with my emotions. To find individual reasons to be patient with those around me and with God. To learn to let go of difficult things and be okay with that. To no longer put on a fake smile so everyone around me thought I was good.

I tried, and if I failed, it was okay and I would pick myself up and try again. I gave acceptance rather than judgment and tried to be inclusive, not exclusive, of those around me. Was I perfect? Absolutely not, but I improved each time I tried and I grew with each step I took. I began to realize my destination was less important in the near term than the direction I chose to take. I learned self-improvement is a never-ending journey, a noble and necessary endeavor I had to learn to embrace, to love, and for which to look forward. I also had to get busy and get going.

Additionally, I had to learn how to optimize resources, whether financial, emotional, or otherwise. I learned to use what I had to fit the need and the circumstance, especially when it came to my personal time and the church. I don't mean that in a negative way—I found myself burning out on life because everyone kept telling me to give more, do more, and to lose myself.

It was as if hyper-activity and hyper-spirituality were medications that were over-prescribed and did not have the intended outcome or effect in my life. I found this type of high-end engagement to not be the answer. I needed to create and maintain enough slack in my life to deal with times of high stress and difficulty. I realized that if I am always acting at capacity, there is no room for the bumps in my life.

Under constant pressure to perform, I was like a driver who speeds to the next stop light only to wait anxiously and impatiently for the light to turn green before racing to the next one. What I needed to learn was that the lights are timed and sequenced, and lowering the speed to match the circumstances was the fastest and most efficient route to get where I wanted to go. I found my life was not a switch that could be turned on and off at a moment's notice, but something I engaged in, something I treasured, and something with which I connected. By doing so, I found out who I really am and what I can really give.

Matthew states as follows:

> Now when Jesus was born in Bethlehem of Judea in the days of Herod the King behold there came wise men from the East to Jerusalem saying where is he that is born King of the Jews for we have seen his star in the east and are come to worship him.[29]

Many lessons are taught and emphasized from the Savior's birth. The journey the wise men made and the gifts they bestowed upon Mary, Joseph, and the Savior have great meaning. While many scholars speculate about these wise men, we do not know their names, how many they were, or from where they came.

Because Matthew later states they came into Mary and Joseph's house and not a stable, and because they found a young child with Mary, many people believe their arrival was several years after the night the Savior was born. Irrespective of the timing of their arrival, what I find noteworthy is that the wise men came seeking God. Perhaps the greatest gift the wise men gave was not the treasures they bestowed, but the sacrifice they made and the time and effort they spent to find and come to God and kneel before Him. Their humble and anonymous journey to find themselves and to find God was conducted without fanfare and without praise, but stands as a shining example for each of us in our lives.

As single adults, we all have a journey to make in this life to find ourselves and to find God. The voyage we all face is not necessarily as far a distance as the wise men traveled, but to come closer to Him through our acceptance of Him and our incorporation of His teachings in our lives. The Savior asks us not to give gifts of gold, frankincense, and myrrh; rather, the treasure He requires of us is a broken heart and a contrite spirit—it is to become one with Him, one with ourselves, and one with each other.

Whether single or married, the gospel binds us together in love and friendship in ways the world will never understand or comprehend. We are each part of a much greater whole without which we would be led to the most terrible loneliness and discouraging despair.

11

The Way Forward: Understanding and Relating to Single Adults

> Therefore, with joy shall ye draw water
> out of the wells of salvation.
> —Isaiah 12:3

I am often entertained when I see articles and videos the church and others release that discuss what should and should not be said to single adults. I chuckle because to me these are akin to the annual continuing legal education credits I am required to attend to maintain my law license. They are like mandatory or necessary sensitivity trainings for the church and its members to better understand the viewpoints and concerns of single adults.

Despite my amusement, I do think these have their place and they are beneficial. They help to educate and inform others regarding the nuances and subtlety of being single in the church. Understanding and relating with single adults is not difficult, but it does require awareness and acumen not found in typical relationships with married members of the church. The Savior's exchange with the woman at the well gives us an important model for how to relate with and talk to single adults, for remember, the woman at the well was herself a single adult. Understanding what the Savior did, why He did it, how He related with this woman, and how He connected with her will help all of us to improve our interactions and increase the quality of our relationships with single adults.

When the Savior departed Judea to travel to Galilee, He passed through Samaria, where He chose to stop and rest at Jacob's well. After sending His disciples into town to procure food, a Samaritan woman approached the well to draw water. The Savior engaged the woman, asking her to give Him something to drink.

Surprised, and somewhat taken aback, the woman asked why a Jew would interact with someone, especially a woman, who was a Samaritan. The Savior replied that if she had known God and He who asked for the water, that she would have asked Him for, and He would have provided her with, living water. Suspiciously, she responded that He had nothing with which to draw water and inquired further how He would even provide such water as the well was very deep.

With some contempt and skepticism, she further stated that Jacob, the patriarch of Israel, had given this well to them and asked whether He was greater than him. The Savior responded that whosoever drank of the water from this well would thirst again but whomever drank of the water He would provide would never again thirst. The result of this benefit would spring forth in their lives, blessing them with eternal life. The woman then sarcastically asked the Savior to give her of this water so she would not thirst and not have to return to the well in the future.

The Savior responded to this request by first asking her to go and bring her husband. She answered that she did not have a husband. The Savior acknowledged this and then followed up by stating she had five previous husbands and the individual who she was currently with was not her husband. Surprised by the Savior's intimate knowledge and understanding of her, the woman began to exercise some faith, recognizing and stating He was a prophet. She then asked an honest and genuine question about the conduct and polices of the church as it pertained to the Samaritans, stating their forefathers worshipped God in these mountains but the Jews believed Jerusalem was the correct place for all men to worship God. In other words, the Samaritans did not have room or place in the Jewish faith and they were ostracized, expatriated, and excluded by and through its practice.

The Savior responded by not disagreeing with this assessment but by teaching that in the future, all men would worship God without physical or geographical constraints. He taught her further that God was spiritual and those who worshipped Him must do so through the Spirit. The woman then spoke about her belief and understanding that a Messiah would come, to which the Savoir affirmatively responded He was in fact Him. The woman then left her pots and returned into town, telling the townspeople and bringing many to the Savior. Sadly, prior to her returning to town, but after her exchange with the Savior, the Savior's disciples returned and were surprised, upset, and dismayed that the Savior was speaking with this woman.[1]

What does this experience mean as it pertains to single adults? Again, it is a reminder to consider thoughtfully how we communicate with and receive single adults in the church. Do we, like the Jews toward the Samaritans, look down on single adults or judge them for who they are? Do we, like the Savior's disciples, judge them against the standards we think they should be following? Do we consider them less for failing in prior relationships or for the lack of or type of relationships they currently have? The Savior's acceptance and treatment of this woman is illustrative and important in helping all to receive each other, to develop greater understanding and testimonies in the gospel, and to provide a means whereby all may come to Him.

Here we have a good woman who was going about the humdrum and routine of her life. She had multiple failed relationships, and she was at that time either not wanting or not able to pursue an additional marriage relationship. I have often asked myself how these failed relationships impacted, influenced, or affected her personal outlook. Was she angry, sad, or bitter? We do not know. We do know, at their meeting, she was at first defensive and suspicious of the Savior based on the fact He was Jewish. At least in part, her defensiveness was related to the tenuous and strained relationship between the Jews and Samaritans. In fact, the Jews often avoided the road through Samaria because they did not wish to interact with the Samaritans.

I like to believe that the Savior's choice to travel that road and the meeting with this woman at Jacob's Well was not a chance encounter; rather, He planned and intentionally chose that route to meet with her and to show her love. To further this point, the Savior sent His disciples away prior to their meeting, knowing His disciples' negative prejudices and attitudes toward the Samaritans. This demonstrated that He wanted to create a safe environment, free from judgment and personal bias, and to provide an opportunity for Him to lower the emotional defenses and to remove the hurt this woman had, so she could receive Him in her life. These actions also show the nature and love of God who stretches out and reaches for us in our lives, who puts aside what is normally thought acceptable for purposes of connecting and helping those who are single. He meets us where we are and helps us individually, based on our needs and not based upon a standardized or an institutional expectation.

I love the fact that the Savior started His discussion with this woman based upon the reason and task she was undertaking, namely to collect and draw water. I am sure this woman came every day to the well and carried that water back for those she loved and for whom she cared. I wonder how much work, toil, and effort this must have been for her. What did she think about as she slowly walked to and from the well? Did she carry the burden of more than just the weight of the water she collected? By asking for water, the Savior showed interest in what was important to her and in what she was undertaking in that moment. His discussion and comparison of the gospel and His atonement to living water show connection and engagement with her at an appropriate and personal level. He also initiated and facilitated her willingness to talk and engage with Him, even if such engagement from her was at first snarky and smarmy.

The Savior did not stop teaching or loving this woman after providing the high-level doctrinal points of the gospel and its effects on our spiritual development; rather, He quickly moved to validate her as a person and as a human being. He did this by discussing her relational status, something that must have been sensitive and personal to her.

I have often thought about why the Savior brought up this topic at that time and in that context. I believe He did this not to prove to her who *He was,* but to demonstrate His acceptance of her and validation of who *she was.* What I enjoy most about the Savior's question is there was no judgment, no condemnation of this woman's relational status nor counsel to change; He offered only acceptance, validation, and understanding of her.

His discussion and recitation of her relational status was to provide safety for her feelings and to demonstrate a personal understanding and deep empathy with her. The result of this was to lower and to remove her emotional walls and defenses so she would accept the important testimony the Savior would later provide. In other words, His discussion of her relational situation wasn't about her situation at all; it was an opportunity to show empathy and compassion. Many times, people will not listen to what you say, or care about what you know, unless they first understand that you accept them and validate their thoughts, positions, and concerns. Knowing this, the Savior provided a safe space for this woman to express her concerns and to be open to learning more from Him.

Put yourself in the position of this woman in today's church. If you were a single adult, how would you react or feel if you had legitimate concerns about the church, had difficulty fitting in, and felt ostracized from the body of the church, and the topic your priesthood leader wanted to discuss related to your relationship status? I am certain it would not be a good feeling for you, and it may set the stage for a negative reaction when a positive one was intended. The topic of relationships and an individual's ability to have them within the framework of the church can be complex and difficult as there are intense feelings and emotions beneath the surface.

The Savior was not bringing this topic up to condemn, to judge, to offer counsel about, or to fix the woman's situation; it was solely to demonstrate empathy, love, and a personal understanding of her and her situation. Talking to singles about their relationship status can be a positive, wonderful, and uplifting event, but if done in the wrong context and for the wrong reason—if judgment, condemnation, expectations, or motivations beyond the welfare and circumstances of the individual are involved—such conversations may have unintended and adverse impacts on the connections between that individual, the church, its leaders, and its membership.

I am not saying such conversations should never occur; however, do we, like the Savior, offer similar opportunity to single adults, in a safe and non-confrontational manner, to express our concerns and to be heard without judgment? Single adults need opportunity both in and out of the church to talk and openly discuss their individual relational situation. Whenever these occur, we should view them as sacred and treat them in the same manner and for the same purpose the Savior did, which was to better understand and to improve our connections and our spirituality.

The next set of questions the Savior addressed were at the heart of this woman's issues and concerns with the church. She knew that as a Samaritan she would have limited or no access to the church. She wrestled with the fairness and inequality this segregation created based solely upon differences in the practice of a common religious heritage. Like many single adults, she felt like she was on the outside looking in. How was she to worship God (to belong and be a part of His kingdom) if this condition existed and persisted?

I think the Savior understood and agreed with this position, for He did not dispute the question nor did He offer any explanation. What He did do was offer her a viewpoint that, irrespective of the current policies and programs of the church at that time, in the future all would have opportunity and all would have benefit from the church. What He gave her was not an answer to her specific question but a response that filled her with hope, optimism, and a sense of belonging and identity.

The most tender and important part of this exchange was when she inquired about the Messiah providing the Savior with the opportunity to bear

His testimony to her of who He was and what was His purpose for her and for everyone. Because of this, she was enabled to lift her thoughts, increase her understanding, and change her perspectives; in short, she gained a testimony. After this, those things that burdened and weighed her down no longer mattered. She left behind the pots—the troubles and the worries of her life as a single adult—and became the instrument that brought many others to the Savior. How beautiful, how remarkable, how important this was for her and is for us.

I often think we misunderstand the lesson and purpose of the Savior's experience with the woman at the well. We look solely at the beauty of the doctrine taught about the wellspring of eternal life and the miraculous insight and explanation of the woman's life, yet miss that the purpose of this exchange was not to provide a high-level doctrinal comparison for scholars to debate and pontificate. It was a step-by-step process the Savior utilized to help, motivate, and encourage a single woman to reach past her traumas, to lower her internal walls, to answer her questions, and to love her enough so that she could recognize the Savior and come to Him. That is the true meaning of this experience, and when it is applied to single adults in the same manner, it will bless the lives of everyone, both married and single, within the church. It will also be the means whereby many are brought back into the gospel, where they may leave behind their individual troubles and find peace in their lives.

I know the Savior lives and He did come and atone for our sins so we may find joy in this life and in the next. He is the center of our hopes and aspirations, and the true author of our salvation. He is in the fine points of our lives, in our families, in our friendships, and in our relationships. He is in the wind and in our trials. He is in the Heavens and the firmament. His love lightens the sun, the moon, and the stars and fills the immensity and loneliness of space. His light and love have the capacity to fill our souls with hope and to make us happy. He loves us entirely for who we are today, yet at the same time encourages us to grow and improve. Our recognition and understanding of that is the greatest worth we have as individuals and as single adults in the church.

As single adults, may we all be a little kinder to ourselves and to each other. May we be more patient, trusting, and forgiving. May we continuously strive to find ourselves. May we all have the peace of mind and peace of heart that is found through the efforts we make to love ourselves and those around us. May we increase our devotion to each other, may we lighten burdens, and may we extend love and understanding no matter the circumstance. May we develop hope in our lives in meaningful ways that allow us all, single and married, the opportunity to come to the Savior. May we all realize just a little more that we are each okay, we have worth far beyond what we may see or feel, and we have the means to find joy both today and in the future.

End Note

I originally titled this book *I'm Single, I'm Mormon, and I'm OK*. Just days before this book's completion, the Church of Jesus Christ of Latter-day Saints issued a styling convention requesting the word *Mormon* not be used. After many years of thinking, writing, and trying to define the issues in this book, the church's policy created a crisis of conscience for me. It came down to the fact I couldn't simply name the book *I'm Single, I'm a Member of the Church of Jesus Christ of Latter-day Saints, and I'm OK*. It didn't sound right, and it didn't even fit well on the cover. In some respects, this experience has given me a better appreciation for those who had to (and why they chose to) abbreviate the brother of Jared's name in the Book of Mormon.

I love this book's original title. It's fun, succinct, and descriptive of what I am trying to articulate to single and married people in the church. After so much time and effort, and a lack of notice on the nomenclature, I wrestled with the decision to change the book's title at the precipice of its publication. I changed it because I didn't want the first thought of those who read this book to be negative or for readers to think I am contravening what the church is asking. I also changed the wording of the chapters within this book to comply with the church's policy; however, not everything could be changed. If concerns arise regarding this book and the naming conventions of the church, I hope they will not be a distraction to the messages contained herein.

I do believe both titles convey a strong message of hope to single adults in the church. This book is about a journey to adapt, to find solace and joy in places that are sometimes awkward or don't always fit as nicely as we would hope. Perhaps this change is in a small way representative of the adjustments we all make to find joy in our lives. The trick is to be okay with those adjustments—irrespective of the impetus for them.

I do hope this book is helpful to you and that it adds to the collective knowledge and understanding of single adults in the church.

Notes

Introduction
1. "Insanity is . . . ," *Quote Investigator*, https://quoteinvestigator.com/2017/03/23/same/.
2. Doctrine and Covenants 28:2–7.

Chapter 1
1. Kathy Grant, "Singles in the Ward Family," *LDS.org*, June 2002, https://www.lds.org/ensign/2002/06/singles-in-the-ward-family?lang=eng.
2. LDS Handbook of Instruction, Section 16.1.
3. Dallin H. Oaks, "Priesthood Authority in the Family and the Church," *LDS.org*, October 2005, https://www.lds.org/general-conference/2005/10/priesthood-authority-in-the-family-and-the-church?lang=eng.
4. Doctrine and Covenants 137:9.
5. LDS Church Handbook, Section 1.3.3.
6. LDS Church Handbook, Section 1.3.3.
7. LDS Church Handbook, Section 1.3.1.
8. Russell M. Nelson, "Salvation and Exaltation," *LDS.org*, May 2008, https://www.lds.org/ensign/2008/05/salvation-and-exaltation?lang=eng.
9. Ephesians 2:19.
10. James E. Faust, "Reaching the One," *LDS.org*, April 1973, https://www.lds.org/general-conference/1973/04/reaching-the-one?lang=eng.
11. Mosiah 12:20–24.
12. Mosiah 15:10.
13. Mosiah 15:10–20.

Chapter 2
1. 1 Nephi 21:16.

Chapter 3
1. Jeanne Phillips, "Dear Abby: Young couple is more compatible when apart," *Times Free Press*, November 28, 2017, https://www.timesfreepress.com/news/life/entertainment/story/2017/nov/28/dear-abby-young-couple-seem-click-better-when/457778/.
2. Kelsey Borresen, "17 Truly Ridiculous Things Couples Have Actually Argued About," *HuffPost*, January 15, 2016, https://www.huffpost.com/entry/truly-ridiculous-things-couples-have-actually-fought-about_n_5699450ce4b0ce4964245e88.
3. Alma 14:8.
4. Alma 14:10.
5. Alma 14:8–13.
6. Alma 15:18.
7. Genesis 2:25; Moses 3:25; Abraham 5:19.
8. Matthew 25:36.
9. Moses 4:13.
10. Moses 4:15; Genesis 3:9.
11. Moses 4:16–19.
12. Mosiah 3:19.
13. Brené Brown, *The Gifts of Imperfection* (Center City, MN: Hazelden Publishing, 2010), 41.
14. Ibid.
15. Alma 36:11.
16. Alma 36:12–13.
17. 1 Nephi 8.
18. Doctrine and Covenants 90:17; Luke 9:26; 1 Peter 4:16; John 2:28.
19. 1 Nephi 8:33.
20. Mosiah: 10:12–17.
21. Genesis 16:2–7.
22. Genesis 16:5.

Chapter 4
1. Joshua 4:1–9.
2. Chuck Hadad, "Dancer returns to stage after losing leg in Boston bombings," *CNN*, April 8, 2014, https://www.cnn.com/2014/04/07/us/boston-bombing-survivor-a-year-later/index.html.
3. John 11:35.
4. Ether 12:27–28.
5. 3 Nephi 12:48.
6. Deuteronomy 24:1–4.
7. 1 Nephi 16:17–32.
8. Genesis 21:10–21.

NOTES

9. Galatians 4:22–31.
10. Deuteronomy 8:2–4.
11. Doctrine and Covenants 24:8.
12. Mosiah 11:6.
13. Mosiah 17:10–12.
14. Numbers 8–13.
15. Matthew 25:14–30.
16. Mormon 6:16–20.
17. Lewis Carroll, *Alice's Adventures in Wonderland*, *Gutenberg.org*, https://www.gutenberg.org/files/11/11-h/11-h.htm.
18. 1 Nephi 17:20–21.
19. Genesis 19:26.
20. 2 Nephi 5:27.
21. Peg Streep, "Why Your Partner May Be Like Your Parent," *Psychology Today*, May 13, 2014, https://www.psychologytoday.com/us/blog/tech-support/201405/why-your-partner-may-be-your-parent.
22. 1 Nephi 8.
23. Joshua 7:3.
24. Joshua 7:5.
25. Joshua 7:7.
26. Joshua 7:10.

Chapter 5

1. Alma 60:33.
2. Ruth 1–4.
3. Ruth 3:10.
4. Ruth 4:6.
5. Mark 14:3–9.
6. See generally Judges 13–16.
7. Judges 14:16.
8. Judges 14:18.
9. Judges 15:3.
10. Judges 14:4.
11. Judges 16:15.
12. Judges 16:28.
13. Mark 8:22–25.
14. See generally Genesis 25–46.
15. Doctrine and Covenants 132:37.
16. Genesis 25:28.
17. Genesis 29:17.
18. Genesis 29:11.
19. Genesis 29:20.
20. Genesis 29:21–30.
21. Genesis 29:31.
22. Genesis 48:7.
23. Genesis 49:30–31.
24. Genesis 31.
25. Genesis 30:1–2.
26. Genesis 30:13–17.
27. Genesis 30:1.
28. Genesis 30:14–15.

Chapter 6

1. "Single and Ready to Mingle," LDS Mid Singles 31–45 (North America) Facebook post, May 17, 2017, https://www.facebook.com/groups/LDSMSANA/.
2. 1 Samuel 8:19–20.
3. 1 Samuel 8:7.
4. 1 Samuel 9:1–2.
5. 1 Samuel 16:5–12.
6. 1 Samuel 16:5–12.
7. Lawrence B. Finer, PhD, "Trends in Premarital Sex," *Public Health Reports*, January–February 2007, Volume 122.
8. Deuteronomy 24:5.
9. See generally 1 and 2 Samuel.
10. 2 Samuel 11:25.
11. 2 Samuel 2:10–12.
12. Robin Saks Frankel, "Ready for romance? A low credit score could mean dating difficulties," *Bankrate*, May 15, 2017, https://www.bankrate.com/personal-finance/credit/money-pulse-0517/.
13. Jamie Ducharme, "This Is the Ideal Amount of Money You Need to Be Happy, According to Research," *TIME*, February 14, 2018, http://time.com/money/5157625/ideal-income-study/.
14. Jessica Dickler, "Credit card debt hits a record high. It's time to make a payoff plan," *CNBC*, January 23, 2018, https://www.cnbc.com/2018/01/23/credit-card-debt-hits-record-high.html.
15. Preston Nibley, *Brigham Young, the Man and His Work* (Salt Lake City: Deseret Book Co., 1936), 128.

Chapter 7

1. "News graphic: The Single Life," *Census.gov*, February 15, 2017, https://www.census.gov/newsroom/stories/2017/february/singles_awarenss_day.html.
2. Casey E. Copen, Ph.D., Kimberly Daniels, Ph.D., Jonathan Vespa, Ph.D., and William D. Mosher, Ph.D., "First Marriages in the United States: Data From the 2006–2010 National Survey of Family Growth," *CDC.gov*, March 22, 2012, https://www.cdc.gov/nchs/data/nhsr/nhsr049.pdf.
3. Kim Parker and Renee Stepler, "As U.S. marriage rate hovers at 50%, education gap in marital status widens," *Pew Research Center*, September 14, 2017, http://www.pewresearch.org/fact-tank/2017/09/14/as-u-s-marriage-rate-hovers-at-50-education-gap-in-marital-status-widens/.
4. Ibid.
5. Copen et al., "First Marriages in the United States: Data From the 2006–2010 National Survey of Family Growth," 9.
6. Ibid., tables 5 and 6.
7. Ibid., tables 7 and 8.
8. Ibid., 7.
9. Mark Banschick, "The High Failure Rate of Second and Third Marriages," *Psychology*

Today, February 6, 2012, https://www.psychologytoday.com/us/blog/the-intelligent-divorce/201202/the-high-failure-rate-second-and-third-marriages.
10. Copen et al., "First Marriages in the United States: Data From the 2006–2010 National Survey of Family Growth," 17.
11. Rose M. Kreider and Renee Ellis, "Number, Timing, and Duration of Marriages and Divorces: 2009," *Census.gov*, May 2011, https://www.census.gov/prod/2011pubs/p70-125.pdf.
12. Ibid., 10.
13. Jamie M. Lewis and Rose M. Kreider, "Remarriage in the United States," March 2015, *Census.gov*, https://www.census.gov/content/dam/Census/library/publications/2015/acs/acs-30.pdf.
14. Ibid.
15. Henry Gorbein, "Why Do Second Marriages Fail? What Are the Major Reasons?" *HuffPost*, November 9, 2010, https://www.huffpost.com/entry/why-do-second-marriages-f_b_779819. See also: Maggie Scarf, "Why Second Marriages Are More Perilous," *TIME*, October 4, 2013, http://ideas.time.com/2013/10/04/why-second-marriages-are-more-perilous/.
16. "2017 Statistical Report for 2018 April General Conference," *LDS.Org*, March 31, 2018, https://www.lds.org/church/news/2017-statistical-report-for-2018-april-general-conference?lang=eng.
17. Clayton Christensen, 2015 Washington D.C. Mid-singles Conference Talk, statistics from personal notes.
18. John Birger, "Mormons and Jews: What 2 Religions Say About the Modern Dating Crisis," *TIME*, August 24, 2015, http://time.com/dateonomics/.
19. Ibid.
20. Ibid.
21. Ibid.
22. Ibid.
23. Ibid.
24. Doctrine and Covenants 88:91.
25. Isaiah 4:1.
26. Birger, "Mormons and Jews: What 2 Religions Say About the Modern Dating Crisis."
27. Lori Gottlieb, "Marry Him! The Case for Settling for Mr. Good Enough," *The Atlantic*, March 2008, https://www.theatlantic.com/magazine/archive/2008/03/marry-him/306651/.
28. Ibid.
29. Isaiah 3:16–26.
30. Ruth 1: 14–17.
31. Genesis 2:18.
32. Mormon 8:5.
33. Hara Estroff Marano, "The Dangers of Loneliness," *Psychology Today*, July 1, 2003, https://www.psychologytoday.com/us/articles/200307/the-dangers-loneliness.
34. 1 Kings 19:13.
35. Mark 12:41–44.
36. *Dictionary.com*, s.v. "poverty," https://www.dictionary.com/browse/poverty.
37. Bernadette D. Proctor, Jessica L. Semega, and Melissa A. Kollar, "Income and Poverty in the United States: 2015," *Census.gov*, September 2016, https://www.census.gov/content/dam/Census/library/publications/2016/demo/p60-256.pdf.
38. Ibid., table 4.
39. John 12:8; Mark 14:7; Matthew 26:11.
40. James 1:27.

Chapter 8
1. 2 Kings 5:9–14.
2. 2 Kings 6.
3. 2 Kings 6.
4. Ether 3:1–6.
5. Deuteronomy 23:5.
6. Moses 5:11.
7. Moses 1:8–10.
8. Alma 18:5.
9. Doctrine and Covenants 58:30–33.
10. Neal A. Maxwell, "Enduring Well," *LDS.org*, April 1997, https://www.lds.org/ensign/1997/04/enduring-well?lang=eng.
11. The Church of Jesus Christ of Latter-day Saints, *Teachings of Presidents of the Church: Brigham Young* (Salt Lake City: 1997), 260–266.
12. Joshua 17:13.
13. Joshua 22.
14. Moses 4:31.
15. Mosiah 23:21.
16. Mosiah 13:29–31.
17. Numbers 13:30.
18. Jacob 1:7.
19. Jacob 1:7.
20. Mosiah 7:15, 23.
21. Mosiah 7:17–18.
22. Joshua 3:13–17.
23. Ralph Waldo Emerson, "Illusions," *The Conduct of Life* (1860), https://emersoncentral.com/texts/the-conduct-of-life/illusions/.
24. Doctrine and Covenants 19:10–12.

Chapter 9
1. Mark 9:17–28; Matthew 17:14–21; Luke 9:37–42.
2. Ibid.
3. Moroni 7:40.
4. 1 Nephi 2:9–10.
5. Romans 1:5–7.

6. Rick Hanson, PhD, *Hardwiring Happiness* (New York: Harmony House, 2013), 22–24
7. Moroni 7:3.
8. Romans 8:24–25.
9. Romans 5:3–5.
10. Leviticus 24:1–4.
11. 3 Nephi 9:14.
12. Helaman 3:29.
13. 1 Nephi 15:24.
14. John 1:1.
15. Revelations 19:13.
16. Moroni 7:41.
17. Abraham 3:24–28.
18. Doctrine and Covenants 67:10; 38:8.
19. Gordon B. Hinckley, "We Walk by Faith," *LDS.org*, April 2002, https://www.lds.org/general-conference/2002/04/we-walk-by-faith?lang=eng.
20. Alma 30:44.
21. Hebrews 11:1–6.
22. 2 Nephi 28:7.
23. 1 Nephi 3:7.
24. Doctrine and Covenants 123:7.
25. Henry B. Eyring, "Act in All Diligence," *LDS.org*, April 2010, https://www.lds.org/general-conference/2010/04/act-in-all-diligence?lang=eng.
26. Doctrine and Covenants 9:7–10.
27. Alma 46.
28. 2 Nephi 21: 4–6; see also Isaiah 49.
29. Romans 1:16.
30. Romans 1:17.
31. Genesis 28:12–13.
32. Doctrine and Covenants 88:99–101.
33. Romans 2:13.
34. Romans 2:14–15.
35. Romans 2:26–29.
36. Alma 34:16.
37. Romans 5:8–9.
38. Romans 6:20–23.
39. Moses 6:59–60.
40. Doctrine and Covenants 20:30–31.
41. Moroni 10:33.
42. Matthew 14:22–32.
43. Mormon 7:45–47.
44. Moroni 10:20–21.
45. Jarom 1:2.
46. Moses 5:5–6.
47. Matthew 19:16–21.
48. Luke 10:25–37.
49. Galatians 2:11–21.
50. Jefferson M. Fish, PhD, "Tolerance, Acceptance, Understanding," *Psychology Today*, February 25, 2014, https://www.psychologytoday.com/us/blog/looking-in-the-cultural-mirror/201402/tolerance-acceptance-understanding.
51. Thomas S. Monson, "Charity Never Faileth," *LDS.org*, October 2010, https://www.lds.org/general-conference/2010/10/charity-never-faileth?lang=eng.
52. 2 Nephi 4:27.
53. 2 Corinthians 2:10–11.

Chapter 10

1. "U.S. Public Becoming Less Religious," *Pew Research Center*, November 3, 2015, http://www.pewforum.org/2015/11/03/u-s-public-becoming-less-religious/.
2. Ibid.
3. Ibid.
4. Ibid.
5. Ibid.
6. Ibid.
7. Ibid.
8. Ibid.
9. Ibid.
10. Ibid.
11. Romans 3:1–2.
12. Ephesians 2:20.
13. Ephesians 1:10.
14. Moses 7.
15. 2 Samuel 6:7.
16. Elizabeth Hopper, "Individualist or Collectivist? How Culture Influences Behavior," *HealthyPsych.com*, January 30, 2015, https://healthypsych.com/individualist-or-collectivist-how-culture-influences-behavior/.
17. Mark 2:1–12.
18. Ezekiel 37:21–22.
19. "Minn. Teen charged in fatal texting while driving crash," *CBS News*, October 20, 2015, https://www.cbsnews.com/news/texting-and-driving-minnesota-teen-kills-father-and-daughter/.
20. U.S Department of Transportation, "Traffic Safety Facts, Research Note," October 2017, https://crashstats.nhtsa.dot.gov/Api/Public/ViewPublication/812603.
21. National Safety Council, "Understanding the Distracted Brain," April 2012, https://www.nsc.org/Portals/0/Documents/DistractedDrivingDocuments/Cognitive-Distraction-White-Paper.pdf.
22. John 17:21.
23. See generally Alma 11.
24. Alma 11:22.
25. 2 Nephi 2:13.
26. Alma 11:22–36.
27. Alma 11:35.
28. Alma 11:36–37.
29. Matthew 2:1.

Chapter 11

1. John 4:3–30.

About the Author

Kevin Baker is a single adult and a member of the Church of Jesus Christ of Latter-day Saints. He currently lives in Minnesota and serves as a counselor in the bishopric of his family ward. Previously he served in various capacities with multiple bishoprics and stake presidencies. As a stake Sunday School President, he was responsible for Sunday School programs at the Utah State Prison. He also served as an institute teacher and volunteered with the Boy Scouts. He served a two-year mission in Zurich, Switzerland.

Kevin is a is a successful corporate attorney and works with large international companies. With nearly 20 years of experience, he is an expert in the natural resource industry and manages controversial issues that have national implications. Kevin graduated from Brigham Young University with a Bachelor of Science in International Corporate Finance and two minors: German and Music. He also graduated from the University of Oregon with a Master of Business Administration and a Juris Doctorate in Law. Kevin is an Eagle Scout, an avid ballroom dancer, and a golfer.

And, if you are single and an incredibly amazing woman, Kevin is an especially nice guy who likes Caribbean cruises, candlelight dinners, and long walks on moonlit beaches!

www.ingramcontent.com/pod-product-compliance
Lightning Source LLC
LaVergne TN
LVHW021559070426
835507LV00014B/1860